Upon Silver Wings

Upon Silver Wings

Global Adventure in a Small Plane

CAROLANN GARRATT

Ben —

It was good to talks
with you during the very first
leg of this adventure.

Blue skies!

CarolAnn 9-24-06

Orlando, Florida

UPON SILVER WINGS
Global Adventure in a Small Plane
by CarolAnn Garratt

First Edition
Editor: Caroline Raboy
Book Design: Janice Phelps

LCCN: 2001012345
ISBN: 0-9753457-5-3

To order additional copies of *Upon Silver Wings*,
please see the order form at the back of the book.

Most of the photographs in *Upon Silver Wings* were taken by
CarolAnn Garratt. Some were taken by David Berelsman, John
Foster, or Jim McLean, and the author would like ot thank them
for permission to use their photographs.

The world map on the cover by
Latimer Clarke Corporation Pty Ltd,
used with permission.

The flight was dedicated to my mother,
Marie Garratt,
who died of ALS/Lou Gehrig's
ten months before my departure.

Dick and Marie Garratt

This book is dedicated to my parents,
Richard and Marie Garratt,
who taught me to work hard,
explore, enjoy adventure, and not to be afraid.

All proceeds, 100%, go directly to the
ALS Therapy Development Foundation
researching a cure for ALS

Seychelles Young Eagle, Pierre-Andre

TABLE OF CONTENTS

Top left: Dave enjoying the Seychelles
Top right: Geoff and PaoChen from Singapore
Bottom: Francine, Isabelle, Gerard, and Lea Bonneau;
the family who took care of me in Sens, France

ACKNOWLEDGMENTS

This adventure and subsequent book would not have been possible without the support and help of aviation professionals and enthusiasts worldwide. I paid for the trip 100% myself and all donations went, and still go, 100% to the ALS Therapy Development Foundation. However, the generosity, helpfulness, and openness of people on the home front and in every port made this a successful journey.

I would like to thank, in alphabetical order: Aero Club de Joigny, Luc, Hubert, Christian et d'autres members; Aero Club de l'Yonne, Christophe et les pilots locales; Airline Flying Club, Ardmore, NZ; thanks Pete and club members; Air-Link, Dubbo, AU; Cliff, Paddo, Geoff, David, Adrian and others; Linda and Bill Alexander, Wood'N B&B, Newfoundland, Canada; American Samoa Tower controllers: Frank Bastis, Greg, Amy and Ella; Aviation Business Center, Cape Town, SA; Dudley and Jenny Lieveaux, Dion, Gert, Jean and Jaco; Aviation Publications Service, thanks David Weiss; Wendy and Paul Barter, Wings N Things, Lanseria, South Africa; Eddie Belle and family, Seychelles; Mark van Benschoten; Dave and Lyn Berelsman; Gerard et Francine Bonneau, Subligny, France; John at Boomerang Software, Inc.; Bourgogne Aero Services, David and Philippe; Pat and Joanne Brown; Nelson Cambata at Starport USA; Sue and Dick Campbell, Northshore Aero Club, Auckland, NZ; Bentley and Jackie Chapman, Paarl, South Africa; Steve Chlavin, Dresser Industries; Goeff and PaoChen Davis, Singapore; Jim, Kelly, EJ, John, John, Mike and others at Daytona Aviation Services; Judy Dickson, in memory of Dave who died of ALS, Halifax, Nova Scotia, Canada; Jamie and Penny Donaldson, Crowborough, England; Gordon and Bridget Donaldson, Stone, England; Earl Colne Airfield, Essex, England, Victoria and Keith; Eric and Stephan England, Hampton-Wick, England; Mike and Janet Ernesta, Seychelles; Far North Aviation, Wick, Scotland, thanks Andrew, Clair and Graham; Rendall Ferrier, Aberdeen, Scotland; Kathryn and John Flynn, Darwin, AU; John Foster and Jamie, Laconia, NH; Wanda Fuller at Kerrlake.com; Greenwood

Aviation Services, Lanseria, South Africa; Ian and Casandra; Ewald Groenewald; FJ Hale; Pat and Janis Hanly, South Africa Mooney Sales and Service; with Dave and Brandon; Jan Harding, Wivenhoe, England; Hardy Aviation, Darwin, AU; thanks Marie, John, Allison, Nick, Mick and Lyn; Nick and Fikirte Heemskerk; along with Haptalmu and Elsa; Richard and Hellen Horrobin, Keri Keri, NZ; Michael Jannine; Johor Bahru Flying Club, Malaysia; Andreas, Norman, Jamil, Terry, Neil, Noor, Yeow Ming, Andreas & others; Kerala Aviation Training Center, Trivandrum, India; Mr.Rajeev, Mr.Prakash and others; Launceston Aero Club, Launceston, AU; Melonie Griffith; Allan and Elsie Larsen, Nuuk, Greenland; Doug Lynch; Valerie and Alasdair MacDonald, Sydney, Australia; Jim McLean; Marathon FBO, Kissimmee, FL; thanks Bob, Jeanne and all the Birks; Hesham and Vicky Mahmoud, Lutterworth, England; Martin Merritt; Rusty and Tricia Miller, Byron Bay, Australia; Jean-Marc and Pat Mollinghoff; Jose' Monroy at Monroy Aero; Nelson Aero Club; Jason, Marc, Craig and Barry; Joe Noah; Northland Aero Club, Whangarei, NZ; Joe, Bevin and other instructors; Northland Aviation, Whangarei, NZ; Mike Chubb, Colleen, Mike, Jason, Rowan; David O'Connell, Lutterworth, England; Out of the Blue Africa Safaris, Lanseria, South Africa, Stan and Barbara; Sharon and Chuck Paradiso; Flemming and Angela Pedersen, Geneva, Switzerland; Donna Pinto; Popular Flying Association, England; thanks Jaqui, Tony, Laurie, Stewart and others; Nick Pride-Hearn; Reed Prior; Peter W. Pruyn; Francis and Pattie Reddan, Birr, Ireland; Brian and Janet Reid, Balmedie, Scotland; Rosemary Rich; Viviane Rochecouste, Cagliari, Italy with Danielle, Ines, Roberta and Nayaghi; Cathy Rosing; Royal Victorian Aero Club, Moorabbin, AU; Rick, Stewart, Paul, Pamela and members; Diane Rozek; Paul and Mary Ryan, Limerick, Ireland; Lori and Chris Saunders, Halifax, Nova Scotia, Canada; Bea and Mel Scherf along with Gil Long and the Early Birds at Sun'N Fun; Shannon Airport, Ireland; thanks Niall Maloney; Shearwater Flying Center, Gene Wertman, Halifax, Nova Scotia, Canada; Timothy and Maryann Seaman at Gran Cru; Arvind Sharma, India; Cindy Sheive; Jim Smith, Laconia, NH; Bob Snape, Leicester, England; Stellenbosch Flying Club, South Africa; Patrick, William and Dean; Stephenville Airport and FBO, Tom, Larry, Tom and Carolyn, Newfoundland, Canada; Dean and Lynn Stevenson,

Lanseria, South Africa; Tayside Aviation, Dundee, Scotland; thanks Stuart, Neil, John, George and Bob; James and Irene Teng, Singapore; Rick and Debbie Terpstra, Melbourne, Australia; Max and Anna Tooley, Manurewa, NZ; Le Tour de Controle a L'Aerodrome de Auxerre, Branches; Wag-Aero, thanks Mary Pat Henningfield; Dee Wakelin, Northshore Aero Club, Auckland, NZ; Phil Waldman and Donna, Mary and Mike of Globe Aero; Mike and Jeremy Ward at Air Desert Pacific, Brackett Field, CA; Wes and Sandy Whitley; Peter and Rita Woodman, Thame, England; Woodstock Aircraft Services, NY, thanks John; Dirk and Amanda van Wyk, Cape Town, SA.

Many pilots and ALS families e-mailed me during my trip with words of support and encouragement. Without them this trip would not have been so special. In addition, their words of praise for the web site and recommendations for a book proved to be enough to move me in that direction upon my return home. Thanks for your support.

Each of the members of my family: father, Dick, brothers, Peter John, Andy, Bill, and Richard; who helped my in the preparation, each in their own special way, and sent e-mails of support during the trip, deserve special recognition for letting me go and not worrying about the hazards of the trip. Without familial support, this trip would not have been possible.

David Berelsman, an EAA Chapter 74 member and friend, deserves special mention, as he joined me for six weeks of the trip, and was helpful and supportive during the preparation, during our time together, and afterwards. He gave me the final "kick in the pants" to get this book started by introducing me to Diane Finney, author, who gave me enough pointers to get going.

Jerry Rooks also deserves special mention for his support and PR activities during my return. He got my presentation schedule started at Fantasy of Flight and continued to raise local awareness of my adventure and cause. Caroline Raboy contributed enormously to "keeping me going" during the editing phase which she volunteered to do.

You have all helped to change my life. Thank you. And, I hope, through this book, we can encourage and inspire others to live life, learn, and share.

Ken, CarolAnn, and Mark in Clarksville, Virginia

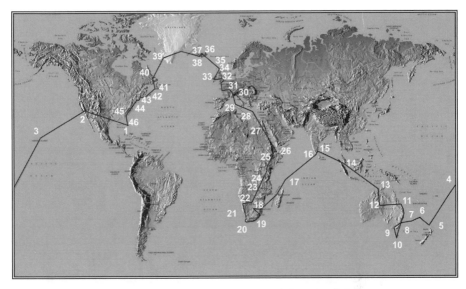

CarolAnn and Mooney being photographed for a
magazine article in South Africa

INTRODUCTION

I didn't realize it at the time, but I guess I was pretty lucky to be raised with four brothers, all very close in age. I did everything they did. When they took judo lessons, I took them as well. When they played baseball and football with their friends in the yard, I played along with them. I was treated equally. When I joined the ski club in 8th grade, they said it was a sissy sport. Then they got started and we all skied together for many years. My dad loved flying and we all took flying lessons, when we could afford it. One brother and I worked at the local airport and got hooked on flying.

When I decided to pursue mechanical engineering in college, no one said that I couldn't do it. It didn't bother me that there were only 2% women in engineering school, but it wasn't a challenge either, it was just the way things were. As I pursued a career in manufacturing engineering, first as a co-op student, I started to understand that not everyone saw things the same way. When I began looking for a company for my first semester's work assignment, one company said that they only accepted male engineering students (this was back in 1973). They let me work for the summer, but not as part of the co-op education program.

As I progressed in my career and in business, I learned that things weren't quite so equal for women. But that didn't stop me. I enjoyed my job in manufacturing, solving problems, and making things work better. I continued to work hard and climb the corporate ladder.

I became a work-a-holic. I loved my job, was moved every three to five years by the companies I worked for, and had many challenging assignments. I lived and worked in Wisconsin, California, France, Illinois, Texas, Utah, Pennsylvania, and Florida. In each new location, I'd work 14 hours per day and weekends during the first year to understand the people, products, departments, job and problems, and start working on solutions. By the second year, I'd be down to 12 hours a day and half-day on Saturday. By the third year, usually things would be running smoother, I'd feel more in control of the job, and I'd be down to 10 to 12-hour days and a half-day on

Saturday. Then a new assignment would come along and I'd start all over again. I still have a great relationship with many of the people in the plants and locations where I worked; a number of them have become friends as well as colleagues.

When I lost my job, I was shocked. Looking back, two-and-a-half years later, I haven't missed it for a day. Life has opened up wonderfully. As they say, when one door closes, another one opens. I would NEVER have had the courage to leave my job; I guess I should be glad that I was fired (or, that my position was eliminated, to be politically correct).

My mother was diagnosed with ALS/Lou Gehrig's disease in March 1999 when I was working in Pennsylvania and my parents were living in Virginia. I hadn't been flying much during my "working years," but I started again that spring. I used to rent a Cessna 152 and fly down to southern Virginia once a month, rather than driving 6 hours each way. In early 2000, I was transferred to a plant in Orlando, Florida. We thought I should buy a plane to continue to fly back and forth each month. I decided a Mooney airplane was the best suited for this long distance travel. It has a small cockpit, which didn't matter, as usually I would be the only occupant. It is extremely cost-effective, with very low gallons-per-hour gas consumption. And it is reasonably fast, 150 knots. Seven months later I was the proud owner of N220FC, white, with gray/silver wings, a solid blue tail, and a red stripe down the length of the fuselage. I bought her sight unseen. John, a very knowledge-able Mooney owner, helped me to find the right Mooney for me, and along with a mechanic, he reviewed the plane and logbooks. With John's okay, I started the negotiations and agreed on a price. Two weeks later, I flew to Illinois, commercially, to fly my Mooney back to its new home in Florida.

I lost my job in October 2001. My mother died in April 2002. I continued flying back and forth to spend time with my dad. I became a flight instructor. I did more volunteer flights for medical patients, Angel Flights. And I did Young Eagle flights—introductory flights for children sponsored by the Experimental Aircraft Association (EAA). Flying and things related to flying became my passion. I volunteered the whole week at Sun 'N Fun and Air Venture, Oshkosh, two big aviation air shows, in 2002.

A friend from France, where I'd worked for eight years, jokingly suggested that I should fly over to Europe and take him and others up for *un baptême de l'air* (an introductory flight baptism). The job market was terrible; I gave up looking for a job, and started planning a flight across the North Atlantic to Europe. While volunteering at Oshkosh, I attended a seminar about flying across the North Atlantic. It turned out the presenter, Mark VanBenschoten, flew a Mooney. I spent some time after the presentation talking with him and other pilots who had completed the crossing. I was getting enthusiastic.

A month or so after Oshkosh, four months after my mother's death, my Dad announced that he wanted to go to New Zealand to visit his sister, Liz. They'd only seen each other once in the last 50 years. They'd each lost their spouse. And they both felt the need to see each other once more. He also had friends in eastern Australia that he wanted to visit. My Dad was almost 81; someone would have to travel with him. Earlier that year, I'd read an article about a Mooney being flown to Australia. Both countries are wonderful for small planes (or so I'd read). I started looking at a globe. If the Mooney could do it, I could do it. Dad loves flying; I could fly him around New Zealand and Australia.

What about Europe? Could I make it from Australia to Europe? I moved from a globe to an atlas. I contacted Mark, whom I'd met at Oshkosh. I'd learned during his seminar that he'd once flown around the world in his Mooney. I started asking questions. Questions got answered, and planning became more detailed. Seven months later, I took off on this wonderful adventure. Nobody said that I couldn't do it.

My objectives were simple:

- Increase awareness about ALS/Lou Gehrig's disease, also known as Motor Neurone Disease in England, and raise contributions to fight the disease.
- Introduce aviation to youngsters in other countries and give them the opportunity to go flying through the Young Eagles program.
- Enjoy one of the greatest adventures of my life!

During the preparation, I had some business cards made up. My motto, on the card, was "Live life, learn, and share." That's what I was going to do during this voyage.

This flight is dedicated to my mother, Marie Garratt, who died of ALS on April 24, 2002.

Sam and Kelly working at the ALS Therapy Development Foundation in Boston, MA

Disclaimer

Statements contained herein are the opinions of CarolAnn Garratt and may contain inadvertent errors. No warranty of accuracy or factual completeness is either expressed or implied. Discussions of flight procedures are meant to be of an informal and conversational nature only and do not necessarily represent the views of the aviation authorities of any government. Furthermore, nothing herein should be construed as ground or flight instruction. Also note that long, transoceanic flying carries with it significant risks necessitating special training and the carriage of sophisticated navigation and survival equipment. Such flights should never be attempted without proper preparation.

CHAPTER 1

The field was plagued with a low ceiling and poor visibility. It reminded us of the films we have all seen of Lindbergh's takeoff from Roosevelt field in NY in 1927.

It felt as if Florida was sad to see her go....

Finally after 3 hours of waiting Carol Ann got her sign... the weather started to lift... She wedged herself into the cramped cockpit and started the engine and idled gently to the runway. A quick check of the motor and she was underway.... after rolling about 2500 ft she lifted off ... and it might have been my imagination, but as she headed out ... the clouds seems to separate and .... if only for a few minutes ... the airport was bathed in sunshine.

She was on her way...
David

Feb. 28th: Florida to California, 1st leg Flight Report

In my mind, my departure for this trip would be on a clear, sunny day with good visibility. Not so. I'd watched the weather as the final week arrived. Everything else was almost completed and I could leave any day near the end of February, as originally planned. Several unfavorable weather fronts had been passing over Texas and through the Midwest and east coast. One front was passing over Florida near the end of the week with scattered thunderstorms and rain, although, during that time, the rest of the south looked pretty good and the west coast was getting relief after several days of rain. So, Friday and Saturday looked to be the best for doing the complete leg, Kissimmee, Florida to Brackett Field, California, in one day. Taking two or more days was still an option if the weather continued to be fickle. I chose a Friday morning, 7 am departure. With friends, we completed the weighing and loading on Thursday evening and did a final ground test of the High Frequency radio. Everything looked good, so I went home to do the final housecleaning (I was renting my house during the eight months I'd be away) and to get a good night's sleep. Which I did.

Brother Andy, a corporate pilot in Atlanta, called first. He'd looked at the weather and gave me his advice. I agreed, departure didn't look good; however, the remainder of the country looked very good if I could get out of Florida. He told me to fly safely, have a good trip, and that he loved me, and we said goodbye.

Brother Richard called next. He would pick me up from Brackett Field. His news was better. The weather had been rainy most of the week, but was forecast to be much better on Friday. It was the best day to fly in. That helped tremendously. Now all I had to do was get out of Florida. He wished me a good flight also, told me that he loved me, and said goodbye. Now, down to the final cleaning and moving all remaining small items into the bedroom/office that I was locking while the house was rented. An hour later I was in bed and fast asleep.

Friday morning I got up early, checked the Internet aviation weather site, and called Flight Service for a weather briefing and to file my flight plan. The nice St. Petersburg weather briefer hadn't had to brief a trip to California before—not too many General Aviation pilots go non-stop. So, 45 minutes later I was fully briefed. It was pretty much as I'd seen the previous day, but he was able to give more specific information on icing in New Mexico and Arizona and where the storm cells were in the Gulf of Mexico. The only problem was the 200-foot overcast and one mile visibility in the Orlando area. I filed for an 8 am departure instead of 7 am and was mentally ready to leave later. I drove down to the airport to meet two friends, Dave and Mike, who had agreed to be there at 6 am to help me pull the Mooney out of the hangar. We talked for about 45 minutes then pulled the plane out, as Mike had to leave for work. I gassed up, 75 gallons on top of the 90 gallons already in the tanks! I'd increased the air pressure in the tires the evening before and they looked okay under the increased load.

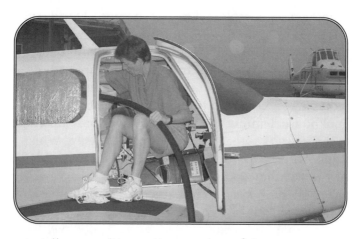

Loading up with gas the morning of departure

After a pre-flight check, Dave and I headed to the local FBO[1] (Fixed Based Operator), Marathon, to look at radar, listen to the Kissimmee airport automated weather reports, and wait for higher ceilings and better visibility. With an over gross weight[2] plane—and this being my first overweight takeoff, I didn't want to have a low ceiling to deal with as well. I wanted a few minutes to see how she flew and handled prior to entering clouds. Actually, the ceiling and visibility got worse before they got better; but, around 9:30 am, they started to improve. Dave and I drove back to the south side of the airport.

I received my clearance to POC, the identifier for Brackett Field, and taxied to runway 15; however, the wind was switching as we, me and my Mooney, taxied. It became northeast, 030 degrees, at eight or nine knots. I really didn't think it would be good to do a downwind takeoff, so Kissimmee ground let us turn around and taxi to runway 33. I went through the checklist very carefully; finally the run-up was complete, and I was nervous. No question, I'd done all the calculations, and the takeoff roll was only supposed to use less than half the runway and climb at 250 feet per minute, but would that be reality?

I held the brakes, added power, and then released the brakes. Talk about sluggish! It took much longer than I'd anticipated picking up speed, but then she just kept on going faster, manifold pressure and RPM looked good, she lifted off at 70k (normally 60k) with the stall warning buzzer screaming. I concentrated on airspeed and looked quickly to see how much runway I'd used, less than 3000 ft, and the numbers had calculated to 2500 ft, not bad. Airspeed was good, climb was anemic, tower advised me that my gear was still down—duhhh. Gear up, flaps up, and the climb was still anemic. Tower wished me a good trip, turned me over to Orlando departure, and I was in the clouds.

The climb was very slow but uneventful; however it was stressful. Orlando departure kept changing headings and frequencies every few minutes. About 17 minutes later I was level at 6000 feet and breathed a sigh of relief; climb rate of 350 ft/min, slightly better than calculated. Orlando approach asked if I was really going

---

1.   FBO — Fixed Base Operator, the airport operation providing gas, parking, maintenance, and office staff to assist pilots at an airport
2.   Over gross — legally over maximum gross weight. This can affect the flight characteristics of any plane.

to POC in California without a stop and how long it would take me? When they handed me over, they wished me a good trip and good luck. Actually several of the controllers did that—very nice of them, they kept me smiling.

About an hour later I was on top of the clouds with only scattered layers above, the flight was smooth, and I smiled for the first time and started to feel good. Now this was more of what I had in mind. I still had strong headwinds and although I'd planned 14.5 hours for the trip, the ETE, estimated time enroute, on the GPS (global positioning system) continued to read more than 14 hours. After the Florida panhandle the winds diminished, the ETE read 12 hours and I felt much better.

In order to get the center of gravity as far forward as possible, I had the life raft behind my seat. After burning off fuel, I pushed it further back on top of the rear 55-gallon tank, moved my seat back, took off my shoes and really smiled! I pulled out the Cheerios and started snacking.

It's over 3 hours into the flight with a blanket of clouds that look like snow below me as far as I can see in every direction (maybe this is to prepare me for the sea of blue that I'll be seeing on the next few legs). There are vapor trails from the jets above and their shadows are on the clouds below. I feel like I have company on this flight experience and yet I feel comfortably alone.

Okay, how to while away the next 12 hours. After the Cheerios comes the pizza. At a meeting with my EAA Chapter 74, I was asked what I would be eating. I said a sandwich, apples, and cookies— good food, not junk food, I said seriously. Well, cold pizza is my favorite and that's what I ate. That took 15 minutes; now what to do for 11 hrs and 45 minutes? Actually, it wasn't that bad. The time passed very quickly. There was always something to do. I'd flight planned the fuel burn at 9 gallons per hour (gph), but had used less in the past. Other Mooney pilots recommended 10 or higher planned fuel burn. Well, using the 55-gallon drum of fuel in the back would be the first test. I wanted to run until it was empty—no use leaving a little and not knowing how much is left. So, at 5 hours (it only has 50 gallons of fuel in it) I started concentrating on the fuel pressure gage and listening to the engine for coughing. Nothing. At 9 gph it should run out at 5.5 hours; still nothing. Six

Ferry tanks in back and right seats

hours, nothing. Finally she coughed at 6 hours and 30 minutes on that tank, an amazing 7.7 gph at over-full load. I'm not leaning too much, the exhaust gases are a nice tan color, just what the doctor ordered. WOW, I'm happy, no problem with plane endurance, only pilot endurance.

I switched to the 17-gallon tank in the right seat, which had 16 gallons in it. Two hours and 3 minutes later it coughed again—yep, I'd had my hand on the fuel selector for at least 15 minutes: 7.8 gph. Now, I'm on wing tanks and 100 gallons to go—let's see, that gives me a conservative 12.5 hours to complete the final 7 hours. I think I have enough reserve. The 55-gallon drum in place of the rear seats and the 17-gallon drum in place of the right seat were certified modifications done in preparation for this trip.

In addition to watching fuel burn, navigating, and talking with Air Traffic Control (ATC), I also had my HF (High Frequency) radio to play with. This was special equipment added for the flight and not usually found in a small single engine airplane. It is mandatory for crossing the Pacific Ocean in order to communicate position reports each hour. Wes and Sandy, sailing and flying friends with lots of HF experience, had tuned the radio, tested the trailing antenna, and installed another piece of hardware, a PTC IIe, that attaches to the HF and laptop computer, and allows e-mail from the air! Because I had to be listening to ATC all the time, I couldn't go off frequency to talk on the HF, but, I could write e-mails on my laptop computer and send them while doing all my other pilot duties. So, I made up my first e-mail as to how the flight was progressing and sent it to my short list of friends and family. Because it uses radio waves, the transmission is very slow. I couldn't send attachments, nor have a long e-mail list. I'd asked that each recipient pass the information along to others. The best part was receiving e-mails. After several hours, I reconnected to send another update, and responses started coming in. Now that made me smile. It was great to hear from Dad, brothers, friends from work, and pilots from my EAA chapter. Later, I asked ATC and received approval to go "off frequency" for a few minutes. This is usually done to pick up weather information or to report weather. I wanted to connect via HF radio to Ben's net, a group of mostly sailors and ham[3] radio buffs that talk every day at 2100 Zulu[4] time, 5:00 pm EDT. I reported in quickly as KE4HBO air mobile, my call sign, and indicating that I was calling from an airplane. We chatted for a few minutes, I reported that all was well, and I signed off to return to the VHF aircraft radio.

West of Dallas the clouds ended and I finally saw the ground. Lots of farm fields gave way to dry barren flat land of New Mexico, then the foothills and mountains of the Rockies. Sometime in there I took my first potty break. I had not been looking forward to this. I've been flying for many years and have never had to use any type of potty. However, with legs of 14 to 16 hours, I knew I'd need something. So, I bought a Little John with Lady J adapter— "designed for outdoor women, pilots, etc, etc." When it arrived, I figured I'd better practice in the bathroom before trying it in the plane—good job I did. I wasn't too successful the first few times. I took it into the bathroom, sat on the stool, as if I were sitting in a plane, and couldn't figure out how this was going to work without spilling. The angle was wrong, there was no way it was all going to go into the plastic funnel. And it didn't. Time to read the instructions.

---

3. Ham is another word for an amateur radio operator.
4. Zulu — Universal Coordinated Time (UTC), also called Zulu time, is used by all aircraft worldwide. Based on the standard time at the zero meridian in Greenwich, England.

Brother Richard doing oil change with Michael and Jeremy from Air Desert Pacific.

I knew that I'd need an oil change in California, then again, 50 hours later, in New Zealand. Actually, I'd planned all the oil changes around the world and confirmed that the type of oil I needed was available, or I'd had it shipped there. I was carrying my own oil filters and had shipped two to France. So, we found a nice friendly FBO and with their approval changed the oil and filter.

All the planning I had done during the seven months of preparation had been technical. Although I'd made a few contacts in New Zealand, Australia, and Europe, I hadn't made any other plans for where to stay or how to get the maintenance done. Amazingly enough, it was the people and the supportive aviation community around the world that made this trip a wonderful experience. Air Desert Pacific Director of Maintenance, Michael Ward, and son Jeremy, were the first two of many, many supportive aviation folks who helped me out all around the globe. They gave me a spot on their ramp to do my oil change and a bucket for the used oil. During the oil change, they strolled over to talk with us about their favorite airplane, the Mooney. When they saw the tank, they asked more questions and the details of the trip came out. They wished me well and agreed that a Mooney is the best plane for this type of long distance adventure.

Spending a few days with my brother, sister-in-law, and beautiful 17-month-old niece was relaxing at first. We went running and hiking in the hills as well as working in the garden. I often work out, but especially before a flight. I run or get a good workout the day before so that my body is tired and doesn't mind sitting all day. As the departure date drew near, I was watching the weather much more closely and calling Flight Service to get additional information on crossing to Hawaii. I was getting geared up again.

Top: CarolAnn gassing up inboard tank, note extra outboard tank
Bottom: People walking across a crater on Hilo, Hawaii

Chapter 2

This is awesome — I received your message while you are still in the air.
Hope you get this response while you are still "up there." I got a note
from Max and he told me he heard from you. Boy, is he excited.

Anyway, have a wonderful flight over to Hawaii and DON'T fall asleep!
Pat

March 5th: California to Hawaii, 2nd leg flight report

W hat a morning, not as planned, again...but mostly sunny this time. I awoke at 5 am and desperately wanted to call Flight Service to get a weather update. I'd been looking at Aviation Weather charts all day yesterday, as well as calling Flight Service three times to get their input on the weather and winds. I'd planned on leaving Thursday in order to spend an extra day with Richard, Di, and McKenna. But when I finally downloaded the current weather charts, things looked too perfect. Tailwinds, a high north of the route, good forecast for arrival at Hilo, I just couldn't wait. If I tried to wait, I'd be worried all day that the high would move off and the low would move in. So, I filed my flight plan and started packing.

When Richard got up, I kissed everyone goodbye and he drove me to the airport. Looking to the south there was fog in the valley; they live 1000 feet higher than the airport. Although Long Beach was clear, Brackett, where I was parked, was IFR (instrument conditions) but lifting quickly. I filed an IFR flight plan from Brackett to Long Beach from the car. Packing the plane and pre-flight went quickly, as not much had been taken out. Big hug goodbye with his wishes, speaking for the whole family and all friends, for a good flight over the Pacific. I had to get to Long Beach first.

It was a normal liftoff from Brackett, as I was going to gas up at Long Beach. We quickly passed through the low mist and were on top in no time. Again I was lucky; practically no one was talking with SOCAL approach. They cleared me via V394,[9] and not long after I reached 4000 feet I was cleared back down again. The 10,000-foot runway was easy to see and I was cleared for the visual approach to runway 30. I gassed up at Rainbow Air. Although gas

---

9.   V394 — a standard charted airway route

prices had jumped 10 cents in one day, it was still the cheapest around. The mechanics started to be interested when they saw the gas hose going into the cabin. They walked around but didn't ask any questions and went back to work. After filling up, I did another quick pre-flight, got in, started up, and called clearance. No flight plan on file...hmmmm. Stop the engine, get back out, go inside and call FSS (flight service station). Apparently some semicolons had been missed and the flight plan was stuck in the system. The flight service person was extremely helpful, recognized that time was important, and worked between central control and me to clear it up while we were both on the phone. He said that he had worked with Steve Fossett[10] during his trip and had learned how to do a domestic flight plan to Hawaii. I thanked him profusely for his assistance and he wished me a good trip.

One more rest room stop, then back into the plane, start up, and call clearance. They have my flight plan, check that I am really going to Hilo, and ask how long it will take. Ground is a little surprised that I ask for the whole 10,000-foot runway; I explain that I'm in an overweight condition and he clears me to the end. During run up, I checked all the tanks to make sure there was no air in the lines. The engine coughed and spluttered on the rear tank, then it cleared—I was thankful that I was on the ground. Tower clears me to takeoff, I'm amazed how little traffic there is; maybe I'm just lucky again and it's a quiet day. Tower wishes me a good trip and hands me off to departure. The climb out feels better this time; maybe it's the sunny day and good visibility; only 14 minutes to 6000 feet. There were several SOCAL approach handoffs in a short amount of time, but each wished me a good trip and one guy said, "Better you than me." Onto the rear tank and wait 6 hours and 15 minutes before changing tanks. I wasn't worried during this takeoff and didn't have time to worry about the trip, but for some reason, my stomach was still tight when I leveled off. The relaxation that I felt on the previous leg didn't happen this time—maybe I was a little worried deep inside.

I checked and rechecked everything. I asked center if I could check the HF radio with San Francisco—it worked fine. So why was this knot still there? I looked outside at the beautiful, calm blue sea

10.   Steve Fossett was the first person to fly solo around the world in a balloon.

and the few puffy clouds ahead. I breathed deeply and asked myself why I was doing this, then I relaxed and smiled. It took a while, but I was finally feeling better. I looked at the ground speed and it was up to 150 knots. I smiled again.

Okay, I'm going to have to do some calculations on this leg, so let's get started. I figured they'd have me on radar and I'd start position reporting at the first compulsory intersection. I set up a chart to calculate distances and times so that I only had to plug in ETA (estimated time of arrival) and ATA (actual time of arrival) for each point. At the first point I made my position report and received a "N220FC, roger." What a let down. I expected cheers for my first report. Well, I patted myself on the back and set up for the next one. I listened to the commercial carriers overhead and modified my words a little to sound more professional. At least I had a good strong signal (thanks to Wes and Sandy) and would stay in touch all the way.

There is a cloud layer below me and I'm in smooth air at 6000 feet. Every once in a while there's a hole in the clouds and I see the sea below. It looks relatively calm. I found myself staring at the gauges. When the oil pressure ticked up slightly and the oil temp did the same, my heart was in my mouth. Everything was normal—quit staring at the gauges, nothing is wrong. Several minutes later the batteries on my noise reduction headset gave up—with the sudden increase in noise, I really jumped. Okay, okay, settle down. Take it easy, everything is ok. Breathe deeply. I wasn't worried at the start, but all of a sudden, a third of the way there, I get the nerves. Almost time to switch tanks. I'm going to do it a few minutes before it completely runs dry this time, so I won't have to worry about the engine coughing. Last time was 6 hr 30 min, so I'll change at 6 hr 15 min. At 6 hr 07 min the engine starts coughing. My hand was already on the fuel selector and I switch immediately, but that was just what I'd wanted to avoid. We'll see if I can do better on the front tank. The back used 8.2 gal/hr. A little more than the first leg, but still less than planned. When the engine runs smoothly, I breathe a whole lot better. I'm back to feeling good.

There's an angry sky to the south. I saw what looked like big storm cells between Hawaii and American Samoa when I was watching the weather yesterday. But this looks too close to be that system. There are higher clouds ahead, but they look pretty thin and there's nothing on the storm scope. Several minutes later I'm in rain. Not much turbulence but we (me and my Mooney) continue in and out of rain and clouds for an hour. It must be the little trough that I saw on the weather chart the last two days. On the other side of the trough, an hour later, it's magnificent. Little puffy clouds, lots of blue water and a tailwind that pushes me back up to 150 knots. I'd been down to 139–142 knots. The charts showed this area and good winds behind it and that's what I got. Clear sailing from now on.

Nine hours down and I have to go potty. No getting around it. Okay, let's try it again. Since I don't have to talk and listen to ATC every minute, taking my headset off gives me a little more head-room for maneuvering. Well, well, well, success. Not exactly elegant, but successful. The sun is setting at 5:35 Hawaii time and it's getting cool. I thought this was going to be a warm trip, but I find myself wearing my only fleece all the time. Hope I'll be warm in Hawaii tomorrow.

As the sun sets there's one big twin flying overhead on "my" airway in the opposite direction. The stars come out and it's clear above with a scattered-to-broken layer several thousand feet below. I have been awake for 13 hours, flying for 10 hours, and I have four-and-a-half hours to go. I can see my destination on the GPS, only 670 nautical miles (nm) ahead of me. Of course, I have the GPS set at 1000 nm range, but it makes me feel good nevertheless. Only four more HF reporting points and I'll be back on VHF, normal aircraft radio for line-of-sight communication. I'm exceedingly happy with the HF reports; each one I've received a "roger" or a read-back of the position. Other pilots that I've heard received "unreadable," "garbled," or "weak transmission." Thanks so much to Wes and Sandy who installed and tweaked the HF system. It's working very well.

The night flying was a little more difficult, as I couldn't use the laptop and wasn't kept busy with e-mail. I had more time to think and not much to do. But, I felt comfortable, not jittery. The time went by quickly. Stars above, clouds below, only 100 miles to go, I just started talking on VHF to Honolulu Center a few miles ago; I'm feeling pretty good. For the last 50 miles a headwind has picked up to 12–15 knots. But, after the tailwinds that I've had for the whole trip, I'm not complaining. A little later, I'm cleared down to 3000 feet and descend through rain and bumpy clouds. I'd heard two weather reports in the last hour: visibility 10 miles, 3800 broken, 4900 overcast, and the latest, few clouds at 2600. Well, I executed an ILS 26 approach down to 500 feet above the ground. It was raining with clouds to 500 feet and maybe 5 miles visibility. Welcome to Hilo, Hawaii!

There was a Navajo ahead of me during most of the trip. They kindly called me by radio from the ground, while I was on final approach, to let me know the actual conditions. They also helped me to tie down the Mooney and we shared a ride to the hotel. I was amazed that they took 12.3 hours to my 15 hours flying time; although their conditions were much more luxurious than mine, having a toilet on board, and room to walk around. At the airport, the tower and FBO were closed but there was one security guard to monitor arrivals (for payment purposes). At least it was warm and I'm sure it'll be sunny tomorrow. Aloha.

The Island of Hawaii, the Big Island

Originally planning on staying only a few days, I took a bus tour of the Volcano National Park and other sites around Hilo. I was hoping that this tour would be worthwhile and it was. The majority of time was spent on volcanoes and at the National Park, but it also gave an excellent overview of the island of Hawaii in relation to the rest of the state of Hawaii. For example, this island represents 60% of the landmass of the state and only has 10% of the population. You know where the rest of the population is! For pilots, there's a reason everyone goes to the other islands; it rains over 240 days a year for more than 200 inches. This is where pilots come for their instrument training. The north and east side of the island is lush and green, the south is barren from volcano lava, and the west, near Kona, is dry.

As we toured around, we saw how the lava has flowed down the hill from above and formed what they call a "bench" or flat area into the sea. The various colors are apparent from old and new lava flows. Some of these flows are only two weeks old.

We didn't see any new flowing lava, but we did see the previous day's flow still red and cooling. It was extremely hot as we walked on the lava and you could see the heat shimmering above the black lava. We could see steam from the lava flowing into the sea. Unfortunately we couldn't get closer. But I would see it again from the air the next day.

Taking the road up the volcano to a point four thousand feet higher, we were at the crater of one of the volcanoes. It is 400 feet deep now, but back in Mark Twain's day, when it was still active, it was closer to 700 feet deep. It was impressively large from near and far.

We learned about lava tubes—holes in the ground through which lava flows. We walked through the one that is over 15 feet in diameter. There are waterfalls everywhere on the island. We visited two on this tour. We also visited an orchid park and a macadamia nut factory—the samples were very tasty.

I thought it would be fun to see the island by air. Unfortunately, I'd learned that there were always clouds over the island of Hawaii and it isn't possible to see the tops of the mountains. When I talked with people at the airport, I found out that it's usually a layer of clouds and it's possible to fly above and see the crater at 13,796 feet.

As I flew around the coast, I could see steam coming from the lava flowing into the sea. This volcano has been erupting and flowing almost continuously for the past 20 years. I climbed to 14,000 feet and saw the top of Mauna Kea volcano peaking out above the clouds. It is a very shallow crater. I thought it was going to be much deeper; but it has filled in over the years.

There are many sparsely populated areas on the coast of this island. After flying over the volcano, I descended and flew along the northeast coast. There are no roads in this area; it is beautiful and untouched. Along the northeast shore there are many waterfalls. Finally, I return down the east coast, call Hilo approach, and land again.

I met some members of a whale survey team who are returning to the northwest shore where there are apparently a great number of whales. After hearing about my trip, they wish me a continued good journey and promised to follow the progress on the web site.

It's time for me to clean the plane and start repacking. I've already checked the satellite pictures once and there is still a major front just to the north of American Samoa. I'll check it again tomorrow.

Unfortunately, my charts for the next leg didn't arrive in time (they were chasing me from California, as I'd left a day early); UPS overnight didn't make it. But the weather wasn't looking good for the next crossing anyway, so I wasn't too upset. Recognizing that I'd have to spend the weekend on Hawaii, I rented a car and took off to visit the rest of the island. I headed north to do a counterclockwise tour. Just out of Hilo, I picked up two students from the University of Hawaii, Hilo: Scarlet and Melonie. They were going to the Akaka falls, just where I was headed, so I gave them a ride. Since they were local, they filled me in on other things to do and see. After the falls, I continued north to an overlook that was majestic. As I was leaving, two young men, John and Mathias, approached me to see if I was headed to Kona. As that was my direction, I gave them a ride as well. Although I don't normally pick up hitchhikers, I felt comfortable with these young people on this tourist island. It turned out that John and Mathias were from La Crosse, Wisconsin, where my older brother, Peter John, and his family lived for 15 years.

I'd met a pilot, Jeffrey, at Hilo who said to visit him at the Hilton near Kona if I made it to the other side of the island. I found the Hilton and eventually found Jeffrey; an excellent bartender, pilot, and adventurer. He runs a company called Advanced Recreation and enjoys flying and training in microlites and hang gliders. He certainly is one happy guy.

The next morning, after a coffee with friends of a friend, Bob and Jeanette, I set off to see more of the Volcano National Park and to do some hiking and camping. I hiked through a crater and through steam fields, and saw lava flowing at twilight. It was fascinating.

After camping overnight, I did two more hikes: first over vast lava fields, then in a quiet forest with rainforest vegetation and birds. Overall, it was a great learning experience that complemented the overview I'd received on the bus tour the first day.

Now, return to Hilo, find my charts, check the weather, and let's get going to American Samoa. I've had five days off and I'm very ready to get back to flying.

I knew the routine, as I'd called Flight Service, FSS, prior to touring the island. They told me to contact the Weather Service, who gave me a wonderful weather synopsis and outlook. However, they finished their report with, "This does not constitute your official Flight Service weather briefing." I asked what does and they said to talk with FSS. When I called FSS, they admitted that they don't brief the Pacific. But they took my flight plan. This was to be the first of many learning experiences—you're on your own from now on. Flying as you knew it in the US, with radar, weather, support and information, ceases to exist.

Vapor rising as the hot lava pours into the sea

CHAPTER 3

I am Scott, AH6BR, located in Kailua, Oahu, Hawaii. I understand that Ms. Garratt has ham radio aboard her airplane, and I would be pleased to attempt to contact her and do flight following from Hawaii.

May I be of assistance?
Scott

March 11: Hilo, Hawaii to American Samoa, 3rd leg flight report

What a frustrating morning...but I'm finally on my way. I got up at 4:30 am and did a final weather check—looked great, no BIG fronts or bad weather. Just like the weatherman said the previous afternoon, a few isolated thunderstorms, easy enough to deviate around. The wind chart on the Internet was missing its arrows (essentially a blank chart), but yesterday it looked like a quartering tailwind. At the airport, I checked everything, ran each of the fuel tanks to make sure all the air was out, and then I called ground when Hilo tower opened at 6 am. Clearance received, beautiful takeoff and climb eastbound, beautiful day, I'm on my way, or so I thought.

Hilo departure asks me to switch to HF to make sure contact is good with San Francisco Radio or they can't let me continue out of their airspace. I think, no problem, HF communication was great all the way over. I switch to HF and nothing. I keep testing, checking wires, and calling for half an hour. The transmission looks strong on the meter. They make me return, and then change their minds and give me another frequency to try. The antenna is reeled in and out twice.[11] I'm exhausted and very frustrated. Finally, after nearly an hour, I return and land, heavy (full of fuel).

It has to be something I bumped getting in or out...I recheck everything. I extend the antenna and check the HF e-mail, as it's

---

11. The trailing antenna was kept on a reel on the floor on the co-pilot's side of the plane and was deployed by unreeling it and allowing it to trail behind the plane. The antenna is usually 80 to 100 feet long. The maneuver requires bending over and sideways and reeling it in and out manually with one hand while tightening or loosening a wing nut with the other hand. It's a little awkward but is usually only done once per flight leg.

the only thing I can hear or receive. The gas guy, Tim, puts the antenna on top of a ladder on top of his truck. Reception is VERY weak. I recheck all the cables and plug in the headset directly (rather than though the plane's intercom system). Then, when turning the power on, I must have hit the transmit button, just beneath. I hear static, finally—what a relief. I know immediately that that was the problem.

I gas up again to top off the tanks. Tim gives me a hug (he'd checked up on me every time I was at the plane and we'd talked quite a bit over the past few days) and says "Aloha Nui." I startup, taxi, and take off. I ask to switch to HF and start testing. No reception. I keep climbing and hear some weak voices. As I climb above 3000 feet I can hear pretty well. I call and SF radio calls back clear as a bell! I'm on my way! I can tell you, it's no fun reeling the antenna in and out while climbing and descending.

Hilo departure gives me vectors to an intersection and clearance to American Samoa. If they lose me on VHF, I'm to call San Francisco radio and check in with them. After 100 miles, I hear Air Traffic Control calling on VHF, but they can't hear my response, so I go back to SF radio on HF and call, and call. No response, my heart sinks. I'm going to have to return again. I switch to the secondary frequency they gave me and SF radio comes in loud and clear. Pheww, I can continue on my way. Ok, now I can get down to flying and position reporting.

There are little puffy clouds all around, then I pass over an open area, and then more little puffy clouds. I'm not looking forward to the thunderstorms, but at least they are isolated, unlike last week when the satellite photo looked red all across my route (see color photo). First position report went okay; I check in with the HF friend I met in Kona, Bob, NH6GB, with no luck; the second position report is okay. Then, while getting ready for Ben's net (the sailors' HF east coast network), I lost static again... uuuhhhh.

Again I wiggle all the wires, no static. I call SF radio, and can hear them over the HF speaker, but not through the headset. As Wes, my HF guru in Florida, knows, electrical stuff is not my forté. If wire wiggling doesn't work, I don't have too many options left. After re-wiggling with no luck, I unplug the headset wire from the VHF/HF interface box and plug it directly into the HF transceiver. I have static again. I call SF radio and all is well. They must think I'm a wacko! It's past Ben's net time, so I switch frequencies and listen. I can't hear anything, but I transmit anyway. AH6BR, Scott, in Hawaii, a brother of a friend of my dad's in Virginia, comes up and we chat for a while. He has to go, so we set 3 pm for another chat.

Back to flying and position reporting...decidedly, this is my day for HF problems. But it keeps my mind off other things, like being bored. Just in case you are wondering, pilots out there, yes, I'm checking the gauges and GPS and instruments while all this is going on! Next position report went fine, almost three-and-a-half hours into the flight, only 12 hours to go. Weather still looks good and I've had a 5-knot tailwind so far. Actually, the oil temperature and cylinder head temperature were slightly higher than their normal reading, not surprising with the engine running a higher rpm. I back off the rpm to 2450 and after several minutes, both gauges go down slightly. I don't want to overheat the poor little engine. Maybe I'm more in tune with the engine as the sun is pouring in the left front window and I'm frying. I don't want to fry and I don't want to fry my engine. Only 180 miles to go and I can make a 10-degree left turn and get the sun off my shoulder. Another good position report; I'm regaining confidence that the HF reception problems are behind me. I really, really don't want to turn around from here. SF radio is sounding loud and clear and it's a joy to hear them each hour.

I'm wondering if I'll see the equator marked on the GPS. Guess I'll find out in several hours. Only 10 degrees 50 minutes north of the equator right now. I'm also wondering when to switch the GPS chip from the Americas to the International chip. I downloaded it before leaving. American Samoa is supposed to be on the new chip, but, so far, the old chip is showing that it knows where Pago Pago, American Samoa, is. Ah ha, she says, after playing with the GPS. I can get there on the old chip, but the approaches will be on the new chip. I think I'll wait until I'm pretty close before I change the chip in the GPS. No sense testing it way out in the middle of nowhere.

Ok, lunchtime, what's on the menu today? Turkey sandwich with lettuce and tomatoes, ginger snaps for desert, Cheerios and an apple for snacking. Healthy! And, by the way, that's dinner as well. Just checked the last leg's fuel consumption, 8.2 gallons per hour and 1 quart of oil. Excellent. My speed is down to 142 knots from

150 knots as I turn more to the south from a southwesterly direction and the wind continues from the east. I still have a four-knot tailwind component and I'm happy with that. What I'm not happy with is the heat; I'm roasting in the cockpit. The outside air temperature, at 6000 feet altitude, is 33C (96F). I have silver reflective shields for my windows, when I'm leaving the plane parked outside on a sunny day. I always fold them and put them in the back of the plane before takeoff. Right now I needed them to shield me from the sun. Unfortunately, I couldn't reach them.

One of the e-mails that I received on this leg was from a previous colleague, who was headed to New Zealand on a business trip in economy class. He wasn't complaining about being cramped, he was wishing he could fly with me instead! Sorry, no room. His e-mail makes me think about where I would be working today...if I hadn't lost my job. I'd probably be behind some desk somewhere instead of flying across the Pacific Ocean. I think I'm very lucky to be where I am, in the pilot's seat, blue sky all around, blue sea below, with time to think and enjoy life.

Wow! Land ho! In the middle of the Pacific, 6 hours and 18 minutes out from Hawaii. I can't believe it. I saw waves through the clouds, and then looked closer. It's not on the GPS. Scott, the Ham from Hawaii, had e-mailed me saying that I might pass over Palmyra Atoll, well, he was right. He also said there was an old WWII runway on it, but I couldn't see the whole island nor any runway on the part I could see. I put a waypoint in the GPS just in case I need to swim back!

After the last position report, the nice radio person followed the "roger" with "talk with you in an hour." Actually, it's comforting to have to talk with someone every hour. It reminds me of why I got my ham radio license in the first place. I was sailing, actually in a motor trawler, from the Canary Islands, southwest of Spain, to Dakar, on the west coast of Africa, in Senegal. We were seven days on the ocean. Not a long crossing for real sailors, but a first for me (I was the third person, invited by Jim and Deb to help out with watches/shifts during the crossing). Jim and Deb had been sailing together for many years. I was happy to be with them and helping out; the trip was fun. But what struck me was that we talked with other people only twice a day. The captain, Jim, had an HF radio and called two nets to receive the latest news and to report how we were doing. To me, not used to this life style, it was like a lifeline to the rest of humanity. After the trip was over, I ordered the ham radio books and started studying. My mother already had her General license and my dad had his Novice, so they sent me all the information and tapes to practice Morse code. Four months later I sat for my General license and passed. I haven't used it much, but now on this trip, it feels like a lifeline each hour. Also, talking with other hams, between the position reports, makes the trip and contacts more personal. They can relay information back to friends and family.

I just made it through the first set of clouds. I'd seen some cumulonimbus clouds developing in various quadrants, but none directly ahead. I had low-level clouds and some cumulus up to maybe 12–15,000 feet. I shut everything down and tied everything down, then the rain started. It wasn't bumpy at all. Half an hour later I was through. Not bad. Last week would have been terrible, if I'd even departed. This is the ideal weather, as good as it gets, (or that's what the weatherman said yesterday). The equator wasn't shown on the GPS, no line, and no indication. I watched the latitude count down to zero, switched from north to south, and started increasing.

Eleven hours into the flight, the sun is just starting to set at 6:30 pm American Samoa time. I've been through multiple cloudbanks, nothing serious, just some cumulus and a little rain. Still clear ahead, no towering cumulonimbus clouds, and I haven't seen any hits on the storm scope the whole trip. The tailwind has picked up and I'm running 158–160 knots. Still four hours to go, but it looks smooth. I tried to reach Scott on the HF radio at 3 pm, but there was no answer. I listened and called every hour; at 5 pm we connected and chatted for a while. We agreed to talk again at 8 pm. Scott kept me talking and awake during the last few hours and I'm grateful to him. After the sun and heat of the day, I wasn't feeling too well.

I'm reaching ELLMS intersection; that's a FIR[12] (Flight Information Region) boundary. I'd seen, read, and heard about

---

12. Flight Information Region — point where communication contact changes, usually with country boundaries.

these during my planning, but don't know exactly what's going to happen when I cross it. I assume SF radio will tell me. As I make my normal position report to SF radio, they take the information and ask me to call Auckland radio, on the same frequency. I call but am unable to reach anyone. I return to SF radio. I'm pretty calm, because this time, there's not much I can do but continue to my destination. I finally reach Auckland radio and he takes my position report and asks where I'm going and where I'm from. I was surprised that he didn't already have this information, but I gave it to him anyway. That's it, pretty simple.

It's time to change the GPS chip. It's not reading any more intersections that are on the chart. Obviously I'm beyond the coverage area of the Americas chip that is in the GPS and need the new International chip for all the detailed information normally provided. But I'm a chicken; I'll follow the magenta line on the GPS to Pago Pago. I can figure out the intersections and reporting points manually from my charts, and change the chip when I've safely got VOR or ADF[13] reception.

One hundred miles out and I'm switched to VHF and told to contact Faleolo approach. I don't have a clue what "Faleolo approach" is, but call anyway. A strong Samoan accent responds. After several repeats, I finally understand what he's saying—to continue to Pago Pago, and asking which approach I would like to use. I put in the new chip and load the approaches. Although there's an ILS[14] in the approach book, the GPS only has two VOR DME[15] arc approaches in the database. Oh well, I load the one arriving from the north, as the wind is light and variable. From reading the Pacific Chart Supplement information, I know there are some mountain peaks, towers, and cables across the bay, so I watch the altitudes very carefully and descend slowly. Finally I'm down, 15 hours and 12 minutes of flying. Time to find GA[16] parking and a hotel! I'm exhausted. The heat in the cabin over the equator really took its toll on me.

---

13. ADF — Automatic Direction Finder — an older, less accurate but more reliable, type of navigation equipment. Also more widely used outside of the US.
14. ILS — Instrument Landing System approach — a precision approach, usually down to 200 feet above the runway. This is the most precise approach a general aviation pilot can make.
15. VOR DME — less precise approaches, usually down to 600 feet above the runway with less precise lateral guidance.
16. GA — General Aviation, small private and business flying as opposed to commercial airline flights.

But it's not that easy when entering another country. I entered the building and found someone willing to tell me where to park the plane. There were no other small planes on the ramp. We pushed the Mooney back off to one side and chocked the wheels. He led me to customs and immigration. After checking my passport, they wanted some paperwork from when I departed Hilo. I didn't have it. I was exhausted. I had my head on my arms leaning on their counter and asked if we could complete this in the morning. Thankfully, they took pity on me, ordered me a cab and called the local hotel.

I fell asleep as soon as my head hit the pillow.

Two days in American Samoa

After a good night's sleep, I went to check on Customs, landing fees, fueling, weather, etc. If I wanted to leave tomorrow, I had a lot to do today. Actually I wanted a local breakfast first...there was none. It was recommended that I eat at McDonalds, down the street. I don't even eat at McDonalds in the US. But, I was starving, so Egg McMuffin it was.

The customs people were the same as were there the previous night. They had had two hours of overtime for a cargo plane that arrived just after me. They relieved me of $50 but waived the overtime charge (that was very nice) and explained that it covered the landing and departure fees also. I still didn't have the departure form from Hilo that they were looking for, but it didn't seem that important to them. Overall, not too bad; next stop fuel.

I walked around and found a Polynesian Airlines pilot named Wade. He was fascinated with my trip but didn't know where to get gas. He suggested visiting the tower for weather information. I hadn't thought of that—thanks, Wade. Next stop, any open office to find out about gas. The first one did it; I think it was Samoan Air. The woman manager called several places, then said that the fueler would meet me at my plane. What service!

I walked to the tower, not really thinking that I'd get in. But Frank, the tower controller, was very kind, answered all my questions, showed me where the weather office was (just below the tower) and told me it was open 24 hours a day. We talked and he reminded me about filing my flight plan early because of advising the next countries' controllers. I retrieved all my charts and flight plan materials from the plane and returned to the tower. We pored over the details, and then filed it directly through his computer. The Tonga controller called to confirm my flight and arrival in his sector.

He shared with me the information he'd received about my arrival the previous day, even though he knew I'd arrive after the tower closed. What looked like an old Teletype page, now done by computer, had the positions of the planes coming his way. It showed my original departure at 1616z,[17] when I first left Hilo. It showed my arrival at Laker, the Pago TCA/FIR,[18] and advised HF communication at that point (a little difficult as Pago doesn't have HF). He and his boss, Greg, gave me a lot of insight as to how communications work between the various Air Traffic Controllers in the different countries in the Pacific. I also learned that Faleolo was the name of Samoa's approach control (similar to Chicago or Orlando for us). I also learned that I'd be speaking with Fua Amotu on the next leg. It helped me enormously to know the details behind a flight plan and HF position reports, as well as local reporting station names. I sincerely appreciated their time and help. I felt better now about crossing FIR boundaries and communicating position reports. By the way, Frank is also an old Mooney pilot, so we chatted about Mooney flying as well. He's been working the Pago Pago tower for 3 years.

I visited the weather office and they let me look at all their computer charts, as well as access charts through the Internet that I'd been looking at from the US. I hadn't looked forward to heading out without a briefing. The last satellite chart I had seen showed two major lows in the area. I was told they were cyclones but that I could pass between them after the first goes by. The newer charts showed that this was a distinct possibility. As this facility is open 24 hours a day, I'll return again this evening and Thursday morning before takeoff.

---

17. 1616z — 6:16 am Hawaii time in Universal Coordinated Time (UTC) used by all aircraft worldwide. Based on the standard time at the zero meridian in Greenwich, England.
18. TCA/FIR — Terminal Control Area/Flight Information Region — both boundaries are at the same point.

With a day off, it was time to visit a little. Frank had suggested taking the bus around, only 50 cents. I walked a little, and then took a bus through a few towns. I'd seen school kids everywhere in various school uniforms. A teacher sat next to me and we talked for a while. There's a big push on education and every child goes to school. Most families speak English at home now, although older people still only speak their native language. I met two schoolgirls who were seniors. Both are planning on continuing on to college.

The trip by bus along the seashore was beautiful. The buses, by the way, were fascinating. Each was different, with different colors (see color photo), interior decorated with cloth, fur, carpets, etc., and all had extremely LOUD music. You just tapped on the roof or back of the seat when you wanted to get off. I had a couple of hours of island tour for $2, not a bad afternoon. The dash is covered with a carpet; when you get off, you toss your 50 cents or $1 on the carpet and step out. If you need change, you put down the $1 and pick up your change. The seats are hard, but they are up high, so you get a good view of everything around. I had fun.

The next morning I'm up at 5 am and off to the weather station. Yes, there's a big gap between the two cyclones; the first is moving at 25 knots and the second at 12 knots, so the gap is widening. But the headwinds are 40–45 knots for the start of my trip and stay at 30-35 knots all the way down to New Zealand. Looks like I'll need to wait a little longer. The cyclones rotate clockwise down in the southern hemisphere, which takes a little getting used to. As the first one is passing, I'll have headwinds behind it, but tailwinds as the second approaches. Timing of this leg is critical if I want an 11-hour trip instead of another 15-hour leg.

Although all went well in the weather office the first few times, I was denied access later the second day. After my delayed departure, due to the headwinds, I had wanted another update on the cyclones and winds. Although they apologized profusely, I was not allowed to look at the weather information, nor would the weatherman give me a briefing. They had been told that it was an FAA responsibility, not the weather service job. This was the same problem that I'd had in Hawaii. A Catch-22 situation in Hawaii and in American Samoa, it appears.

The weather in American Samoa is very hot and humid. It rains often, very similar to weather in Hawaii, but it feels more humid, if that's possible. The hotels, however, are not on the same level as Hawaii. I'm paying twice the price I paid on Hilo, $79 per night in American Samoa, for a room about a third the value. Although I have international TV, with BBC and CNN, there is mold everywhere, the towels are exceedingly thin and there are no other amenities. Each day I try to negotiate for a better rate, but no deal.

While it was raining outside and I was waiting for the cyclones to advance and the winds to diminish I watched BBC World News in my hotel room. An Italian football (soccer) team is being investigated for drugs and their relationship to an unusually high rate of Lou Gehrig's disease among its players. Over the past 30 years, 32 team members have come down with ALS, Lou Gehrig's disease, which is more than coincidental. Doctors are investigating the link between drugs and the disease.

As I talk with people on this trip, I'm still amazed at how many know someone who has or had ALS. The Head Bellman, Allan, at one hotel in Hilo, had a friend who had died of ALS. When I met some whale surveyors at Hilo airport, as soon as I said ALS, they said Lou Gehrig's disease and knew how devastating it is. I'll meet with different groups as I travel, especially in Europe and Canada, to help promote awareness of ALS/Lou Gehrig's disease, and also to solicit donations for the ALS Therapy Development Foundation that is researching a cure for this terminal disease.

But for now, I have to make it to New Zealand.

CHAPTER 4

Having stumbled across your website, and enjoyed following your progress so far — I just wanted to send my best wishes and wish you the best of luck for the rest of your journey.

Your logs are a real inspiration. I'm a only a new PPL living in the United Kingdom (having trained in San Diego) with just 50 hrs total time. However, you have me hooked on the idea of a round the world trip — what an achievement it would be!

Anyway take care, and I look forward to reading about your further adventures on your website...
Shane

March 14–15: Pago Pago to Auckland, New Zealand, 4th leg flight report

I'm on my way again—after another difficult morning. I guess I should expect problems and I'll probably have even more in other countries, as I don't know all the rules and paperwork requirements.

I got up early, walked to the airport, and the nice night weatherman let me use his equipment—he was sleeping on the floor and moved outside to smoke a cigarette while I looked at the weather. The winds are 10 to 15 knots from the west, much better than yesterday. The first cyclone has passed and the second looks bigger, but still off to the northwest of New Zealand. Auckland forecast is for clearing by my arrival time. Time to get the plane ready.

As I head outside, it starts pouring rain. I decide to do the customs paperwork first. When I'd passed by the offices, all the lights were off and the doors locked, even though I'd been told the day before that someone would be there. A security guard found me, assured me that someone would be there, and knocked on the door. We heard rustling, and the customs person came to the door. I explained that the previous customs person had told me to come here to get my paper stamped prior to leaving. I showed him the paper (it was the receipt from arrival). He said that was the wrong form and that I needed a customs declaration form to be stamped before leaving. I said that I didn't have one, I wasn't a company, and I was a private plane. Despite much discussion, he wouldn't accept anything but the proper form, which he told me to get from Samoan Air. I trotted over to Samoan Air and finally found a pilot, Carrie, who took me into the office and printed me a blank form. Carrie is an American pilot flying for Samoan Air; I thanked him profusely and he wished me well.

Back to customs—he was smiling when he saw that I had the right paper and was happy to stamp the form and wish me a good flight. He was amazed that it would take 11 hours and hoped I wouldn't get too tired.

It had stopped raining; time for load, preflight and startup. I called Amy and Ella in the tower (I had met them the previous day also) and they got my clearance and let me start taxiing. They gave me the HF frequencies and I took off with a very slow climb. They asked if I had stopped by the tower this morning; I explained that I had received the weather report, therefore didn't stop by. It was unfortunate because they had prepared a "care" package for me. Now I was sorry that the weatherman had let me in. I was a little short of food for this flight. Thanks, Amy and Ella!

There were isolated storm clouds all around and some cloud-to-cloud lightning, but nothing on the storm scope. As I was climbing through 1000 feet, the engine coughed. I gulped, but it caught and I kept going. A few minutes later there was some serious coughing and spluttering. I turned around and headed back to Pago Pago. I called Ella and Amy and told them I was going to head back and continue climbing, that the engine was coughing a little, and I wanted to be closer to land while I climbed. They okayed the maneuver. I climbed to my enroute altitude of 6,000 feet while circling the airport. I could have landed and looked into things, but probably wouldn't have found the problem. As long as the coughing stopped while I was climbing over Pago Pago, I felt it was safe to continue the flight. I called Amy and Ella when I was outbound again. They wished me a good flight.

Communicating position through Faleolo (Samoa) approach went sort-of okay, after talking with Auckland radio, a Polynesian flight doing a relay, and Pago approach again. Everyone wanted to know where I was. When I was switched to Fua Amotu (Tonga), that was more difficult due to interference on the HF, but we talked, so I continued. I wasn't sure they received my next position report, so I reported through Auckland also. Auckland sent me back to Fua

Amotu (Tonga). I'd learned from Frank and Greg that New Zealand was the "big dog" in this airspace. So I figured if they knew where I was, I was okay.

I had about a 9-knot headwind at the start, which increased to a 20-knot headwind after two hours. I wasn't too worried; it should reduce, and then become a tailwind. Even if it didn't, I had enough gas to make it—I just wasn't looking forward to another 15-hour flight. The sun came up and beat in through the pilot's window. I put up my silver reflective sunscreen (that I'd kept up front with me) and sat happy and cool this time—I wasn't going to fry a second time.

It IS a BIG ocean. Tonga is still 183 miles away even after 2 hours and 40 minutes flying. The islands are quite far apart. I just calculated the last leg's fuel consumption at 8.23gal/hr and I'd used 2 quarts of oil. That was right on track, as planned. Because I'd used 2 quarts and only had one extra with me, I had to leave one quart low. This concerned me slightly; at least it stayed in the back of my mind. Unfortunately, although they had aviation gas at Pago Pago, they didn't have any piston oil, only jet oil, and I was only carrying one quart spare. Think I'll carry two quarts from now on.

Communication has gone from position reports once an hour to talking at specific times on specific frequencies, I don't know if it's just me or if that's how they do it in Tonga airspace; anyway, it seems to be working.

I don't know why, but I can't relax on this leg. The headwinds are up to 30 knots and I'm just feeling "jumpy" about everything. I have a knot in my stomach. All the gauges and instruments are okay. Hopefully I'll settle down. Having the left window covered from the sun makes me a little claustrophobic (like my mother always was), so I keep looking out the right window. If the winds keep up at this rate, I'll still make it in 11 more hours. I'll make that decision over Tonga. Even the seat doesn't feel good. Many people have asked me if my butt gets tired during these trips. I had never had any trouble with "saddle soreness" during my previous, short, 4- and 6-hour trips. And, happily, I can say that I had absolutely no discomfort on the first three legs of this adventure. The seat is extremely comfortable. I think it's my general unease that's also being felt other places today.

But it's a beautiful sunny day, very few puffy clouds; let's breathe deeply and enjoy the trip. I think I can spy the first island of Tonga ahead. The water seems to be turning a lighter shade of blue. Yep, click, first photo.

As I approach Tonga, I start talking with them on VHF and tracking inbound on their VOR. Looks like I won't get a picture as there is a cloud layer just below me. The airspeed is sneaking up— 113, 115, now it's 117 knots. I think I'll be getting out of the headwinds and hope to be catching tailwinds as I approach the next cyclone. Not TOO close, mind you.

South of Tonga, the airspeed is up to 120 knots and I'm only 250 nautical miles from Auckland airspace. I feel good, finally. Only 9 hours to go. As I was tracking inbound to Tonga, a Beach, N500MK, heard my transmission and called to say hi. He was headed to another island and thought I was stopping at Tonga. Unfortunately, his second communication radio wasn't working, so we couldn't chat on 123.45 (frequency often used for plane-to-plane communication). But it was nice to hear a friendly voice. I tried the HF nets this morning and thought I heard someone on Ben's net, but my reception was very weak. It would have been nice to chat. I couldn't pick up Scott in Hawaii either. Nor could I connect to send e-mail. Oh well, a day without much contact. I should be able to reach Sydney HF stations to transmit e-mail, as I get closer.

I thought I'd lose a day when I crossed the International Date Line in a few hours. But the time zone zigzags east of the 180 degree parallel to 172 degrees 30 minutes. So it's already tomorrow! Time to change my watch. I've been in the clouds a lot this leg. The tops are just above me at about 6,100 feet and I'm at 6,000. Actually, it's cooler out of the sun, so I'll stay here. When I do come out, there isn't much to see except other cloud layers all around. At least there are no thunderheads anywhere. The wind is now off my right side at about 10 knots, but neutral to me. I'm up to 141 knots with only 5 ½ hours to go. I just switched to the front tank and it's beginning to feel like a short trip. I don't even jump any more when my noise-canceling headset clicks off—as it just did!

Feeling good, I'm up to 150 knots and the wind has swung around to the northwest, just as forecast. I'm at 27 degrees south latitude and the cyclone center was at 26 degrees south (but well off to the west) 10 hours ago. As I continue south, the tailwinds should increase. I'm up to 160 knots now, and smiling.

The clouds start to get thicker and it's raining. It reminds me of our trip to Alaska and when we couldn't cross the Rockies due to clouds and icing, we returned to Ft. Nelson through two hours of this stuff. This seems to be in waves, or so I thought, so maybe I'll come out from time to time. Two good things about it: it keeps the plane clean, and at 20 degrees C there's no icing. I tried climbing to 8,000 feet, but I'm still in it. A couple of hours later, my stomach is in a knot, I'm still in rain, and it's very heavy at times and bumpy. I'm not comfortable and I'm getting worried. Less than 3 hours to go and landing in daylight are the only thoughts that comfort me.

The tailwind had me up to 180 knots at times, but I'm back down to 150, so I must be further south of the cyclone now. I keep thinking that it seems lighter on the horizon, but the clear air never arrives... Now it really does look like it's clearing ahead. I see a layer of clouds below and some layers above; I'm not in solid cloud any more. I can even see water below. I'm still in a very light rain shower, but smooth air. As I'm traveling further south, it's actually getting cooler; I just closed the air vents! It's quite different from the last leg across the equator, where I roasted. The outside air temperature is down to 5 degrees C. Only two hours out, I'll be switching to VHF in half an hour. I haven't been able to contact anyone by HF this trip, unfortunately, it's been pretty lonely.

And there she is, New Zealand. I spy the islands off the northeast coast. It's been a long two weeks, but now it's worth it. The planning was GREAT, the flying was very good (with a few frustrations and worries) and landing in Auckland is terrific.

After landing, I was directed to the apron and parked in slot 83, right in the middle of the "big boys." As I was taxiing, the ground controller actually told a United 747 to wait for me to pass. I was dumbfounded. While I was stuck inside the cabin for 5 minutes decontamination, I took pictures of the Air New Zealand 727 next to me. I wanted to kiss the ground when I got out, but resisted the urge. The customs people were already waiting for me. We unloaded my luggage and took it inside to be x-rayed. I was stamped in by immigration (as crew), paid my landing fee, and saw my plane listed on the arrivals screen. I was IT001, which I learned is what they use for non-scheduled traffic. We are called itinerant aircraft, thus the IT. At least they listed me as "on time."

Before leaving Florida, I had made contact with Max, a colleague from my previous work life, who lives in Auckland. He's a pilot and we'd talked non-stop flying when we met a year previously. I advised him that I'd probably be tired and would spend the

Parked next to a Boeing 747 in Auckland

night in Auckland prior to flying to his strip, Ardmore Aerodrome,
only a few minutes away. However, I was ecstatic and found my
second wind. So I loaded up the plane and asked for clearance to fly
VFR[19] to Ardmore. Ground and tower cleared me. It was early
evening, but still light enough to see everything. I plugged Ardmore
into my GPS and it was only a 10-minute hop away. I saw the
runway, circled looking for the windsock, and landed into the wind.

From above, I saw lots of hangars and buildings. Where was I to
go? How would I ever find Max? As it was evening, many places
were already closed, and I didn't see anyone around. I finally taxied
towards one building and shut down the engine. I got out and
walked around. I saw people in the building next door and walked
over to talk with them. They said that I was welcome to park on
their ramp and that we'd call Max after I was tied down. As I headed
back to the plane, I heard my name called. There was Max.
Somehow, he'd seen me and driven over to where I had taxied. He
gave me a big bear hug welcome to New Zealand. I later learned
that we'd missed each other by two minutes at Auckland. He'd
come looking for me, had seen my plane, and had gone into the
building. When he came out, I was gone. We had a wonderful
evening catching up.

---

19.   VFR — visual flight rules. Flying clear of clouds with reference to the horizon
      and visual indicators outside the plane.

CHAPTER 5

Just had a chance to read up on your website. WOW. Pretty cool, girl.
Keep it up and I think it is wonderful what you are doing. Not many would
attempt to fly around the world in a single engine aircraft. I started
flying about the same time you did, the late sixties, early seventies, but
never got past single engine instrument rating. I later lost interest and
much later, never seemed to have the time.

Have a great flight. I'll keep reading. Good luck.
Robert

Flying around New Zealand

What a beautiful country from the air. It reminds me of England, so lush and green. The small islands you see when arriving from the northeast have rolling hills and sandy beaches. They look very appealing.

There are significant differences in the VFR charts and procedures between the US and NZ. Luckily, Max sat down with me for about two hours going through the specifics of NZ charts and airport operations. They have MBZ areas outlined by blue diamonds. These are Mandatory Broadcast Zones. You need to broadcast your position, altitude, and intentions in these areas. If there are specific reporting points, you must report over those, otherwise every 5 to 10 minutes; or if you hear another plane, you must advise your location. The Delta airspace is more often an oblong shape covering the runway directions rather than a circle as in the US.

There is a Visual Flight Guide in NZ that contains all the airport information, details of each airport operation, arrival and departure routes, communications, runways, and services. It's very complete and very necessary for flying around NZ. The NZ charts do not include communications frequencies or airport altitudes. Correction: the new charts just came out this week, with significant changes, including communication frequencies and airport elevations. I sincerely appreciated Max's time and information, without which I would probably have broken a few flying rules in New Zealand airspace. Luckily, I'll be meeting a flying friend when I arrive in Australia, and will definitely spend some time learning their rules before venturing too far on my own.

Although I'd put over 50 hours in my logbook and on the Mooney, I really hadn't done much flying. The autopilot had handled all the enroute flying and I'd only done six takeoffs and landings in the past two weeks. So we took the right tank out of the plane, put the seat back in its rightful position (instead of traveling in the luggage compartment), and Max and I took off to do some approaches into Auckland. We'd called ahead of time and they approved the instrument practice. They were a little busy, so we stayed out of their airspace with me under the hood and Max giving me headings, altitudes, and turns. He really put me through my paces. Finally they had less traffic and gave me vectors for the first approach. We did a total of three. I got the practice I needed and Max had a great view of the city. He said that he never gets to fly over the city normally and this gave him a great opportunity to see things up close.

My first VFR flight in NZ was from Ardmore Aerodrome, just SE of Auckland, to Whangarei, about 80 nautical miles northwest. I had already learned that Ardmore was New Zealand's busiest Aerodrome, and uncontrolled at that. The Sunday after I arrived, Max, Anna, and I went out to do some work on the Mooney and were impressed by the display of aircraft out for a Sunday afternoon flight. We saw a deHaviland Dove, T-6, T-28, Stearman, Pitts Special, Extra 300, PBY Catalina, Tiger Moth, a French jet trainer, along with the many training Cessnas, Pipers, and others. It was extremely busy. I was surprised on the Monday afternoon I went to leave for

Max and Anna with Bobbie their dog

Whangarei; the pattern was still very busy. I checked and rechecked everything, then sat at the end of the taxiway waiting for a gap to allow me to depart.

The flight north to Whangarei was beautiful. I could have snapped 100 pictures, but they still wouldn't have captured the beauty of the rolling green hills and scalloped cream beaches. I made my reports in the MBZ, landed without trouble at Whangarei, and taxied to the local Aero Club. There's an Aero Club on just about every airport that acts as FBO and club/bar/social meeting place. They all seem to have helpful and friendly people.

After spending a day with my Aunt preparing for my dad's visit, I returned to the Whangarei airport. I needed to do an oil change and this was a nice, quiet place. The Aero Club instructors recommended that I see the Airport Manager, who had a maintenance facility next door. Mike Chubb welcomed me, listened to my story, accepted my payment for landing and parking, and happily let me change my oil in front of his maintenance hangar. He and his crew lent me a bucket and plenty of rags. Also, it was close to 100 hours since my annual inspection had been completed three months ago. My Mooney has one AD[20] (Aircraft Directive) that recurs every 100 hours and needs to be signed off by an appropriately certified person. After reading the wording on the AD, he realized that it was the same as their requirement in NZ. His chief mechanic checked out the AD, looked over my engine, and said that everything looked to be in good shape. He signed my logbook, and I enjoyed a nice cup of tea while chatting with the group.

The return trip was almost uneventful. I couldn't believe it; on final approach into Ardmore I was alongside a Tiger Moth landing on the parallel grass strip! I wish I could have taken a picture. It was amazing to look out and see an old biplane beside me. There are actually five of them based at Ardmore, and they fly regularly on weekends.

In an effort to obtain a little media coverage for my trip and donations for ALS, I'd contacted several US flying magazines prior to my departure. However, since I was slightly "phobic" about the

---

20. Aircraft Directive — mandatory inspection point on an airplane. Must be signed off in the logbook by a appropriately certified person, which can sometimes be the pilot.

Pacific, I'd asked them not to publish anything until mid-March at the earliest, at which time I'd be across the Pacific. While in Auckland, I started receiving e-mails from pilots, ALS families, and ALS patients themselves, many related to pilots or flying in some way. Some pilots told me that I was "living their dream." Others were from Singapore, South Africa, Belgium, Greenland, Nova Scotia, and other locations where I would be traveling. Many of them invited me to their homes and sent me information to help with arrival at their local airports. The support and helpful invitations were unimaginable. The ALS families told me their difficult stories, usually shared their passion for flying, and gave me support and best wishes for my continued journey. The outpouring was overwhelming. From this point on, helpful e-mails, from people I'd never met, continued to arrive throughout my trip.

The following day I flew with Anna, Max's wife, to Tauranga, an hour southeast of Auckland. The beaches are immaculate and there is one "mountain" at the harbor entrance, sticking up 800 feet. Before landing at Tauranga, we flew around Rotorua and the remains of Tarawera Volcano. When the volcano erupted, it burst wide open and is now a small jagged crater.

After staying with Anna, her daughter, and her sister for one night, I flew south down the North Island, past Lake Taupo, Mt. Ngauruhoe, and Mt. Ruapehu, over barren mountains to Wellington and across the straits to the Marlborough Sound, and on to Nelson on the northern tip of the South Island.

It was a magnificent flight and I couldn't stop taking pictures. The Marlborough sound has land peaks sticking out of the water— some large and inhabited, many small, tree-covered with no habitation. Some barren. The water was blue, blue/green, turquoise, and always different depending on the sunlight, depth, and shadows. So much changing terrain in such a short distance was amazing; only three hours of flying and I'd covered snow-capped peaks, volcanoes, lakes, barren mountains, farm land, and beaches.

I found the NZ tower controllers exceedingly precise with VFR traffic, much as the US controllers are with IFR traffic. The pilot is expected to read back every instruction. If you don't, you are reminded, usually politely. When you report receiving the ATIS (air traffic information system, a recording giving local weather and airport information), you also report the QNH (pressure in heco-pascals or millibars). The Visual Flight Guide gives you VFR approach and departure information. It's good to be familiar with this prior to arrival because each tower gave me arrival instructions per the VFG. Not knowing a location was not an excuse, as it is written in the Guide and on the chart. I found Pepin Island without a problem and reported it to Nelson Tower, who then cleared me to continue and join downwind for runway 02. "Joining" is the term used here for "inbound for landing." "Circuit" is used for "pattern," and "line up" for "position and hold."

The winemaking region is on northeastern coast of the South Island and the Marlborough region is known for excellent Sauvignon Blanc. So I had to do some taste testing. I went to a little town called Mapua just west of Nelson. There was a wine store/restaurant that had wine-tasting from the local wineries. I enjoyed a selection of several wines with a cheese plate and bought bottles of the wines I preferred. They were some of the fruitiest white wines I'd tasted, without being too sweet. They were most enjoyable.

As it turned out, today was the start of the Gulf War, so I tasted wine while watching CNN and BBC coverage of the initial bombings of Baghdad. I felt that I was about as far away as anyone could get from the war. However, I'd be flying closer as my voyage continued.

The next morning, the instructors at Nelson Aero Club, Marc and Craig, gave me recommendations for VFR flying in their area to get the best sites. It was magnificent; but I think I've used that term before. The seashores and bays were mostly uninhabited and natural. On the west coast, the mountains were untouched. I climbed to 7500 feet and flew over them on my way northeast. I flew past Nelson and the Marlborough Sound again, then across the strait to the North Island and on up to Tauranga. What a country!

I had been contacted by a young girl named Amelia, who had seen my web site, was interested in aviation, and wondered if I would be stopping by Tauranga when I was in NZ. I told her when and where we could meet. I met 15-year-old Amelia and her dad at the Tauranga airport and took her flying. She had a great time. I did, too. I always enjoy the enthusiasm of the kids and young folk that I'm able to take flying. Her dad is going to start taking lessons and probably Amelia will, too. I then picked up Anna and we returned

First Young Eagle in New Zealand, Amelia

to Ardmore. Although Amelia was my first New Zealand Young Eagle, during my time at Ardmore, I was able to take up three other youngsters and give them an introduction to aviation.

Speaking the lingo and understanding what's been said is not always easy. North of Auckland there's a VOR, Whenuapai. I'm sure no-one understood me when I tried to pronounce it as spelled; and I didn't understand when they talked about "Fen-oo-a-pie." I always had to think before saying Whangarei as it's pronounced Wong-ga-ray or Fong-ga-ray. I'd include my full registration, N220FC, when first contacting Air Traffic Control. That way, they knew they were dealing with an American plane and pilot, new to the area. I'd get shortened to NFC, November-Foxtrot-Charlie, after the first exchange. They use ZK as the international prefix in New Zealand (the same as US plane registrations start with the prefix N); but usually use only the last three registration letters in Air Traffic Control calls. So, NFC fit the NZ system well and I finally got used to saying NFC instead of zero-Foxtrot-Charlie.

Max had contacted the *New Zealand Herald* to tell them about my flight. The day after I arrived, I met the journalist, Rebecca Walsh, at the airport and she wrote a wonderful story about my flight for ALS. A number of pilots contacted me following that story. One couple, Sue and Richard Campbell—Mooney pilots, owners, and enthusiasts—invited me to visit North Shore Aerodrome, just north of Auckland. I was nervous about my landing because I saw people standing around the club house balcony, and my last few landings at Ardmore hadn't been that great. After too many 10,000-

foot runways, these narrow 3,000-foot runways were making me work at my patterns and landing precision again. But I got lucky and this landing was a good one. I was welcomed over the radio and asked to taxi to the clubhouse. There were people everywhere. I felt honored. Many were students and instructors who were headed out for lessons, but had waited for my arrival. After the hellos and a look and the plane, tanks, HF setup, etc., they headed out to train. A small group of us went upstairs to talk and eat Sue's delicious muffins.

There were new and experienced women pilots along with Dee, an instructor, judge of the London-Sydney air race, and Air New Zealand pilot. I'd actually met Dee a few days earlier at Ardmore where she also instructs. Most of their questions were requesting elaboration and more details of some of the more nervous moments I'd written about. They were also interested in how I stayed awake and if I took naps or not. I didn't. Sue and Richard have flown their Mooney to Australia (all the way to Perth) two times and are planning another trip next year. They were exceedingly helpful with how to cross the Tasman Sea, where to stop and stay, and what to do. They also lent me their Australian VFR charts to get me started over there. We went to their hangar and they showed me their completely rebuilt Mooney 201. It's a beauty. They had to completely disassemble and rebuild every part.

Richard and Sue with their rebuilt Mooney

What a job, but what a great result. This is their fourth Mooney, and they've enjoyed each one.

I had a full afternoon of talking and learning about NZ aviation and flying in Australia. It was fun and ended too soon. The aviation family has been very open and extremely helpful to me in Auckland and all around NZ; and it's been a pleasure to meet so many women pilots.

My dad arrived in Auckland the following Monday. To keep him awake, in order to get over jet lag, we visited the planes at Ardmore Aerodrome. We found a Hawker Fury and a deHaviland Dove, as well as a DC3. Dad had flown in a Dove on business when he worked for David Brown Tractors in Meltham, England, in the 1950's. After a day's rest, we said a fond farewell to Max and Anna, and took off for Whangarei. We did a big loop around Auckland first, to see the hills and sheep farms to the south and the rugged west coast. We then took the VFR corridor across Auckland, and started to fly up the east coast. All went well until we were half an hour north. The weather moved in quicker and lower than forecast. Although we were only 25 miles from Whangarei, we couldn't get through. We turned around, landed, filed an IFR flight plan, and took off again. Now the landscape looked even more like England with clouds and rain over the green hills and valleys. We finally made it to Whangarei, took a cab to the hotel, and reunited Dad and Liz for only the second time in 50 years.

While we were in Whangarei, it "bucketed down" for three days with howling winds. Low clouds, mist, rain, green rolling hills, JUST like England. My Mooney was tied down outside and I wasn't sleeping well each time I heard the heavy rain pounding down. Mike Chubb of Northland Aviation offered to put the Mooney in his hangar, and he, Mike, Jason, and Rowan pushed it in. Thanks guys! I finally got a good night's sleep!

Brother and sister, Dick and Liz Garratt, reunited for only the second time in 50 years

Dad and Liz talked non-stop for two-and-a-half days, and then we went driving the third and fourth day, just to get out and see a little. It's a beautiful area; and we drove to the farm where Liz and her husband raised their children when they first moved from England to New Zealand after World War II. The waterfalls and the Whangarei Heads are attractions to see when visiting the area, so we toured all around.

The low pressure moved to the south and the sun came out on the fourth day. Dad finally felt warm and was looking forward to seeing more of New Zealand. After a heartfelt goodbye, Dad and I left Liz in Whangarei, and flew up to Keri Keri and the Bay of Islands region. As the name indicates, there are small islands off the shore in the bay. It's a great sailing area; but then, so is most of New Zealand.

We met Liz's son Richard and his wife, Helen. I'd met them once before when I'd traveled to New Zealand in 1990, but Dad had never met his nephew. We toured around Keri Keri for two days and enjoyed their stories of life in NZ and their trips to Australia. Then it was time for us to move on.

Dad in front of the volcanoes on Lord Howe Island

CHAPTER 6

March 31–April 1: Keri Keri to Norfolk Island to Lord Howe Island to Sydney, 5th leg flight report

As I spoke with pilots in New Zealand about crossing the Tasman Sea to Sydney, without exception they told me to visit the islands along the way instead of crossing in one hop. There are two islands between New Zealand and Australia: Norfolk Island is 481 nautical miles north west of the North Island of NZ, and Lord Howe Island is 484 nm to the southwest of Norfolk. Then Sydney is only 425 nm southwest of Lord Howe Island. Three hops of 3 ½ to 4 hours with one overnight stay, instead of one long 10-hour flight. Dad and I decided that this would be much more fun.

Monday morning, after a delightful weekend with Richard and Helen in Keri Keri, it was time to get the flight plan filed and get ready. This was my first international flight plan from a foreign country by myself. Each previous trip I'd had local help from an aero club, pilot, instructor, or a meteorological office next door. From the hotel I called for a weather briefing in Wellington. The person said that he'd need several hours to prepare such a meteorological report, and it would cost $25, and if I could give him a MasterCard number he'd start the preparation. I said I'd call back. I'd already watched the weather for the last several days, the low was moving to the south, a high was moving from Sydney to the east and there was a high further to the north. It certainly didn't take much more to know that the weather was okay. I called the Norfolk airport manager to advise him of our arrival (they needed to notify customs and refueling) and asked for the current weather and forecast. This confirmed scattered clouds and variable winds. I faxed my flight plan and received the return fax confirmation. Richard and Helen drove us to the airport to gas up.

There was a broken layer of clouds at 2500 feet, although that thinned out to scattered as we moved north. Since I only had 100 gallons in the wing tanks, the takeoff from the 3500 foot runway was not over gross and proceeded normally. We flew northwest directly over the North Island to the tip of NZ (see color photo). Along the west coast is a 90-mile-long beach that looked like an untouched strip of orange sand from the air. I'd not had a good night's sleep in anticipation of this leg and I had a knot in my stomach that wouldn't relax.

I'd hooked up the HF radio again, and it was located under Dad's knees in front of his seat. That made it a little difficult for an 81-year-old to get in and out, but Dad got better at it with each entrance and exit. I had to reach around his knees and under his legs to set the frequency and reach the volume knob. It was a sunny day with a broken cloud layer. After half an hour, we were over the northern tip of NZ. I asked Dad if he was okay to continue. He replied, "Okay to continue." The knot in the pit of my stomach wasn't for the flight; I was worried about Dad. It's one thing to do a trip like this alone, it's quite another to be responsible for another person. Dad had a life vest on, just in case. We certainly didn't need to be fiddling with that if anything happened. I told myself that I couldn't hold my breath for three hours, therefore I should try to breathe and relax. It still didn't work. I was uptight for the first half of the flight.

As I'd seen before, there were waves of cumulus clouds with clear areas in between. No towering cumulus, no storms, and only 12- to 15-knot headwinds, as anticipated. The HF communications with Auckland proceeded hourly without a hitch. It should have been a comfortable ride, but it wasn't.

Finally, about 100 miles out from Norfolk Island I began to feel better. From 60 miles out I could see the island and cancelled the flight plan. Auckland prefers them to be cancelled once you are on the ground; however, I explained that I had a trailing antenna and wouldn't be able to report by HF from the ground, so they cancelled in the air. I was already in contact with Norfolk unicom and proceeded inbound. I reported every 10 miles with distance, altitude, and arrival time. Not that anyone else was on the air; but that's the procedure. The airport manager would respond each time with a double click of the transmitter.

The island looked majestic sitting out there with a crown of clouds over it. There was a smaller uninhabited red rock to the southwest and the main island had one large hill and lots of trees. The runways are HUGE and very well kept. I taxied a long way to the terminal building and gas pumps. The customs people arrived and handed me a decontamination aerosol through the window. I closed up, sprayed, and waited for 2 minutes. This was the same procedure as in Auckland except for the shorter waiting period.

After that we moved into the customs office to complete the paperwork while the refueler gassed up the tanks. He'd asked ahead of time if I had Australian dollars and was disappointed when I said not yet. He agreed to meet me the following morning for payment. I found everyone to be as nice as that throughout the stay. The customs people, after completing the paperwork, called the hotels and stayed with me until I'd found one that had a vacancy and would come and pick us up. Even though I was the only customer in the terminal, they ensured that everything was ok before leaving. Even the janitor showed me where to go, what to do, and who to call if I needed to return to the plane. This was customer service at its best, and it continued everywhere on the island.

The hotel room came with a car and we drove to the old penal colony—the major attraction that we'd wanted to see. It was well maintained in typical colonial style. If the prisoners had been able to look over the walls, they'd have had a magnificent view of the beach. I didn't have time to go swimming, but was tempted. We drove up the hills to the other side of the island; there is a small jetty on each side, but no deep water for large ships to dock. The island was immaculate, not one piece of paper or rubbish anywhere. The town was very touristy, not my cup of tea, but driving around was interesting.

I drove to the meteorological office, which was next to the airport, and spoke with Pat. He assured me that they would be able to give me all the latest weather in the morning and showed me some of the charts that were available, and where the current lows and highs were moving. I wanted to take in a dinner show because they gave a flavor of the history of the island, but there were several large groups in town and everything was booked full. So, dinner and an early night were on the menu.

After a little rain during the night, the morning was bright and clear. I prepared my flight plans to be faxed in when the hotel office opened. Then I went to see the weather station again. David, the morning shift weatherman, was most helpful. He had just launched a weather balloon and had real-time wind reports at all altitudes. 6,000 feet was optimum for my flight, as the winds increased at 8 and 10,000 and turned to a more westerly direction. The satellite images showed a small storm cell to the southwest, moving southeast, that could easily be passed by traveling slightly west prior to turning southwest. As it was isolated, it would also be clearly visible and easy to fly around. The isobars were far apart and winds would be light. This is significant for landing at Lord Howe Island, because it is notorious for high turbulence when the wind whips around the volcanoes on the south side of the island. It looks as though we'd be ok for landing there later in the day. I had enough gas to continue on to Sydney in case the winds were worse than predicted.

At the airport, the refueler showed up for his payment and the airport manager, Rob, dropped by to see if I needed anything. He'd

Approaching Lord Howe Island from the northeast

call Lord Howe Island, after I departed, to pass on my flight time, so that they knew when to expect me. Everyone was exceedingly helpful from arrival to departure on this small independent island.

We took off from the immaculate runways and circled the island before departing to the southwest. I was rested, relaxed and felt good. What a difference from the previous day. I enjoyed the short 3.5-hour trip, detoured very slightly around the buildups and, as we got closer, was transferred from Auckland to Brisbane radio. I asked for and received permission to descend, but then couldn't reach them to close my flight plan. Lord Howe radio, I think it was the meteorological office, gave exceptionally detailed wind reports at both ends of the runway: winds were generally 130 degrees at 10 knots. At runway 10 threshold they were 110 to 140 degrees at 13 gusting to 25 and at runway 28 threshold they were 10 knots gusting to 15. After passing the runway 10 threshold one was in the lee of the volcanoes and the winds died down. A second person got on the radio and explained the approach and what to expect. Both people were very precise in their information. It was a great help.

We were both in awe of the two volcanoes on the south side of the island as we approached. It was a magnificent site. Too late we noticed the rock spur to the southeast; however, we'd fly around it after departure. It also was magnificent. Lord Howe Island and Ball's Pyramid rock spur, standing 1811 feet high, were definitely the high-lights of the crossing—and every pilot and visitor to the island that I've spoken with agrees. Wow, we were grateful to the pilots who recommended this trip. Island hopping was definitely the way to go.

There were an amazing number of houses on the island and I learned later that 350 people live there. The customs officer, Stan, was born there, as was his father. I passed Australian customs quickly and efficiently and took some pictures of the island and volcanoes (see color photo). Unfortunately, we couldn't rent a car to drive around or take a taxi, so we continued on our way. Once again, the met[21] office was extremely helpful, providing winds aloft, TAF[22] for Sydney, and the weather enroute.

---

21. Met — short for meteorological
22. TAF — terminal area forecast

Ball's Pyramid, 1811 feet above water, highest rock spur in the world

The final leg was happily uneventful. I was communicating with Brisbane radar 100 miles out and they had me identified, so no more position reporting was required and I reeled in the antenna. I had attempted several HF contacts with Hawaii and e-mail connections, both without luck. Propagation doesn't seem good during the day, but position reporting works extremely well with Auckland and Brisbane radio.

As we passed over Sydney, I snapped a picture of the bridge and hoped that the Opera House would be in it. I looked and looked for Bankstown airport, but I was looking west into the sun and haze. I couldn't see it, even with its three parallel runways. I heard a chuckle as approach told me to turn right and I'd see it under my wing—there it was, I was right over it. I think I heard another chuckle when I talked with tower. But they cleared me to land on runway 11 left and I followed an airport vehicle to a customs waiting area. I explained that I'd cleared customs at Lord Howe, but their instructions were for me to get cleared again. When customs arrived, they explained that more paperwork was necessary. I filled out a crew document and, most important, a plane document. If I stay longer than 2 months, I'll be required to pay tax on the value of the aircraft...think I'll be on my way in a month.

Dad in front of the Sydney Opera House

Dad with Valerie and Mac, who took care of us in Sydney.

Chapter 7

Dear Carol Ann
I have just looked up your position report and
you look as though you are in the middle of nowhere.
Just wanted to wish you all the very best and to let you know that you are often in our
thoughts. I still remember every second of our flight in Sydney with much pleasure.
Stay safe
Michael & Marta

Flying around Australia
Week 1: Sydney, Melbourne and Tasmania

Sydney is an amazing city with a very large and complex harbor area using boat taxis and ferries to get people moved across the harbor. It's fun to commute that way. Dad's friends live on Elizabeth Bay. Using their home as a base, we visited the Aquarium, Darling Harbour, the Opera (of course), Manly Beach, Kings Cross, and the downtown areas of Sydney.

After several days in Sydney I left Dad and flew out of Bankstown, the General Aviation airport serving Sydney, for Moorabbin, the GA airport serving Melbourne. It was a beautiful sunny day, so I flew VFR and didn't file a flight plan. Rick would be waiting for me at the other end, but still, I learned a lot about "designated remote areas" and search and rescue (SAR).[23] I started out weaving my way below and around control areas. Once clear, I climbed to 6500 feet and looked further ahead on the charts. I was headed straight to and through Canberra airport control area. So I called and asked for clearance through their area and over their airport. They gave me clearance then asked if I was really going "direct" to Melbourne or taking a southern route. I said that I was going to Moorabbin, near Melbourne, and yes, direct. They cleared me direct to Moorabbin.

I felt some hesitancy on his part and wondered what I was doing wrong. Once I met up with Rick, at the other end, I learned that most pilots file VFR flight plans with SAR times. We filed them on the next two legs! After Canberra, I was getting close to a moun-

---

23. SAR — Search and Rescue

tain range, so I asked for and received clearance to climb to 8500 feet. I would have preferred 10,500, but that was not available as Australian IFR altitude starts at 10,000 feet.

For an hour and a half, I continued over the mountains. There was almost nothing, just mountains and valleys. Sometimes, the valleys were green with lakes and some houses. Most times, there was nothing. It was pretty desolate. There are very large areas on the charts listed as "designated remote area." There is nothing there. Now I know why people file VFR flight plans with SAR times. Close to the end of the range, I found a ski area; apparently there are a few in these mountains. The highest mountain in Australia, Mt. Kosciusko, is in this mountain range just south of my flight path.

I arrived at Moorabbin and was directed to the Royal Victorian Aero Club building and told to park in front of it. There were a lot of people on the patio and in the building. Rick came forward and introduced himself, then introduced me to many of the club members. As it turned out, he was sitting at the club, listening to his handheld radio and preparing his next flight plan to Brisbane for an hour or so prior to my arrival. People started asking what he was doing and little by little it came out that he was waiting for me. As the story spread, the members decided to wait and meet me. There were many congratulations and handshakes. Then Stuart, the club president, presented me with an honorary membership, the club wings, and club shirt with their insignia. I was proud and very happy to agree to return the following day to meet and talk with

Members of the Royal Victorian Aero Club
in Melbourne, Australia

other members. Although I had planned to leave for Tasmania, how could I pass up this hospitality?

Rick was finally able to extricate me and shepherd me to his home to meet his wife, Debbie, and teenage sons, Matt and Nick. I had been introduced to Rick by e-mail via my best friend's cousin who knew Rick and thought he might be able to help me. We'd been e-mailing each other since January and he'd prepared and sent me information on flying in Australia. It's amazing and warming to see how friends of friends of friends have gone out of their way to help me with this trip. I owe many, many people a debt of thanks for all they've done for me.

The next morning, with Rick as my right seat pilot, I did two approaches, one NDB (that wasn't in my Garmin/Jeppesen database) into Moorabbin and an ILS into Essendon, the major airport next to Melbourne. We requested to do approaches at Essendon while still on the ground at Moorabbin. The local tower makes the request with the other tower. Due to arrivals and timing, they couldn't take us immediately, so the Moorabbin tower recommended an NDB at their airport. I said that I'd like to, but didn't have a copy of that approach (at this time, I only had the DOD[24] approaches to major airports). The tower controller ran down the tower steps with their copy so that we could do the approach. What service; thanks, Tony! Then I discovered that the approach wasn't in my newly updated Garmin database. I did it the "old fashioned" way and it went well. We received our missed approach instructions to proceed to the IAF[25] for the next ILS approach. Great, Essendon was going to let us in. That approach went very smoothly—I love ILS approaches. I was very happy to have done a total of five approaches this month and was determined to do more during this trip. Rick had the same reaction as Max in NZ: "Wow what a view, I never get this view flying VFR because we can't fly over the city." And I missed another great view!

After the flight, we visited the Moorabbin Tower and talked with Warren, Tony, and Chris, the controllers on duty that day. I

---

24. DOD — Department of Defense — provides airport information, world wide, for airports with runways longer than 6000 feet.
25. IAF — Initial Approach Fix — assigned point for starting the approach procedure.

always enjoy visiting towers and seeing the views from up there. We talked about how the operations work, the use of parallel runways, and training procedures. It was fascinating to learn that years ago a group of Australian air traffic controllers had toured a number of US airports and determined that the safest and most efficient airport design would be to use parallel runways and have one for takeoff and landing practice and the other for arrivals and departures. That's the way all their airports are designed and operated. I must say, from my short time in Australia, it seems to work well.

Later on, Rick and Debbie took me out on the Melbourne bay for a boat ride and lunch. We toured the huge 50-mile-diameter bay. Many sailboats were out on this sunny Sunday. Although, comparatively speaking, the area is so large and the population so small that nothing is crowded on the beaches or the bay.

In the afternoon, Rick and I returned to the Royal Victorian Aero Club to meet and talk with more members. I enjoy telling my story and answering questions. Pamela and Stephanie, two women pilots, talked with me about the Australian Women Pilots' Association and how any member would be glad to help me out wherever I am in Australia. Pamela knows many pilots in various areas and wanted to ensure that I had support and aid everywhere in Australia. She wanted to give me all the information and contacts in all my planned destinations. I also had offers from the club maintenance engineer to help me with my plane or engine if necessary, or anything else I needed. I enjoyed showing my plane and the modifications required for the Pacific crossing. The 55 US gallon drum in the back seat astonished most pilots. Just a simple 44 Imperial gallon drum! I explained that a custom-designed 68 US gallon tank had been built, but the STC for the Mooney was for the 55 gallon drum and that's what was mandated by the FAA. It's empty for my local trips and the plane is within standard limits. It's only for the long crossings that I fill all tanks. They were also interested in the trailing antenna and the HF radio.

Sunday evening Rick showed me how to get weather and file a flight plan through the Internet. We weren't sure that the system would accept my American registration, N220FC; but wrote a note in the remarks to explain the situation. Rick told me that he'd receive a phone call within 2 to 3 minutes of sending it in, if there was a problem. I laughed and said that the flight service people must be just sitting around waiting for flight plans to come in if they called that quickly. Two minutes after we sent it in his cell phone rang. We both laughed, and it WAS flight service! They just wanted to check on the registration. I am still amazed that they are on top of all flight plans that quickly.

There is much less communication in the air and on the ground than in the US, but that's to reduce congestion of the airwaves. There is no flight following, but reporting your position and route when entering center's coverage area is acceptable. Also, reporting position and requesting airways clearance prior to entering controlled airspace is required.

Monday morning early, Rick and I took off for King Island and Tasmania. As in NZ, when I explained where I was headed, the locals recommended what to do and see along the way. In this case it was a stop at King Island on my way to Launceston, Tasmania. King Island is an island off the northwest coast of Tasmania's main island, and is notorious for its cheese. Since I love cheese, this became a mandatory stop. We had an 18-knot tailwind from the north. First we followed the coastline and gorgeous beaches, then turned left and made the short crossing to King Island. Although it is normally a lush Irish green, it was only an average, unhealthy green as we flew over. It was later explained that the rain had missed the island all summer.

As we arrived, a King Island twin overtook us and landed first. I'd heard him on the radio when he was behind and above us. We talked as he descended below and ahead, then landed. We followed him in, and then another arrived. As we tied down, two more planes landed. It was rush hour at the airport. There are several twins that ship crawfish and cargo to Melbourne and others that ship people and crawfish each morning. When we returned from touring the town and sampling the cheese, the airport was its normal empty shell. So, arrive any time but 9 am and you'll have the airport to yourself.

The cheese shop was luscious. I could have stayed there all day. After a 10-minute video educated us about the island and its history and kelp industry, it concentrated on the manufacture of cheese. My mouth was watering by the end. Luckily that's when we were led to the tasting room. After sampling more than 20 cheeses, I settled on buying my four favorites.

We took off again and flew over the rougher, more rugged, south end of the island, then over the sea to the northwest tip of Tasmania. We flew down the west coast that changed from flat lands to beaches to mountainous terrain. Halfway south, at Strahan, we turned left, inland, to Launceston. This took us over the mountainous region with many lakes and no roads. It was very rough terrain, yet majestic and wonderful to see. After half an hour, we saw the escarpment and descended from our crossing altitude of 7500 feet to airport altitude of 562 feet. It was a wide, green, farmland valley between the mountains we'd just crossed to the west and another range to the east.

It had been a fantastic morning and we'd had lots of fun. Rick had done all the flying and I had plenty of time to see the sights for a change. But, it was time to split up; Rick took a QANTAS flight back to Melbourne, and I rented a car to tour Tasmania.

I drove south, through the farmlands to Hobart, where I stayed overnight, then drove up the east coast. There are many small villages along the road that had housed the convicts on their way to prison in Hobart in the 1800s. Convict labor had been used for much of the construction in these villages. It was nice and peaceful touring through these small villages and stopping as I felt like it. It was also a time for reflection. I'd come a long way, and this was almost my first time alone since reaching NZ. It had been a great trip so far. It was also approaching April 24th, the anniversary of the death of my mother. I wanted to write a tribute to her on my web page and have it uploaded prior to that date. My time here and in the hotel would permit me to get some writing done. The following is what I wrote while crying my eyes out in a hotel room in Hobart:

"As we approach, remember, and move on past April 24th, I'd like to take a moment to pay tribute to my mother, other ALS patients and victims, and still others for whom this date is special:

First, I'd like to remember my mother, Marie Garratt, who died one year ago today. She was strong during the 3 years that ALS slowly took her body, but not her mind. And she had a beautiful face and smile until the end. ALS is a terrible disease that attacks the body while the mind is still fully functional. It is to her that I dedicate this trip. She would have been terribly worried the whole time, but proud. She would have had sleepless nights, but bragged to her friends of my accomplishments. She would have cheered me on; but wrung her hands in worry behind my back. We all love you and hope that you are in a better place. I've heard these words from others during my trip; others whose family members or friends have also died or are suffering from ALS.

Steve wrote to me because April 24th is his birthday and also because his brother died of ALS. My heart goes out to him too.

Max and Anna, who took me in and cared for me in Auckland, remember April 24th because their son Allen died on the same day 2 years earlier. He died of cancer. My heart goes out to them and their family who remember Allen today.

It's Dave's birthday in Utah also. His mother died a few years ago and one of his daughters died of cancer. We hiked and talked together often and he doesn't know how much he helped prepare me for the eventuality of my mother's death by talking of his daughter and mother. Thanks Dave.

Mark from my dad's town in Clarksville, VA wrote to me and wrote a story for the Clarksville newspaper about my trip. He also had a family member who died of ALS. I thank him for the article and support so that we can all raise awareness and donations for the ALS TD Foundation.

James wrote me about his niece who contacted a child's form of ALS at three and died at age 16. What a tragedy when it strikes someone so young.

Jill's father died of ALS and she lost her mother three weeks later. In reality, she lost both parents to ALS. It takes its toll on the caregiver as well. I wish her well in her struggle to overcome her loss.

David wrote to me as he had purchased his Mooney from a pilot, Al, who lost his medical certificate when he had ALS. Al just died a few weeks ago and David flew the Mooney to Al's wake. I'm sure Al would be happy to know it was there and that it is in good hands.

Alex's wife Diana lost her dad to ALS when she was only 6 years old. It can affect a family for a lifetime after it takes the patient's life. I wish Diana and Alex well.

Herb's youngest son, Tom, was diagnosed with ALS in 1996 and is completely handicapped at age 41, requiring a ventilator and caregivers around the clock. He was a pilot and a doctor. His brother is a 12,000 + hour pilot with the airlines and Herb is also a pilot. They know first-hand how devastating ALS can be to a family. My thoughts go out to them and to Tom who will hopefully write a book about his medical practice and ALS.

Many other people wrote to me and I thank them all. I thank also those companies and people who have already generously donated to the ALS Therapy Development Foundation. It is through your support that they will eventually find a cause and cure to this terrible disease.

If you are enjoying this website and haven't yet donated, please consider a gift that goes directly to the ALS foundation. There's no middle person. I'm paying for the trip; all donations go directly to ALS. Thank you for letting me remember April 24th."

Week 2: SE Coast, Woolongong, Dubbo, Sydney

Time to move on. It was a cold, 7C/45F, but sunny morning in Launceston as I prepared the Mooney for our next leg. The weather was questionable, so with the help of Melanie, an instructor and commercial pilot at Launceston Aero Club, I filed an IFR flight plan and looked at the weather for the southeast coast of Australia. There would be a layer of clouds at 5000, but good visibility below, with some widely scattered rain showers. I had purchased the east coast enroute and approach charts in Melbourne, just in case the weather got bad. I had chosen not to purchase the Jeppesen charts before leaving the US, as they would be out of date by the time I needed them and I didn't need all of Australia. The Airways Australia charts are very similar to the NOS charts in the US and less expensive than the alternative. So, I had current charts and felt good about the trip.

The tower gave me my clearance and told me that no other IFR traffic was in the area. I asked if I needed a transponder code and he gave me one, but normally they don't assign that until getting closer to the radar coverage areas. I learned a lot about IFR flying in a non-radar environment on the next few flight legs. As with the ocean crossings, they wanted position reports and ETA at future reporting points. As I was climbing out, they told me where to look for other IFR arriving traffic and told the traffic where to look for me. With no radar, the pilots sometimes talk directly with each other as to their position and altitude. I cleared the traffic, climbed over the mountains to the east, and leveled off at 7000 feet. I was on top of a cloud layer and didn't see anything—bummer. I knew I'd be

*Office in Launceston, Tazmania where Melanie helped
me file the IFR flight plan*

flying over Flinders Island and had wanted to see it, but couldn't. I did, however, report it, as it's a mandatory reporting point.

As I was checking the gauges, the fuel pressure gage suddenly dropped out of the green and below the red line. My heart jumped and I hit the fuel boost pump switch. The fuel flow was immediately back up to normal. After a few seconds, I turned off the boost pump and the fuel flow stayed in the normal range. I didn't understand what had happened or why. I continued monitoring the gage very closely and saw it dip a few times, but it had done that before, just never below the red line. I began to relax again and had no further problems.

On reaching the coast, I wanted to see a little of the area, so I requested and received "No IFR traffic reported" to descend to 5000. This was probably not a good decision. I was just in the base of the clouds, and it was bumpy and rainy. Oh well, only an hour to go to Wollongong. I got a few photos of the many beaches and expansive shoreline, but also got bumped around. "N220FC identified" is how ATC tells you that you are now in radar contact. But then I received a transmission to contact the next frequency and to stay clear of their airspace. I was entering a military airspace area and apparently permission is given directly, not through the preceding ATC. Approval was given on first contact, and I continued without any

Dad with longtime friends, John and Edna, in Woolongong (see the escarpment behind)

slowdown or change of direction. I descended to 3500 feet, then went over the 2000-foot escarpment and down into Wollongong. It was a beautiful semicircular area with a long beach on one side and the escarpment on its circumference. By then I was in its MBZ and reporting my position for approach and landing. I met up with my Dad and his friends, and we all had a delicious lamb lunch together.

Off to Dubbo, or so we thought. When climbing out, I usually back off on the throttle and watch a reduction in manifold pressure. Not so this time. The engine was performing correctly, but not the gage. So I broadcast my intentions, did a U-turn, and landed again at Wollongong. I took off the cowl and checked the connections; all looked okay and I didn't see any leaks in the hose or tubing. With Robert, an instructor at Wollongong, we looked at it and discussed options. There is no mechanic on the field; I would have to go to Bankstown or another field to get a mechanic to check the gage.

So, we took off again for Dubbo. I had planned to fly along the coast from south to north to view Sydney and the harbor area. But without a working manifold pressure gage, I didn't want to do that at the 500-foot VFR altitude, so I went directly to Dubbo at 7000 feet so that the manifold pressure would remain below the engine rpm. We left the flatlands near the beach, climbed the 2000-foot escarpment, and continued over mountains with fires burning due to the dry conditions, and rugged cliff and valley areas. On arriving at Dubbo, I spoke with Cliff, the supervisor at the Air-Link hangar and he said that someone could look at it the following morning. I felt better already.

Dubbo is over the mountains and into the flat arid lands an hour to the northwest of Sydney. Six hours by car. Dad and I settled into a nice "farm stay" bed and breakfast that also provided dinner. After touring the cattle auction in the morning (now that was fascinating), I went to the hangar and Paddo, the mechanic, had already repeated my inspection from the previous afternoon and found nothing. Once he got inside the cockpit and looked behind the instrument panel, he found the loose connection immediately and tightened it. I didn't even have to buy a new gage. With a smile on my face and profuse thanks to Cliff and Paddo, we left for the Dubbo Zoo. That kept us occupied for most of the day; then we went to learn about boomerangs—with ailerons! Actually there is only one aileron per boomerang. But, they have left- and right-hand boomerangs.

I'd read books about Australia, and the characters always talked about the weather and rain. Well, that's exactly how it is out here. The main topic is the drought, when they last had rain, the impact on the cattle and sheep, and when the next rain will come. So, when I got up on Friday and it was raining, I didn't complain to anyone, I knew they'd all be celebrating.

The Air-Link manager, Geoff, let me use their computer to file my flight plan and check weather. I was in the middle of that when a crew returned and the pilots helped me with the standard route to Bankstown and what to expect in terms of arrival and radar coverage. David, Adrian, and the other pilots were a great help, as they'd just returned from Sydney and gave me the latest weather. They were also interested to hear about my trip and where I was going from there. I gave Geoff the web address, thanked him for letting me use their equipment, and went to pre-flight the Mooney.

I called Melbourne Center from the ground and received "no IFR traffic reported." So I made my MBZ calls and departed. On climb-out I again contacted Melbourne Center and gave my position and time to reporting point. I think I'm getting the hang of this non-radar environment reporting. After half an hour, the clouds opened up and the sky was blue. We descended through some clouds to get back into Bankstown, and I was switched to VFR as soon as possible. David from Dubbo had warned me about that and Geoff had shown me the VFR arrival procedures book with Adrian explaining what to look for and the 2RN tower. Thanks for the preparation—you helped me enormously!

The rain had done a good job keeping the top surfaces of the plane clean; however, after two oil changes, it was time to degrease the underside. I'd left Dubbo early to give me enough time to clean the plane prior to being picked up by Dad's friends. I cleaned out the baggage compartment and reorganized the interior. Lying on the grass, under the fuselage, it only took 45 minutes or so to get the underside looking as good as the topside.

My planning and chart logistics were working. When I returned to Sydney, I found that a FedEx package had arrived with my next set of charts. As this trip duration was over seven months, chart expiration dates were a big problem. I'd planned to have charts shipped to various destinations in different countries on specific dates. Also, the total volume of charts for the whole world was enormous and heavy. I had planned to discard or return my old charts at the points where the new charts arrived. The first shipment arrived as planned in Sydney.

Time now to prepare for the next legs. Dad would be flying home commercially and I would pick up a long time friend, Jim, and visit more of Australia with him before continuing my journey to other countries.

After seeing my dad off in Sydney, I gave Mike, a "not-so-Young Eagle," a flight. He is an English doctor and pilot who hadn't flown in about 20 years. He loves aviation, but had concentrated on being a doctor and helping many unfortunates for the last few decades. His eyes and smile gave him away—he really missed flying. He had no trouble remembering checklists and maneuvers. He had flying back in hand in no time at all. His aviation world was opening back up to him again—he couldn't help himself, like so many other pilots, his love of flying was going to take a front seat again. The same thing had happened to me; I'd stopped flying for 14 years while climbing the corporate ladder. But January 1st, 1996, I started again (with a New Year's resolution) and I haven't looked back. Good luck Mike—I know you'll be solo again soon.

A week previously, I'd given my oldest "Young Eagle" a ride. Valerie, who hosted Dad and me in Sydney, was a flight attendant in early life. She loved flying and especially takeoffs and landings. She had a sparkle in her eyes for my plane from the day Dad and I landed. One Sunday, we took off for a sight-seeing flight. "Wheeee" she said as the wheels left the ground; she was having the time of her life. Her eyes sparkled as we flew around the local area, over the hills and the reservoir beyond. Time to return for a landing, but she was on cloud nine the whole time. This gives truth to the old saying, "You can land, but you never come down."

Week 3: Byron Bay, Barrier Reef, Farm stay

Leaving Sydney on a sunny Sunday morning felt comfortable and uncomfortable at the same time. Bankstown was an airport I had come to know after four arrivals and landings and I was beginning to feel that I knew the ropes with both IFR and VFR reporting points. But it was time to move on to another unknown region and airport.

It was only going to be a 3-hour flight up the coast to Byron Bay, the eastern-most point of mainland Australia, but the weather indicated a cloud layer and possibly lower clouds on arrival. Although I wanted to fly over the coast, I decided to file IFR and fly higher through the numerous Terminal Control Areas along the coast. I met Jim at the airport and off we went. Unfortunately there was a cloud layer between us and the coast, but that just stopped me from clicking another 60 photos of the beautiful scalloped beaches with very few people on them. They are gorgeous. There are hills to the west, relatively close to the coastal areas, with a little farmland between the two. Jim is a long-time ham or amateur radio operator, and used those skills daily during his many years sailing and boating in the Bahamas and Mediterranean. So it was logical for me to fly and for Jim to play with the radio. As I was under instrument flight rules (IFR), I stayed on VHF and we separated the HF system to Jim's headset. He was able to talk with Tasmania and Texas during this first trip.

The clouds cleared and I dropped lower for a better view of the coastline. There are a few towns and villages along the coast, but many miles of untouched shoreline. I made my mandatory broadcasts and heard another plane landing on runway 06, which made sense with the on-shore breeze. I landed at Ballina airport, taxied to the grassy aircraft parking area, proceeded to an empty spot and as the pace slowed I added power. The grass was looking decidedly wet and soggy. I turned so as not to go any "deeper" and stopped over the tie-down wire. After getting out, I walked all around and found it very wet, but relatively solid underneath and more solid by the wire, where the wheels were. "Well, the sun will dry it out" I said to myself and proceeded to tie down the plane and get our bags out.

Rusty and Tricia, friends of Jim, picked us up and took us to their home after a tour of the area and town. The hills overlook the beaches, a lighthouse is on the eastern-most point of Australia, the waves are long and rolling and inviting, and I knew that being three hours north of Sydney, the water would be warmer. First thing the next morning Rusty had us on the beach. While he was giving a surfing lesson, daughter Taylor went off surfing, and Jim and I walked over the hills and snapped pictures of beaches, surfers, and dive boats. After we returned to the beach and took a swim, Rusty's student lesson was over and he took me by the hand for my first lesson.

He patiently explained that the most important move in surfing is getting up on your feet from the lying down position on the board. We practiced this multiple times on the beach before even entering the water. On the first lesson, Rusty did all the timing and pushing and all I had to do was concentrate on getting up and staying balanced. We got oriented, Rusty timed the wave, pushed, and off I went. After getting the feel of the wave the first time, standing and immediately falling the second, I actually stayed up for a bit on the third and fourth waves. I was ecstatic. Although exhausted from battering my way through the waves to get out each time, I felt good about having stood up and stayed up at least for a short time. Little did I know that each of the following days would follow the same pattern. Up early for a walk with Tricia and Java (the dog). Load the surfboards and head for the beach. Swim, walk and surf, rest, surf, etc. Go and have a late breakfast or brunch. What a life. I could have stayed there.

CarolAnn learning how to surf

Jim and CarolAnn on the most easterly point in
Australia, Byron Bay

Actually it was Easter weekend and Byron Bay hosts a five-day Blues and Roots festival each year—it's huge and fun. We went one night, saw more than eight bands, and had a great time. It was a terrific week of meeting and talking with a number of local families and surfing with Rusty and Taylor. Among all the memories will remain that of the "squeaky" beaches. The sand squeaks as you walk barefoot on it. I'd drag my feet in the sand to make it squeak louder. It was the first time I'd run across this phenomenon. A Byron Bay beach called The Pass squeaks louder than most. I just found out that it's due to the silica content of the sand. The higher the silica content, the squeakier the sand. I'm sure going to miss this wonderfully relaxing location and great people. It's time to move on, but first, a new Young Eagle flies.

Taylor, Rusty and Tricia's daughter, almost didn't get to become a Young Eagle. On our first trip to the airport the winds were strong and gusty and I explained that we might not be able to fly, depending on the direction of the winds and runway. As we walked out to the plane, we saw that the wind was perpendicular to the runway—well, almost—and very gusty. After looking at the Mooney, Taylor and her mother, Tricia, said, "You crossed the Pacific in this?!" In their minds, my plane was a little bigger. We went to the airport manager's office and Jake talked about the weather and let us look at the conditions and radar. The winds were 180 degrees at 16 to 22 knots gusting to 34 knots. The runway is 06-24. I explained about crosswinds and how they affect the plane on landings. Taylor understood and we both hoped that the wind would die down over the next few days. Two days later we went back to the airport. The winds were still strong with some gusts, but right down the runway. Off we went. Taylor had a great big smile. She enjoyed every minute, flew around her house and the local town and got us back to the airport. Well-done, Taylor!

Good news arrived during the stay: my Indonesia over flight permit had been granted! Yeah, I was now sure of a continued trip. I hadn't been too worried as I set off from Florida, because the paperwork was in process and I had two months ahead of me. As time passed and the May 2nd flight date from Darwin to Singapore drew closer, I started to wonder whether I would be able to continue or not. When the Indonesia permit came through, I breathed a sigh

Taylor, an Australian Young Eagle

of relief. I didn't need a permit into Singapore, I knew the India permit was in process and I already had a Seychelles permit. Two days later, I received confirmation of my permit over Madagascar. Great! That meant that my flight was clear all the way to South Africa in early June. I still needed the African countries, Ethiopia, Sudan, and Egypt to complete the trip. But those permits were in process and I still had time.

For now, we continue around Australia, next stop Great Keppel Island at the southern end of the Barrier Reef. There is an unlicensed airport on the island, with an 800-meter bitumen (blacktop) runway 12–30. What hadn't been explained to me was that it sits between two hills and the wind swirls around both ends, making the approach and departure very difficult. It was a beautiful sight on the approach, but as we got closer, the Mooney had to be tightly controlled all the way to the ground. Two planes were lining up to take off as I arrived, so I waited my turn before landing. I found out on landing that there is only room for one at a time and only parking for 3 or 4 planes, so we'd all have been in trouble if I'd arrived any earlier. I'd called ahead and booked a landing time, but didn't realize that space was so tight.

After landing, we found the choice for accommodation to be a resort or hostel/camping facilities. After paying a $100 landing fee, we chose the hostel at $23.50 per night instead of $120 per night for the resort. The large tent structures were fine for a few nights and shared toilet/shower facilities were adequate. Mass-produced dinners and breakfasts at $10 each were ample. The rest of the day was spent swimming, snorkeling, and hiking the many trails on the island. At the end of one 3-hour hike I came to a beach with three people that I could see in the far distance at one end, and two

Landing at Great Kepple Island

swimming near where I entered. That was it; the whole beach was almost untouched. I went a few hundred yards away and changed into my swimsuit. With no one around, changing was easy. I swam and lounged about in the warm sun.

After two nights and one full day, we were off again for a ranch stay and a taste of farm life in the almost outback. I'd called the Myella farm two times and received confirmation of a local Ambulance airstrip, 800 meters long, bitumen (blacktop), only 16 kilometers from the farm, near a town called Baralaba. There was nothing there but the strip and they would pick us up at 10 am on the day agreed. I found the town but not the airport on the charts. It was with much faith that we departed Great Keppel Island for an unknown point. I plugged the latitude and longitude coordinates for the town into the GPS. I checked the roads and other visual check points that I'd be looking for on the charts and we departed.

While on Great Keppel Island, I'd been told that many planes take off downwind and down the runway grade because the winds are so swirly at both ends. I checked the windsock and decided on a normal upwind takeoff. I thought staying a little lower between the hills and gaining speed would help before entering the turbulent zone. It turned out to be a non-event, very little turbulence and a normal takeoff and climb out. After a quick trip over water to Rockhampton, while talking with the tower, I transited their airspace and was set on my own again. Over the first set of hills with the highest tower topping out at 2486 feet and us flying at 2500 feet, it was easy to spot and avoid.

Continuing to the valley beyond, the farm was going to be in these flatlands before the next mountain range. I found and crossed the "major" north-south road and continued. I saw some cattle below in the large, relatively green fields. Before too long, I saw a group of buildings that I thought would constitute a town, roughly where the GPS said Baralaba would be. I looked to the southeast and saw a long blacktop strip in the middle of farm fields; no buildings, no hangars, only the strip. That was it. I descended and found the windsock at one end, joined the downwind and made a smooth landing on this long, beautiful strip...in the middle of nowhere.

We searched for tie-downs; but there were none. We tried getting pegs into the ground, but it was impossible. A truck arrived; it was Peter, from Myella, 15 minutes early. He said we could make tie-down weights at the farm, so we loaded up and drove away. Well, all the way to the gate at the end. The strip is completely fenced in with a gate near the road. Then we drove to the farm for a wonderful, tiring, bruising, but great fun two days and nights. Great food, great company, riding horses, riding motor bikes, bringing in cows for milking, feeding hens, playing pool volleyball, cracking whips, stroking kangaroos. It was a wonderful combination of relaxation and working muscles that haven't been used in years. The food was plentiful, home cooked, and tasted great. The homemade beer in the evenings hit the right spot at the right time. Star gazing before bedtime was interesting and educational. We left two days later stiff and with bruises, but feeling relaxed.

Week 4: Longreach, Ayers Rock and Darwin

Next stop Longreach, home of the Stockman's Hall of Fame and QANTAS Founders Outback Museum. Peter dropped us off at the barren airport. No worries—no one goes there. Everything was as we left it. There are now two cans filled with gravel that can be used as tie-downs for the next plane; just bring your own ropes and call Myella for a pick-up before departing. We circled over the farm and the airport to take pictures, then took off to the west. With tailwinds, the trip was shortened to 2 hours and 20 minutes. There is a range of mountains to go over; 4500-foot altitude took care of that. Then the green started to give way to some red and brown. I was amazed at the number of small lakes, water holes, and other water filled areas. Peter had explained that their last rain had been in February, two months earlier, and they'd received 12 inches; but still the number and level of the water holes was more than I'd ever imagined. As we passed over the town of Emerald, there was a relatively large lake to the south, on the map and in reality! It wasn't dried up as in Canberra.

Continuing west, there seemed to be rows, layers or strata of green, orange, and brown; but very sparse. There aren't many roads, but lots of tracks, red and brown, in very straight lines. Off to the left is the town of Alpha with an airport, or at least a long blacktop strip. The next town is Beta! Later on the same road there's a grass strip by another small town. It's a beautiful day with blue sky, clear as a bell (that's more for sound than sight, but it's clear) with 60 kilometers' visibility at least, and a few puffy clouds. As we continue, the earth is getting redder and it's BUMPY. For the last 50 nautical miles it's very bumpy. I hear other planes checking in, both IFR and VFR, for arrivals at Longreach. I announce my arrival time and see the airport from 20 miles out. Someone else is landing before me, so I know they are using runway 04. I announce my arrival and downwind position. Jim sees a huge Boeing 747 on the ramp—I didn't realize that big jets came in here. After landing and taxiing in, I saw that the 747 was behind the fence and parked; it turned out to be part of the QANTAS museum! The BP refueler drove over to welcome us and ask about avgas. I asked for a fill up the following morning, and also received the local information. Three choices of hotels were across the street from the airport. The Hall of Fame was down the street within walking distance and the QANTAS Founders Outback Museum was next door to the airport. All we needed right here—great!

The QANTAS 747 had been delivered to the museum in

November '02 commemorating QANTAS' 82nd birthday. The jet was QANTAS' first 747, received in 1979; it had carried 5.4 million passengers, flown 82 million kilometers, more than 2,000 trips around the world. The rest of the museum told the fascinating story of how the company was started by two WWI Aussi pilots who had just completed a land survey between Queensland and the Northern Territories and believed there had to be a better way to get around Australia. What a great story.

On the way again, up and away at 9 am leaving Longreach and headed west. It's pretty desolate as I look around while climbing. You can see green lines where the rivers flow during the rainy season or floods. After seeing the Stockman Hall of Fame and reading about the pioneers, it's easy to imagine the hardships they struggled through as I look down on the barren landscape. From here I wonder if they followed the "path of green" down the rivers, but they didn't have the vantage point that I have. As I continue, there aren't even any tracks across the landscape; now that's a lot of nothing.

The browns give way to more red earth; that's what I was expecting to see. I look on the map and it's an extensive area called Simpson Desert, which looks inhospitable. There will be an end to it, in another 150 miles or so. I sure wouldn't want to go down in

First QANTAS 747 at Longreach,
home of QANTAS Founders Outback Museum

that—very hot and dry and no towns around. Earlier, to the east, I saw just a dirt track, and by golly, it was marked on the WAC chart. I've been plugging in NDBs and have cross-checked my progress with their bearings and the latitude/longitudes in the GPS. I'm glad I'm not an 1850s pioneer.

With 130 miles to go, I thought I saw Ayers Rock sticking up in the distance. It looked like a dome shape, but it also looked too far south of course. As I got closer, I found that it wasn't Ayers Rock, but Mt. Connor, another lonesome rock. At 50 miles out I spotted the real Ayers Rock; it had the right shape this time and was just slightly south of course, as the airport is north of the National Park. I called the airport and was told of other traffic, started to descend, and looked at a huge red dome that was just sitting there. Wow, what a sight. There are specific flight paths shown in the guide that a pilot needs to follow to fly around the Rock. I was too tired after over five hours of flying, so I decided that I'd do that flight on leaving the area. It was too hot and bumpy to do it now.

Ayers Rock was a fantastic site, and the walks and talks by the Ranger were fascinating and informative. During the sunrise tour, you see the changing colors of Ayers Rock as the sun comes up. It truly is magnificent (see color photo).

I've seen enough red sand to last a while. Red sand and Ayers Rock were two of the sites I was looking forward to seeing after spending the first three weeks on the east coast. But five days of it are enough. One last shower to wash out the red tinges on the legs and arms and I'm ready to go to the airport and head north. There's one other point people forget to mention—the flies. At Longreach and Ayers Rock the flies are ALL over you. Many people wear head nets; unfortunately, I'd left mine in the plane. Early morning and late evening when it's cool, they aren't around, but during the day they are all over your face and body. An unverified statistic is that there are 2 million flies for every Australian. It's the only disagreeable point in the whole stay; but the cool mornings and evenings without flies are terrific.

Up and get the plane ready for the final Australian leg. We're going to fly around Ayers Rock, the Olgas, and Kings Canyon prior to heading for Darwin. There is a specified flight route for scenic flights around the rocks, with altitudes and position reports. Although no one else was around, I followed the procedure and made the callouts. Wow, they are magnificent from the air!

The trip to Darwin took six hours with a slight tailwind for most of the trip. Even at 8,000 feet, I couldn't reach Melbourne Center, so I couldn't set up a SAR time (for Search and Rescue); this felt a little uncomfortable. After about three hours, the ATC coverage changed to Brisbane and the receiver was only 60 miles away, so I made contact and set up a SAR time. Whew, I felt better. There is a lot of nothing down there; red soil, some hills, no water, no roads, completely deserted. Finally I saw tinges of green and then real green and trees and this started only 100 miles from Darwin. There was one major road, Stuart Highway, and apparently there will soon be train service between Darwin and Alice Springs, to the south.

Approach and tower efficiently handled our arrival at Darwin. I landed straight in runway 36 and taxied straight to GA parking and picked out a tie-down spot. While I was tying the plane down, Kathryn Flynn arrived. Kathryn had been informed of my arrival by Dee from Auckland, NZ, and had made contact by e-mail several weeks earlier. She is Governor of the 99s Australia Section and a member of the Australian Women's Pilots Association. She is a commercial pilot and held a job as a corporate pilot for many years. She and her husband, John, and family hosted us for four days while I prepared my Mooney for the next crossings.

The first day, with many thanks to Marie (same name as my mother) and John Hardy, I was allowed to use their hangar and maintenance facility to do my oil and filter change, air filter change, spark plug clean and check, and compression check. Everything checked out 100%. Nick helped me to get the work done correctly. The same day I received the Aviation Laboratories results from my last oil change (e-mailed by my dad) and they were all within normal limits.

During a trip to the Met Station on the other side of the airport, I talked with Brian and Jason, looked at several satellite images, winds, water vapor and prognostic charts, and all looked good for a Friday crossing to Singapore. With the plane, engine, and weather in good shape, I could now relax and see the sights.

We visited the Aviation Heritage Centre and saw all about the invasion of Darwin during WWII. Not much is written in the history books about this, but it was five times more destructive than the attack on Pearl Harbor. The next day we visited Kakadu National Park and I saw wetlands for the first time, and the birds and vege-

Kathryn next to a monument commenmorating the first flight from London to Darwin in December 1919

tation that thrive in that habitat. There is also Aboriginal rock art, drawings on rock walls, over 2000 years old.

During the week we also took time to publicize the trip and talk about ALS. The local radio station did a live interview during one of their morning broadcasts. This was my first radio interview and live to boot, so I was a little scared. But, it all went well. I didn't stumble or mumble too many times, and we were all happy with the results.

With one more day to take care of the final details, ship back 15 pounds of "stuff" that I don't need, get a haircut, and file a flight plan, I'm ready to go. Many, many thanks to Kathryn and John who were a tremendous help taxiing me around and taking care of us in Darwin. Also, thanks to John and Marie who allowed me to use their facilities for my flight planning and preparation.

After six weeks in NZ and Australia I'm getting itchy feet to start moving again. It's been a wonderful time, but I'm ready to get more flight hours under my belt and get further around this wonderful world. Tomorrow, Jim will fly commercially to Sydney and I'll take off for Singapore.

CHAPTER 8

I am a Portuguese wheelchair aviator, Earthrounder (1995) flying "solo." I went through
your site and I wish you all the luck of this world to get home safely. I am planning to
FAW "solo" again next 9 August (eastbound) in order to attend the Earthrounders
meeting in Perth.

Anyway I hope you will have very strong winds.
All the Gods will help such a brave woman, like you.
All the best
Antonio

May 2: Darwin, Australia to Singapore, 6th leg flight report

Four hours down on this leg and I'm exhausted already; it's been a heck of a morning after not sleeping well last night. I wasn't worried about the trip, we'd prepared everything and the plane and engine checked out 100%; I just tossed and turned a lot. I wanted an early departure when it was cool, so decided on 5:30 am local. Kathryn, who did a noble job taking care of me during my stay in Darwin, got up at 4 am to take me to the airport; that was really above and beyond the call of duty. She spends a lot of time helping women pilots and I vow that I will do more as I continue and when I return home.

When we arrived at the airport, the FBO we were using wasn't yet open. Customs were going to arrive at 5 am, so we called security to let us through the gate. They gave us the code and we let ourselves in. With two of us, the preflight went very quickly. Customs came and executed the paperwork efficiently. One last trip to the toilet and I'd be off. A big hug and many thanks to Kathryn and I climbed aboard again.

Clearance delivery gave me my clearance right away. I guess I'd been a little worried that something would go wrong with the paperwork or the Indonesian over-flight permit and I'd not be allowed to depart. I gave a big sigh of relief and smiled when I read back the clearance. I asked for progressives[25] for taxiing to the runway; "no worries," they helped me out. I had to wait for a

---

25. Progressives — step by step taxi instructions to get to the runway or else-
    where at an airport

QANTAS airbus to depart plus three minutes for wing tip vortices, and then was allowed to takeoff. It was dark, only 5:45 am, so I gave extra concentration to my instruments, not having flown that much at night. Wheels up and climb about 250 feet per minute, pretty much the same as previous climb outs. Departure steered me on to my course, then turned me over to center.

There seemed to be some clouds to the right of my course, but nothing ahead or to my left. Tailwinds were excellent, 25 knots for a ground speed of 170 knots, wow! At that rate, I'd be there in 10 hours; but the winds were supposed to weaken near the equator, so I knew it wouldn't last. I wanted to establish HF contact early, so I asked for and received an HF frequency to contact Brisbane Radio. I called several times but reception was weak. I tried the second frequency, and reception was a little better.

When center called me to confirm contact by HF and to hand me over and terminate VHF contact, I went to reply and found no push to talk (PTT) button. My finger kept moving over where it should be, but it wasn't there, nothing. As it was still pretty dark, I put the flashlight on the yoke and saw that it wasn't there. In moving around and putting things away, I must have hit it with something. Now what, go on or go back? I'd have at least 10 hours on HF to find a solution. I pushed my ballpoint pen tip into the broken end of the PTT button and the transmit light went on. I replied to center that I'd established contact with Brisbane radio and HF was working. He terminated VHF contact. It worked. I wouldn't be able to fly and talk like that at the same time, but I'd figure something out.

As it got lighter outside and inside the cockpit, I looked at the situation. I had a PTT button on the other yoke, but it had been disconnected when the yoke was removed to fit the tank in. However, maybe I could exchange the buttons. I got the tools and started to disassemble the yoke. Then, on the other side of the yoke, I saw my extra PTT for the HF radio. It plugs into the microphone (mic) chord and I'd used it in planes without intercom systems. I unplugged it from the HF and plugged it into VHF; the transmit light went on. Solution found! When I terminate my HF communication, I'll plug it into my VHF mic wiring and will be able to talk and fly at the same time. In the mean time, if I have any VHF communications, I'll use the tip of the ballpoint pen.

I was approaching the second waypoint where I would change over from Brisbane to Bali radio and climb from my great tailwind altitude of 6,000 feet to the obstacle clearance altitude of 14,000 feet. I got my oxygen prepared and put on the cannula.[26] I didn't turn on the oxygen because if I could see all the peaks, I didn't really want to climb all the way to 14,000; but stop at 10,000 and descend back to 8,000 feet on the other side.

The chart showed the obstacle clearance for the sector to be 13,300 feet and the next sector to be 9,600 feet; but the visual charts showed only a few peaks. After passing 8,000 feet I was above the haze and cloud layer and could see clearly. Wow, the mountains to the east were HUGE. Straight ahead and to the left, they were much lower. I asked for clearance to stop at 10,000 feet and descend to 8,000 on the other side of the island. Brisbane had to relay to Bali, but finally I received the clearance. Speed had dropped to 130 knots at 10,000 feet and was back up to 140 to 145 knots at the lower altitude. Position reports went well and I was able to stay between the peaks. What a view: rugged little islands with tremendously high peaks and beautiful empty beaches. There were a few houses on the hillsides and near one beach. Also, I saw one road through the hills to the west side, but nothing in the high peaks to the east.

Four hours down and I have to go. The morning coffee went straight through me. The previous departures each had minor problems to let me relieve myself multiple times before takeoff. We were just too efficient this morning. Well, the Lady Jane worked perfectly, I feel better, and the sky ahead only has little puffy clouds and no cumulonimbus buildups. Less than eight hours to go and I'm ready for a snack. Cereal will do for now. Mmmm that feels better too. Now, clean up the cabin, put the oxygen away, and get ready for the next position report.

I've been turned over to Bali control, a VHF frequency, but am unable to reach them. I chat on 123.45 with another American up at 28,000 feet. At first he doesn't realize that I'm a Mooney at 8,000 feet, then asks where I'm headed to and where I came from. He tries to relay, but says that communication with Bali center is hit and miss. We talk a little more, then he says that he'll monitor the frequency in case I have any trouble. I thank him and try calling

---

26.   Cannula — thin, clear, plastic tube system that fits around the head, to feed oxygen from the tank into the person's nose.

Bali center a few more times. Much, much later after no reception, I return to HF. The controller gives me another frequency and I make contact immediately. After checking the chart, it looks like I'll be back and forth between HF and VHF as I cross various control areas. Not the best leg to lose my PTT switch, but the ballpoint pen is working fine. Speed is above 150 knots consistently now, great, and still only one cumulonimbus cloud building off to the north, nothing in my path.

This is nice being in VHF contact during the trip, now I can send HF e-mail while monitoring the control frequency. I just received an e-mail from our EAA Chapter 74 back in Orlando. In addition to the monthly Young Eagles' Saturdays, they have an annual Air Fair each April at Orlando Executive Airport, Showalter FBO. This year they flew 340 kids. Great going, team! I'll be there next year to help you out.

I don't know if I explained that I have a watch on my belt with UTC[27] time on it. The last two time zones have been on the half hour, not a full hour different from UTC. It's not easy for me to calculate UTC in my head, so I keep the watch on my wrist on local time and the second on my belt on UTC. I now set Singapore time on my watch and I'll be only eight hours ahead of UTC. I just checked a map, and on the next leg, I'll be half way around the globe from my starting point in Florida. Probably not yet half way in mileage, as I have to cross the equator two more times and go further south to South Africa, then further north to Greenland. But still, it seems to me that after this and the next leg, I'll be half way home! I've been traveling for just over two months.

My meal planning this trip would rival the commercial airlines in the US: a cold ham and cheese sandwich with more bread than ham and cheese, barely a slice of each, plus a cereal bar and an apple. It really reminds me of the airlines. Anyway, it's enough to keep me going for three-and-a-half more hours. I'm over Borneo and in and out of clouds. It seems very wet and soggy down there. There are several buildups that I go through with some moderate turbulence, but it doesn't last long and the rain cleans off the plane.

---

27.   UTC — Universal coordinated time also known as zulu time, is the standard time in Greenwich, England. It is used for all aircraft departure, enroute, and arrival times, worldwide.

Geoff, James, David, Jamil
and Norman welcoming
me to Seletar Airport in
Singapore

It's pretty hot outside, 19 degrees Celsius, but I have the silver reflective shade on the sunny side and the cockpit is livable—much better than when I crossed from Hawaii to American Samoa.

The last few hours were uneventful. The hand-over to Singapore Radio was expectedly efficient. While I had to call and call other radio frequencies to report positions, Singapore Radio anticipated my crossing, asked if I was there, and what time my next position report would be. They were highly efficient in all respects. Singapore approach was busy with major commercial traffic coming into Changi, but vectored me around to the northeast and directly to Seletar, the General Aviation airport. There was no one flying at the airport, or at least I didn't see or hear any other planes. I had expected a lot of planes in the pattern; although it was a Friday afternoon, so most people would be working, not flying. I landed and taxied to a parking spot where Geoff, James, and David were awaiting my arrival. I received a "red carpet" welcome and we unloaded and started the paperwork. One form required seven copies and there were five other forms to fill out. Geoff acted as my handling agent and it was the easiest customs and immigration process I went through. Thanks Geoff. Five minutes later we were headed out to meet the other pilots, Norman and Jamil, and go out to dinner.

Two quick days in Singapore and Malaysia

Friday evening we had an introduction to Little India in downtown Singapore. We had a variety of foods that were hot but tasty. I learned that the food would be even hotter and spicier in India, but I'll get used to it little by little, I hope. Another pilot, James, who flies a Trinidad, with his wife Irene, kindly hosted Dave and me for the weekend. Dave, an Orlando EAA Chapter 74 member and friend, was very interested in my trip during the planning stages and volunteered to help out or join me anywhere in the world. Due to the weight of gas necessary over the Pacific, those legs were not possible. However, shorter legs started at Singapore and we decided to meet there and fly to India and the Seychelles together. Dave brought over the new Jeppesen charts for this area of the world and for Africa, keeping us up to date with the most current charts for the next legs of the trip.

Together we prepared and filed the flight plan to Chennai (previously Madras), India. It has to be entered into the system 72 hours before arrival. Since we were spending Sunday in Malaysia and staying the night there, our departure had changed to Johor Bahru airport from Seletar. When I was doing the original planning, months previously, to get the India entry permit I'd given Seletar as my departure point. While communicating with Geoff by e-mail, I'd done the paperwork to get the India permit revised to depart from Johor Bahru. The new permit arrived by HF e-mail during my Friday flight to Singapore! Great timing.

James helped us with weather sites on the Internet for satellite weather and wind information. In the afternoon, an old colleague came by for a visit. I'd worked with Ming Y. during the mid 1980s and again in the early 1990s when we were both Operations Managers for our respective plants. We'd always got along well, and we had a good

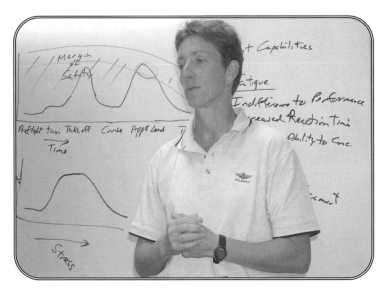

CarolAnn giving an Aviation Safety Seminar in Singapore.
For photo of the Seminar Group, see color photos

few hours reminiscing and catching up.

We went out for a local lunch and toured a little. You'd never know that there was a SARS outbreak; life seemed to go on as normal. After all the news and cautions about travel, I expected to see fewer people on the streets and masks everywhere. There was no external indication of a problem. The only difference was a temperature check with an ear thermometer at the airport upon arrival.

Geoff had planned an Aviation Safety Seminar for the local pilots on Saturday evening. There were over 40 pilots in attendance from Singapore and Malaysia. After an explanation about the Wings program, Geoff started the presentation on the subject of Pilot Fatigue and Exhaustion. He'd done some research, and presented the main topic, including the contributors to exhaustion and recommendations for what to do. Geoff had coordinated with me by e-mail and asked me to present my experiences with fatigue during my long flight legs. I was happy to participate. After my short explanations and stories, the pilots were interested in my flight details and asked many questions. Several among them had done some ferry flights and added their perspectives.

Going through arrivals processing at Johor Bahru Airport, Malaysia

We had dinner before the meeting and took a group photo afterwards (see color photo). It was an evening of fun for all. One interesting aspect of the meeting was the number of nationalities and cultures represented. The pilots in this region represent not only the local countries but also many expatriates from all over the world including US, Europe, Scandinavia, South Africa, Australia, and India.

We'd planned to meet Sunday at Seletar airport to show the Mooney to those interested in seeing the modifications. The HF setup was the item most pilots wanted to see and talk about. Then we would depart for Johor Bahru (JB), Malaysia. All went as planned. Four planes set off for JB. Dave was with me on this short leg, so I took the opportunity to do a practice approach, a full ILS, as JB doesn't have radar. Prior to the approach I practiced holding. As four planes had departed from Seletar in Singapore for the short half-hour flight, the ones after me had to hold prior to executing their approaches. There usually isn't much activity at Johor Bahru, so this might be the first time they've had to "stack" planes in the holding pattern.

The trip is a little different from a domestic flight in the US, as each person has to go through customs and immigration at both airports. Ten of us trooped through the processes, including an ear temperature check for SARS at Seletar. Then all of us trooped through the empty terminal in JB and repeated the process with the Malaysian authorities. For a half-hour flight, our administrative time was probably one-and-a-half hours.

Then we swapped around passengers and three planes set off for Tioman Island, a small island off the east coast of Malaysia. It has a great one-way-in, one-way-out approach with hills on three

Final approach into Tioman Island, Malaysia.
There is a hill to the left, straight ahead and behind us.

sides. The downwind leg is almost to the first hill; turn right before the coconut tree. The base leg is almost to the next hill, then turn onto final, slow down, land, and stop before the 300 foot sheer tree and rock wall.

The experienced pilots got us all down safely and I was happy to be a passenger. We had great views, but I'd only try it if my plane were lightly loaded. It was a great day: flying, eating Malaysian food beside the beach, swimming in warm seawater, and enjoying the warm sun. After a while we had to return. A quick trip to the tower to say hi, and we were off to JB again. The other pilots returned to Singapore; but Geoff and PaoChen, his wife, stayed to make sure all went well for our departure the following morning.

As we returned to JB, the tower called us to say there was a slight problem with the flight plan. It was better to discuss it in person, so we trooped up to the tower with charts and fight plan. David, the tower controller, greeted us and explained that Chennai control (in India) wanted N220FC at 8,500 feet minimum airways altitude early in the flight. I explained that with full fuel it would be

In JB tower
communicating with
Kuala Lumpur and
India for altitude
required on next
day's flight

difficult to attain that altitude too early. He communicated with
Kuala Lumpur (KL) control and finally I spoke with them directly.
After many calls back and forth, because Velu, in KL (whose
brother, he told me, is an EAA Chapter president), had to coordinate
with Chennai control, we finally accepted to be at 8,500 at the
ANOKO intersection, which gave me enough time to burn off fuel
prior to climbing. Phewwww, now we could go to dinner.

Geoff had checked us into the JB Sofitel at an expensive $35 US
per night for a wonderfully appointed room with king-size bed. I
figured I deserved it, as this was probably going to be my last
comfortable bed for a number of weeks.

CHAPTER 9

I got to know about your flight from a dear friend. I am based in a city called Bangalore (south of India). Please mail me your flight schedule through India. Do let me know what assistance I can provide for your flight.

Would you need help with Directorate General Civil Aviation, Airport Authorities, technical assistance or any other thing? Please let me know. I have attempted a similar journey and thus would like to assist in any way possible.

Best of luck and happy landings.
Regards,
Arvind

May 5: Johor Bahru, Malaysia to Chennai (Madras), India, 7th leg flight report

U p for an early start again. Geoff drove us to the airport and got us through the gate with our manifest. All had been prepared the previous evening, so the preflight was easy. As is the custom from now on, I asked ground for permission to startup the engine and, this time, received it immediately. This was a good sign; if they hadn't had my clearance, startup wouldn't have been granted. Clearance okay, run-up okay, back taxi 5,000 feet down the 10,000-foot runway—I want full length when I'm loaded with fuel and heavy. Dave had not had a good night's sleep. This was to be his first long flight over water and he was a little apprehensive. He asked if I had a ritual or anything that I did before takeoff. I didn't. He needed something to "cast off." So he said a sailor's farewell, mentally cast off the lines, and off we went. It was a smooth liftoff into a sky just starting to get light; there were patches of fog between the hills and flashes of lightening in the cumulus clouds to the left. The air was smooth and the climb rate was a normal 250 feet per minute. I believe this was the best climb out so far.

I had to make a left turn after reaching the VOR five miles from the airport. This didn't put me directly in line with the thunderstorm clouds but not far enough off for me. I asked for and received a deviation to the right by five miles. Then ATC asked me to climb to 8,000 feet. I couldn't believe it, after all we'd been through the previous evening; here we were starting again. I explained that I was heavy and could not climb to 8,000 feet immediately, but could later on. They wouldn't relent and I said I'd try. Slowly, ever so slowly, at 100 feet per minute for the last 1,000 feet, we finally made it. I leveled off and switched to the rear tank. There were still thunderstorms around, and I asked for and received additional deviations.

I was over Kuala Lumpur and took a photo of the enormous airport. Then ATC was back on my case again, asking me to climb to 12,000 feet. I explained again that I couldn't at this time. They conferred with Chennai and we finally accepted 8,500 feet immediately and 12,000 feet at the intersection we'd discussed the previous day, ANOKO. How would they ever know? I would be out of radar range and it was only what I was telling them. But I wouldn't feel right telling them that I was at 12,000 feet when I was actually at 8,500 feet, so at 50 miles before the intersection, I started a slow climb. When I reported ANOKO and my position report, I was at 12,000 feet and chugging along at 140 knots. After three-and-a-half hours I had eight hours to go and was finally at peace. The HF was working and reception was good.

Four hours later with four hours to go, all is calm, especially the water below. I haven't seen it this calm anywhere. Barely little ripples on the surface. I had the silver reflective shades up to keep the sun and heat out; Dave wanted to see the view. I told him there was only blue water, but he'd come to see the sights and absorb the trip, so we compromised. There are small puffy clouds everywhere, but nothing large or menacing.

I couldn't reach Chennai Radio in the last two hours and was starting to get irritable at 12,000 feet (but my fingernails weren't turning blue); I wanted to get lower and breathe some oxygen. I tried Chennai Radar on VHF and got through 200 miles out. They kept us at 12,000, much to my dismay. I took the time to clean up the cockpit and put on my flight suit. I'd learned that in India and other countries the customs and immigration people pay more respect to pilots/captains in uniform than those wearing shorts and T-shirts. I chose a flight suit instead of a white shirt with epaulets, on which I could have put captain's stripes, but now I think the white shirt might have been cooler.

I requested and was finally approved to descend to 8,500 feet. It was hotter, but I started to feel better. It was extremely hazy as we were finally descended to 6,000, then 4,000 feet. I flew over the airport, elevation 47 feet, at 4,000 feet. At five miles out, I was finally descended to 1,700 feet, turned on to final, and cleared to land. Two jets were holding for takeoff while I slowly finished the last three miles on final. I took the first taxiway and called ground, who directed me straight ahead to holding area 45. Suddenly three voices came on frequency for N220FC to stop and follow the "follow me" truck. I stopped and laughed to myself; this was only the beginning of the arrival experience. I had heard that it could be exasperating; we waited for the various parties to decide what they wanted us to do. Finally I turned around and followed the "follow me" truck. They parked us on a separate apron, another truck arrived, and six people approached the plane. This was the beginning of two hours of fun.

When I thought they were asking for "papers," they were saying "purpose" of the visit. I said a pleasure trip to visit India. They smiled and were happy to hear that, but said that we would have to be parked elsewhere since we were staying for 14 days. We got in again and followed the "follow me" truck to another ramp. Now we had ten handlers and two armed guards helping determine what to do next. We were parked behind a disabled jet airliner, which was chocked and looked like it was there for maintenance. There were no tie-downs. I explained that I needed to tie down the plane. One person was sent off to get cement blocks. I started unpacking the plane to buy time trying to remember where I'd put the General Declaration forms. We had only made out enough for Malaysia departure and didn't get one stamped for the next port of entry; I needed to make one up for my arrival. During most of these discussions, the Indian rep would address the questions to Dave. Dave would indicate that I was the captain and I would answer the question. The next question was again addressed to Dave, who again pointed to me and I answered the question. This was the way things would continue in this and other countries while Dave was with me.

Air India offered to act as my "handler" in the absence of anyone else. I explained that Cambata[28] had helped with my permits for India but didn't have a presence on this field, so Air India said they would do the handling. There were many comings and goings as I unloaded, looked for paperwork, and continued asking about tie-downs. It was 39C (108F) on the ramp, and I was in a full fight suit. I was hot, sweating, and irritable after a 12-hour flight at 12,000 feet, and trying to be as patient and charming as possible. While I was in the cockpit, I felt a bump against the plane and jumped out quickly to see what was happening. One person had put a huge jet chock in front of my wheel. I looked at it and laughed as I asked for a larger one—we both laughed. I finally remembered where the forms were, and as Dave kept them occupied, I filled it out. They asked if the aircraft had been decontaminated prior to departure and could I show them the empty spray can. I explained that no it hadn't but if they had a can, we could spray it now. They said that we wouldn't be allowed entry if I couldn't supply a spray can. I said again that I didn't have one but maybe they could provide one. They said that the health department wouldn't let us in. I said that we weren't flying back.

At the Aviation Safety Seminar in Singapore, an Indian Air Traffic Controller, Ram, had introduced himself and offered his services and those of his dad, located in Chennai, to help out. As I was stepping out of the cockpit, I noticed a person walking toward our large group: it was Ram's dad. He introduced himself and helped where he could. The Air India representatives came up and explained their services and prices. Although the normal price was $990, they could help us for $330. I joked with them and asked what it included and said that Ram's dad was my counsel, and then we all agreed. I gave them my newly found General Declaration and our passports and we all hopped on a transit bus; yes, a bus just for us and them, and went to arrivals. First stop health inspection.

The doctors, nurses, and aids were milling around "holding up" the counters. Some were wearing masks and others had them draped around their necks. On hearing that we were coming in

---

28.   Cambata — an Indian airport handler and services company; also with offices in the US.

from Singapore, actually Malaysia, they all donned their masks. I put my hand over my mouth and laughed. When they learned that we hadn't been sprayed on departure they said it was impossible for us to enter the country. That's what one pays a handling agent for. After 15 minutes it was decided that we could get a spray can, return to the plane, spray the plane, and all would be okay. I returned to the plane, accompanied by two health workers and two Air India handlers. We sprayed the inside of the plane and returned. An Air India handler asked what I did for work and I explained that I had lost my job a year previously but had helped build some of the equipment used by his company on the ramp. We chatted for a while about this and discussed the equipment and competitors' equipment. He seemed happy that we had something in common.

We returned to the health area, filled out the SARS declaration form, filled out the immigration paperwork, and proceeded to the next desk after smiling and thanking the doctors, nurses, and aides. With ten people surrounding the immigration desk, the agent could barely see Dave and me to ask questions, but managed to ask if this was my first trip to India. I replied yes and that I was looking forward to visiting his country. Stamp, stamp, stamp, and we were cleared through. Next stop customs to check luggage, but we walked right through.

Next stop the Air India office and more paperwork. After sitting down, we were offered a coffee or tea. I accepted tea, but several minutes later they explained that tea could not be made because they had lost electricity; it was also the reason the air conditioning wasn't working. They took about 30 minutes over the paperwork and also ordered the hotel bus. The airport manager walked in and they all stood up immediately. I was introduced and shook hands; unfortunately, I had dropped the top of my flight suit to get into my shorts pocket for cash, and so I was standing with my sweaty T-shirt on and flight suit half off. I apologized and they all waved away the problem and said it was hot without air conditioning.

Two of the Air India personnel explained once again what was covered in their fee. I explained that I would need to get back out to the plane the following day to drop off some luggage before we set off. Oh no, that would be too difficult, impossible. With heightened security it would not be allowed to return to the plane before departure. Ten more minutes of discussion, with Ram's dad helping, and it was decided that he could take us to the permit office the following day and possibly/possibly not a permit might be arranged; but probably not. He would also take us to the landing and parking office to find out those charges. I said that with Ram's dad doing all this work, he should get 10% of their fee. They all laughed and said they were from sister companies and worked together.

Finally we trooped out of the office, through more guarded gates, to the taxi and bus stand outside. It didn't look as foreign as I'd expected. There weren't beggars all over the streets (so far at least). The hotel bus arrived and we were whisked away.

Norman, Geoff, CarolAnn, Dave, Andreas, James and Neil, in front.
Pilots from Singapore and the Johor Flying Club.

CHAPTER 10

My daughter Maggie and I read the article about you in the Orlando Sentinel (May 11). Your trip is very inspiring to both of us and we wish you the very best of luck and Godspeed.

Maggie thinks that "it's really cool that you're flying solo around the world and that it must take a lot of courage to do what you are doing." Maggie is 10 years old.

Your Mom is very proud of you. We will be following your adventures on line.
Cathy & Maggie

Two Weeks in India

I'd talked with other pilots who had done this trip and, without exception, they said that if they could have avoided India they would have. It is one of only two stops for gas when crossing the Indian Ocean and the bureaucracy is practically unbearable. Sri Lanka is also an option that some pilots have taken, but most choose, and hate, stopping in India. During the planning, I kept going back and forth between India and Sri Lanka and finally decided on India. With the fighting in Sri Lanka, it is not recommended for American tourists. Since I HAD to stop in India, I really wanted to see the Taj Mahal. I figured this would be my only chance, my only visit to India, so I decided to spend two weeks traveling in the country. It was my most worrisome country and I was very glad that Dave was traveling with me. I'll cut to the end before going into the details—it is a most wonderful country with so much diversity, rich in culture, religion, and history that I will definitely be back. I'm thrilled to have been able to see as much as we did and can't wait to see more on a future trip.

On the first day we just took a taxi tour of Chennai (previously known as Madras). The driver showed us many Christian churches, including St. Thomas' church on a hill outside Chennai. It turned out that our taxi driver was converted to Christianity by a sister who he believed saved him when he was sick, taking much medication, and not improving. Walking between one church and a Hindu temple we passed through a back street where families were living in corrugated steel shacks and cooking fish curry outside on the "street." This was our first introduction to the poor streets and it was difficult to walk back to the car through the smells and sights. At least these people had something and weren't begging. Later we would see worse.

We visited a beach that was deserted. There were wooden stands for cooking and what appeared to be handmade children's "merry-go-rounds," made of pieces of broken toys, but no people. The driver told us that it's too hot during the day and people only come out in the evening. Later, in each city, we saw that things liven up at night and there are people all over the streets. It's cooler and more comfortable to be outside then.

We planned to take a commercial flight to Delhi with the objective of doing the "golden triangle" tour of Delhi, Agra, and Jaipur. Then we were going to head to the Himalayas and visit Shimla, a town recommended for summer tourists. So we repacked our bags to carry only one backpack each and left the rest at the hotel for pickup ten days later. Next stop, Air India to check on the Mooney and airport fees. Our first challenge was to get into the terminal and get to the Air India office. Due to the crowds, only ticket holders are allowed through the doors into the terminal. We didn't have a ticket and thus couldn't get through. The ticket sales and baggage offices all have windows to the sidewalk where people queue up to buy tickets or ask questions. We asked what to do and showed our Air India Handling Agent receipt and were told to go through arrivals to the second floor Air India office. We showed the door guard the receipt and he asked for passports, then finally let us through. On the second floor another person questioned what we were doing, looked at the receipt, and escorted us back down to the first floor through another guard station to the Air India office. We were finally where we needed to be.

We explained that we wanted to know the landing and parking fees and would like to see that the plane was okay and tied down (the previous day they had said that a third tie-down would be added, but I wanted to make sure it had been done). They said that we'd have to talk with the Airport Manager about fees. We went back through the guard area (showing the receipt) to the Airport Manager's office. He escorted us back to the Air India office and said that it was their responsibility and not his. Unfortunately, it was shift change time at Air India and they asked us to return in half an hour. Also they were in the middle of moving to new offices down the street, so not many people were available. We killed time by going to the Domestic terminal and buying our tickets to Delhi. Upon returning, we found a most helpful manager who made all the necessary calls to find out about the fees. It looked like about $50–60 for landing and parking plus some airways fees. Not too bad.

The next issue, to get on the ramp to see the plane, was MUCH more difficult. Without a special ID badge it was next to impossible. Since we weren't leaving and didn't have a flight plan, they couldn't get us onto the tarmac airside. We explained that it was necessary to see that everything was okay with the aircraft before leaving for ten days. They decided to walk us through the departure steps (rather than try to get a pass) with the explanation of what we needed. At each point, getting into the departure lounge without a ticket, immigration, security, etc., the initial reaction was no, check with manager, no, maybe, let's see, lots of discussion, well okay if they are accompanied all the way. The Air India handlers got us through and got a bus to get us to the plane. Everything looked great. A tail tie-down weight had been obtained and put in place. All the sun shields were in place—my big worry, with all the heat. Now I could leave knowing that all was safe.

I changed $200 to Rupees.   Little did I know that I would receive a one-inch thick wad of notes. 9,300 Rupees in 100 R notes. Where was I going to put all those?

Security boarding the flight to Delhi was pretty "standard" at first, they send men through one check point and women through another—each person gets "wanded," all your pockets are "hand-checked" and you must walk through a metal detector. During boarding, there is a second bag check and "pat down" process. Each time, the hand luggage ticket is stamped and, before boarding the plane, the ticket is checked for all stamps. As we taxied across the ramp, I looked out the window and there was N220FC! I waved goodbye and silently said "See you in ten days."

The Yatri Guest House in Delhi was basic, clean and comfortable. At 1,500 R per night, $30, it met our needs and became our home in Delhi. The next morning we took our first "auto rickshaw" ride to the Tourist office. These are three-wheeled rickshaws with room for a driver up front and two passengers in the back. The engine runs on compressed gas. They were to become our best means of city travel at 20–70R, 50 cents to $1.50 per ride, with a story to tell with each trip. The Tourist office informed us that the city bus

Typical street scene in Dehli, India
(For picture of rickshaws, see color photos.)

tour had been cancelled due to lack of tourists; our only other option would be to take a car, driver, and tour guide for the day at a cost of 1,200R vs. 350R each for the bus tour. We took that option, as we wanted to see the sights. It turned out to be a fantastic day.

Mr. Tewari was an extremely knowledgeable guide who spoke excellent English and enthusiastically shared with us the history, culture and religious aspects of Indian life. We enjoyed the day so much we asked if he could accompany us to Agra and Jaipur, which he did. Although all the sites were fascinating, the most notable was the Jantar Mantar, a group of astrological instruments designed and built in 1725 AD to measure the movement of the sun and planets, forecast the eclipses, as well as tell time. It was an amazing accomplishment for that era. We also saw Parliament House, India Gate, and a number of tombs that were a great preparation for the Taj Mahal in Agra the next day, as they served to amplify its magnificence.

When I walked through the gate and looked at the Taj Mahal, it literally took my breath away; it is 100 times more exotic than anything else we had seen (see color photo). We took the obligatory pictures, then walked closer, took off our shoes, and climbed the steps to visit the inside of the tomb. It is splendid from all angles,

One of the many structures in the Astonomical Observatory in Dehli, India. A photo of the Taj Mahal is in the color photo section.

close, far, inside, and out. The inlaid gems in the tombs were unbelievable. It's no wonder the structure took 22 years to build. This is what I came to India to see and it was worth the trip. I didn't want to leave. We sat silently for a while, and then finally had to continue our tour. From the Red Fort, which we visited later, there was a splendid view of the Taj Mahal. This was where its builder, Emporer Shah Jahan, was imprisoned for the last seven years of his life by his youngest son in order to stop him from building an identical structure, in black marble, on the opposite shore of the river.

We moved on to Fatehpur Sikri, the ghost city, which was built by an emporer in 1571, lived in for one generation until 1585, and then deserted to move the capital back to Agra. In the middle of nowhere was this city with all the accommodations and supplies to support about 1,000 people. The whole city, including a wall of 27 kilometers around the city, had been built of local red sandstone in less than three years. We then moved on to Jaipur. The forts on top of the hills had kept these Mogul emperors free for many generations. We rode an elephant up the hill to the fort and toured the numerous buildings and living quarters (see color photo). Throughout the four days, each time I'd have trouble understanding why something was done a certain way, Mr. Tewari would look at me and say, "You know what your problem is? Your problem is you are too Ultra Modern." If he said it once, he said it ten times. But we had some lively discussions on life, history, culture, and religion. It was a fantastic tour of all the cities and sites. I wished we had more time to see other areas.

Unfortunately, we had to see some of India on our own, so we said goodbye to Mr. Tewari when we returned to Delhi. We went to the train station to book a ticket to Shimla in the Himalayas. Bad luck, it was tourist season and there was no place on the train. A car and driver could be made available with a complete package deal with hotel for $325 for three days. Not what we wanted, but since it was the only way to see the Himalayas, we accepted the deal.

One more night at Yatri Guest House, our same room, and we'd leave the next morning. Actually, we had several memorable auto rickshaw rides that evening (see color photo). One driver wanted to take us to a shop. We only had to look for five minutes, we didn't have to buy anything, but if he took us there, he'd receive some food that he needed for his family. We accepted this one stop, although we were both tired. He drove like a mad man on the way there. We looked for five minutes and came out. He asked why we hadn't bought anything and really badgered us about it. He said that he'd take us to another shop. We said no, straight to the hotel. He drove wildly again, then stopped and said that he'd take us to another shop. We both told him no, exited the rickshaw, and walked away. No question, that was the most memorable ride. On other rides, we either had drivers who didn't know where they were going and stopped to ask people along the way, or had engines that stopped and wouldn't restart, or drivers who told you about their family and children in the hope of getting a bigger tip.

After an hour-and-a-half in the car on the drive to Shimla, our driver said that we were passing his village, that he was sick (he actually looked and sounded very bad), and would we accept his brother driving us to Shimla instead of him. Dave and I looked at each other; we thought that only auto rickshaw drivers had these kinds of stories. He assured us that his brother worked for the same company, had all the papers, and it was okay. We said that we'd call the company and let them know. He wavered and said that it was his job to do that. We said yes, and we'd do it too. He said that was okay. Really, I just wanted to see if he was okay if we called the company—it was Sunday and we had no way of reaching the correct person. So, we accepted the switch. Aside from the A/C going out, it was uneventful during the seven-hour drive. It was extremely hazy in Chennai and Delhi and I was expecting the air to clear in the mountains—nope, still hazy all the way.

As we got into the mountains, the terraces for the crops and gardens were amazing—up the steep slopes (see color photo). When we arrived, the houses and hotels built on these sheer slopes were unbelievable. I don't know how they were anchored in, but just hoped that they stayed there for another few days. We turned left off the road and drove onto the roof of our hotel—that was the parking. Then we walked down five floors to the room. Everything was straight up and down. We got to know the streets and the way to the "mall" where all the tourists went; we walked all around the town. There were Indian tourists everywhere. It was extremely crowded, certainly not my cup of tea. I go to the mountains for peace and quiet, not crowds. Dave was okay with it, but I had to get away.

The next day our driver took me away from the town and towards a resort in the valley. On the way it was peaceful and the scenery was majestic. I finally realized that he was taking me to another crowded tourist destination, so I asked to get out and walk in the hills. We agreed where to meet, he drove away, and I walked, sat, read, took pictures, and walked some more. When we met, I asked for another hour, so he drove three kilometers up hill and I set out for another walk. It was beautifully calm and relaxing; I didn't want to return to the crowds and noise of Shimla.

The next day we had planned to take the scenic train from Shimla to Kalka, where the driver would pick us up and take us back to Delhi. What a nightmare! With double the number of people squashed into half the number of wooden seats for a seven-hour trip it was not the restful, scenic trip that we had imagined. The views were good, but I'd seen better the day before. I'm glad that we tried it, but it's not a trip that I'd repeat. Back in Delhi we were at home at the Yatri Guest House for one last night before returning to Chennai.

In Chennai, the day before our intended departure, we started the paperwork "battle" that I heard about from other pilots. These

The seven hour train ride, pure torture

stories included one departure bureaucratic nightmare that took the pilot 24 hours before being allowed to depart and a second that took six hours. Again we had trouble getting through airport security and back to the Air India offices, but after that they were most helpful. With the paperwork in hand, we walked one-and-a-half kilometers to Air Traffic Control to pay our fees and prepare the paperwork for departure the next morning. ATC was extremely helpful also. There were four main stops that had to be signed off: fees and permit, communication, met (weather) office, and briefing. The met office would be completed the morning of departure, but the others were happily completed that afternoon. The employees shared a cup of tea with us and joined in our photograph sessions. We all had fun.

Actually the clearance we received in Chennai was just for a three-hour trip to Trivandrum on the southwest coast of India. By preparing the paperwork the previous day, we assured that the morning of departure was relatively painless. We'd allowed two hours, arriving at 5 am in the Air India office, for a 7 am proposed departure. The stamps and approvals through customs and security proceeded relatively well. We got the met briefing and paid a minor adjustment in the parking fee, then went to the plane for fueling. I was happy when the fueler arrived on time at 6:15 am. Unfortunately, they couldn't start refueling until the "accountant" showed up, which took another 45 minutes. After that, refueling proceeded well, we paid in dollars, and shook hands all around.

The Air India representatives had done a noble job of getting everything done.

We jumped into the cockpit, enjoyed the peace and quiet, and prepared to startup. Due to a potential lack of avgas at Trivandrum, I'd loaded up at Chennai, so the takeoff was long and the climb-out in the 30-degree Centigrade heat was slower than "normal." But it was good to be in the air again. This short leg was to reduce the distance to the Seychelles. I also hoped that since Trivandrum is a smaller airport, the paperwork could be handled quickly for a 6 am departure in three days' time.

Upon arrival we met with ATC directly. Knowing the ropes in Chennai helped the process in Trivandrum. We calculated the landing and parking fees immediately to get that out of the way. I submitted the flight plan to get that into the system. I talked with the met office to get the briefing prepared for Monday morning while Dave went to the Airport Manager's office to get a pass that would allow us to get back onto the ramp to get to the plane during the weekend. Things were looking good and we both felt more positive about a relatively speedy departure.

An Indian pilot, Arvind, had contacted me by e-mail and helped me to get gas in Trivandrum. He had contacts at the Kerala Aviation Training Center who could provide avgas for topping off

One of the many signatures needed to depart India

Gassing up in Trivandrum, India

before the next long leg. I got a clearance to taxi over to the other side of the field and met Mr. Prakash, Chief Flight Instructor, and Mr. Rajeev, the Administrative Officer. They happily completed the paperwork and with the help of the chief engineer, Mr. R. Babu and his mechanics, supplied 100 litres to see me through the next leg. I sincerely appreciate all the help, especially that of Arvind, whom I didn't get to meet.

More on ALS

While in India, I was reading a *Time* Magazine dated May 12, 2003, and found an article on ALS and soccer/football teams. It was very similar to the BBC news show that I saw while in American Samoa. They have found an unusually high number of older professional football (soccer) players who now have ALS. Doctors are now looking into any possible link with drugs or painkillers and ALS. The month of May is ALS awareness month in the US and I hope other articles and news programs were published and broadcast to help increase the awareness and contributions to find a cause and cure.

Also while in India, I received an e-mail from Jackie in Australia. Unfortunately she didn't find out about my web site until after I'd left; I would have liked to meet her. This 40-year-old woman who has had ALS for 15 years and is completely in the care of others, 24 hours a day, wrote me a long e-mail in early April about herself and ALS awareness in Australia. She's not on a respirator, but needs others to do everything for her. Once her hand is placed on the trackball, she can type an e-mail and look at web sites, painfully slowly. Her doctors had given her 18 months to live 15 years ago. She believes that God has something else for her to do, and I'm sure He does. I very much appreciate her e-mail and her support and that of others as I continue on this journey.

Rickshaw driver waiting for a customer

Top: From the window of the train as we depart from Shimla
Bottom: Terraced fields on the Himalayan slopes

CHAPTER 11

We have so much in common, except I'm not a pilot...... Saw your article in the Orlando paper on mother's day, and GOD BLESS YOU, your mom, your plane, your journey! U are a serious inspiration. I live in Florida now and will share your website with my daughter who one day will fly. We are Cessna offspring.

Are you going to the Greek Islands? I liked Crete and Santorini the most. I think the latter is Atlantis lost.

Keep in touch and we will roast some coffee for you when you return. Bummer you don't have a Citation to fly with around the world, next time?

Blue Skies to ya!
Michael

May 19: Trivandrum, India to the Seychelles, 8th leg flight report

The Seychelles airport closes at sunset (at least that's what the internet web site said); so an early departure is in order to complete the 12-hour flight during the daylight. By starting the process at 4 am, we hoped to be in the air at 6 am. But what a frustrating morning it turned out to be. The airport was just opening at 4 am and there was no one at immigration, our first required stop. Some people were reading paperwork at the customs desk, so I wandered over there to talk with them. I'm not so sure that was a good idea. The man at the desk wanted to know all about my trip. He looked through each page of my passport; he looked through every paper in the departure folder, even though some were unnecessary. He asked a million questions about the whole trip. I was getting very irritated. After 30 minutes there was still no one at immigration. Each stop, immigration, security, airport manager, and ATC continued the same way: all interested in the trip and lots of unnecessary questions. I took to repeating that we had to be off by 6 am. That didn't speed them up. Although we had paid the parking invoice the previous evening, the Airport Manager's office found an error, recalculated it three or four times and required that it be paid, in the tower, prior to departure. Dave and I split up. He headed for the tower to handle the parking bill; I headed for the doctor's office for his signature on the Health

Declaration. A guard had to wake up the doctor, and I had to explain about our flight to the Seychelles, but finally it was signed. I made it to the plane and did the preflight, praying that Dave would be arriving soon. One of the officials walked over to wish me a good flight and to ask more about the plane and trip. I was painfully polite and exceedingly happy when he shook my hand and wished me a good trip. I was very frustrated at the end of it all, but Dave arrived and we were only 30 minutes behind schedule—not really all that bad.

We took off at 6:30 am. We both breathed a huge sign of relief. It was a slow climb as usual. Trivandrum is on the southwest coast, so we were over water immediately and climbing to 4,000 feet. I wanted about two hours to burn off fuel before climbing to 6,000 feet. The headwinds were less than forecast and we stayed above 130 knots on the first leg to the Maldives. There were a few cloud buildups, which we deviated around, but nothing major. At first I couldn't raise Chennai radio on HF, but finally they came through and confirmed our current position and future position estimates. There was one ominous looking black cloud ahead, but it was only rain. On the other side we were in the clear. Two hours later and we were over the beautiful green blue Maldive Islands. There are hundreds of them—some inhabited, many not (see color photo). It was a magnificent sight. Malé center (Maldives Airport) was coordinating commercial flight arrivals without radar and was asking each plane for its distance and altitude. We stayed at 6,000 feet and out of everyone's way. One plane announced 356 passengers—that's a big jet going into the Maldives on vacation. Later on, a second plane reported 337 passengers. What a tourist destination—and it's easy to see why. It looked beautiful from the air.

Take a right turn at the Maldives VOR and we are headed 245 degrees, west-southwest. The headwind picks up and we're down to 123 knots. Sometimes up to 130 knots but mostly down. That's what we flight-planned for, but I'd hoped for better. Oh well, eight-and-a-half hours to go. I had had a bad night's sleep and had caught a cold during the last two days in India, so I was sniffing, coughing, and generally feeling poorly. Each time the ground speed picks up I feel a little better and when it's down I don't feel so good. This was not going to be one of my better flights. After a position report about

297 miles from Malé, we were out of their airspace and Malé radio told us simply to "contact Seychelles" when we got within range. I thought that was weird at the time, but didn't think anything more of it. It was about 244 miles (almost two hours) to the next position report. At that point, I tried Malé, no contact; I tried Mumbai, no luck; I tried Chennai, they said we were weak and to try another frequency, but I couldn't raise them on that frequency. I could hear a few position reports from other pilots, but none clear enough to do a relay. I tried the HF e-mail and that worked fine, so it wasn't our radio or transmission that was the problem. I wasn't comfortable with the situation because no one was answering and, in the highly unlikely event of any problems, we couldn't immediately contact anyone. This was not a good place to be out of radio contact. Phil, who had done my tanking in Lakeland, Florida, had told me that out here over the Indian Ocean, no one even cared. He said that if we went down, no one would come looking for us. What a great thought; but now I'm here, I think he was right. I was probably safer over the vast Pacific than here over the relatively smaller Indian Ocean.

Another 368 miles (2.8 hours) and we were over the next reporting position, but still no contact with Mumbai radio through any HF frequency. We tried every frequency on the chart multiple times. We were getting close to the extended range VHF of the Seychelles, so I tried calling them instead. Actually, the chart has a note saying that it is imperative to contact the Seychelles on HF 20 minutes prior to entering their airspace. I still couldn't reach anyone and thought: "Oh well, what am I supposed to do, circle around out here until I'm out of gas?" I kept on going right into their airspace; let them slap me on the wrist when I arrive. Finally I heard another pilot on VHF. I asked him to relay to Seychelles control for me, which he did. No problem, they said, just contact them when in range. I felt better; they knew where we were and when we'd arrive. Only 180 miles to go.

The winds had come around to easterly as forecast and our speed was up to 140 knots, which was good, but I was actually feeling worse even though I'd eaten some food and had taken plenty of water. It's okay I thought, I can concentrate for one-and-a-half more hours and get us onto the ground. I already had a bad

Final approach into Mahe Airport in the Seychelles

headache and all the attempted radio contacts for the position reports, with HF static in my ears, had made it worse. Unfortunately I'd left the aspirin bottle in my luggage in the back, behind the tank. No way to get to it. Next time I'll remember to bring it up front with me. Finally I could hear Seychelles control and talked with them directly. They asked me to give them the times I had crossed the last two position reporting points—nice, I thought, just fill in the paperwork after the fact instead of being in communication with the pilots when they are over the ocean. I guess I was a little tired and impatient. I later learned that their HF had been out that day. The clouds were scattered and down to 2,000 feet. We dropped through them and saw the island from 20 miles out. It looked similar to the Samoas, a lush island with a high ridge down the middle—beautiful. The 10,000-foot strip was a welcome sight as I turned downwind, base, and final, and then settled onto the runway.

The weather was warm and humid, but when I opened the door, a cool breeze came in and it felt like heaven. I taxied to the parking location, stand 2, and saw two people, one wearing a mask, walking in our direction. The SARS Team. The masked lady asked if we needed a disinfectant spray can, but I told her we had already sprayed ourselves on departure and showed her our health declaration. She handed over the SARS declaration forms that we filled out, indicating I had a cough from my head cold, but no fever. She took off her mask and said it was okay to de-plane. WHEW. I headed to the bathroom immediately. After five minutes outside and some cool water on my face I felt slightly better. Mike and Eddy arrived. Mike is a friend of a friend, Peter, in Houston, who had responded to my e-mails, reserved a hotel, and offered to help us on arrival. They were both exceedingly informative and helpful. The paperwork, customs, and immigration were a breeze—only 10 minutes. What a difference compared with the two-and-a-half hour Indian bureaucracy. Fifteen minutes later we were headed to the Guest House, and in another 10 minutes we were listening to the sounds of the waves breaking on the beach and the birds chirping, and were handed a glass of fruit juice. What a difference. We were in heaven.

Mike and Eddy who helped us greatly in the Seychelles

Four wonderful days in the Seychelles

Paradise doesn't get much better than this. The surf on the beach, soft white sand, a breeze blowing through the open bar, comfortable chairs, and a SayBrew beer—Life is GREAT. But I was very tired, and getting sicker; I think the last meal I had in India was getting to me. I was feeling worse as the day wore on and the following morning I was still not feeling good. Dave was feeling fine; we'd each had different meals on the last day.

We decided to go for a walk, thinking that I needed exercise. It was a beautiful walk over to the other side of the island. Then we went to the airport to check the plane over and start figuring out the paperwork necessary to depart. After meeting with the Air Operations people, the Met office, and the Avgas Company, it looked like a bit of time at the airport on Friday afternoon would take care of all the details and payments and I could be off with very little trouble on Saturday morning. The Met Office was particularly good with satellite pictures, wind charts, everything I needed—it's GREAT to have all the information available prior to departure.

The next morning I went for a swim at our beach and had a lovely hot breakfast; but I was still not feeling up to par. I'd changed my plans to come to the Seychelles instead of Mauritius due to lack of avgas at Mauritius, but I hadn't done the detailed planning for the flight from Seychelles to South Africa, so that was my morning job. Once I reviewed the charts, I discovered it was going to be longer than I originally thought, 16 hours; but at least the winds would be favorable. If not, I can still land and gas up when I cross the coast at Maputo, Mozambique.

We took the bus to the main city of Victoria, to find a local Internet café and get some e-mails off (it cost $7 per e-mail from the hotel, so it's worth a trip). And, I'll look into the paperwork to get duty free avgas if possible. We were walking to the government building to check into Customs and Duty exclusions when we ran into our friend and helper, Eddy. He immediately took control of the situation, called around, and told me where I needed to go. But it was lunchtime and the office would be closed, so he arranged for us to have lunch with his friend Gerard, who is from the Minister's office and is in charge of transportation, including the airport.

David in front of a Cocoa de
Mer. This plant grows only in
the Seychelles

We had a wonderful lunch and talked about airports, yachts, travel, and vacation destinations. I told him about the Seychelles website showing that the airport is closed at sunset. He said that the facility is open 24 hours a day, but only staffed when a flight is expected. He said that he'd look into it. It's amazing how much everyone in the Seychelles makes it their business to take care of the tourists. Besides Mike and Eddy, and now Gerard, many people ask how our stay is going and how we like the Seychelles. They really seem to care about how we are treated on their island. The bus drivers are very helpful and it's easy to get around by public transportation. By mid afternoon I'm beginning to feel better; and it's good to feel like myself again. Now...back to the paperwork chase and seeing if I can get some duty-free avgas (at $3.80 per gallon every deduction helps).

That evening, after another swim, we sat on the chairs on the beach with a beer, listening to the waves on the reef. The wind was blowing from the east and the air was perfect. It was like being in the Bahamas (but with mountains): peaceful, relaxing, wonderful. The mountains are granite, not volcanic. That means that they have always been there, and not under water, and give majestic and breathtaking land and seascapes. The flora and fauna are different from volcanic islands and they have some plants that exist nowhere else in the world. The Coco de Mer, a type of palm tree, has the largest seeds in the world and takes over 25 years to flower and reproduce. There is a world heritage site as well as many nature reserves, which total 46% of the land area of the Seychelles. They are home to the world's largest population of giant tortoises and provide nesting grounds to great numbers of spectacular ocean-going birds as well as to the last remaining flightless bird in the Indian Ocean.

During the week, we gave Eddy's children, Kalsey and Pierre-Andre, a Young Eagles flight around the Island of Mahe (see color photo). It was fascinating for me to see the island from the air and they both loved it. Dave was ground crew for the Young Eagles operation and handled the certificates and paperwork. When we were finished, we did a radio and newspaper interview about our trip around the world and our stop in the Seychelles.

The Seychellois are hospitable people who are a fusion of a number of cultures, which has produced a multifaceted community. As they were both a French colony and a British colony, one finds both cultures in many parts of the lifestyle. There is Creole food, which is exceptional, as well as three languages, English, French and Creole. The Seychelles has long been at the forefront of environmental protection, and started eco tourism in the 1970s before it became a buzzword. Spear fishing was banned, shell collection was restricted, and plans for building hotels higher than the surrounding vegetation were disallowed. All this helps to preserve the Seychelles and its tourist dollar, and keeps the waters clear, the beaches uncrowded, and the hillsides verdant. It's truly a magnificent tourist destination.

CHAPTER 12

Green with envy is the first thing that springs to mind, but awe and envy have little consideration to your fantastic achievement thus far. I live in Johannesburg RSA and my wife and I would welcome you to contact us on your arrival. If there is anything that we could do to assist in making your stay more pleasurable, please do not hesitate to contact me. Life is a journey, enjoy the ride.
Dean

Where are you? Seem to have lost you but presume you couldn't find anywhere to plug in on the islands, so maybe I can catch you in the air. Lousy wet weather here hope its better where you are. Love Dad

May 27: Seychelles to Lanseria, South Africa, 9th leg flight report

Sometimes things go wrong; and unfortunately, this time they did. I was flight planning from the Seychelles to South Africa, and it looked a little tight. Although winds were mostly favorable, if anything changed, I'd need a stop in Maputo, Mozambique, for gas. I e-mailed the person doing my permits and asked if I could stop in Maputo. He informed me that we didn't have a permit for Mozambique and it took seven days to get one. I looked at the airspace and there was no way around Mozambique. MMmmm, now what? He started working on the permit and I got in touch with the local DGCA, Director General of Civil Aviation, to see what else we could do from this end. After a day, while that was still in process, I checked with the Met Office to see what the weather forecast was doing. Things looked good everywhere except southern South Africa, where a front was coming across in the next few days, and a huge high pressure south of Madagascar was putting out 40-knot westerly winds—that would give me considerable headwinds. Now, there was no question, I had to stop in Madagascar for gas. I had an overflight permit, but not a landing permit; so we started working on that one also.

Sometimes problems create opportunities. Since it would take several days to obtain the permits, I had the weekend in the Seychelles with two wonderful families. We put Dave on an Air Seychelles flight to South Africa, as originally planned, and I traveled around the island, swam at the beaches, saw the water reservoir and desalination plants, had more wonderful Creole food, and enjoyed the whole experience with Mike and Eddy and their families. It's a magnificent island and get-away. It's a long way from anywhere, but I hope I'll be able to return.

I spent all Monday at the airport with the DGCA and met office. The weather was looking good again; the winds had died down, another benefit of delaying the departure. Unfortunately, the permits had not come through during the weekend. Dave had arrived in South Africa and was working with Dean, who had e-mailed me and invited me to spend some time with them when I arrived. They were working with Mozambique to obtain that permit verbally so that I could cross their airspace. Finally, at 4 pm the Madagascar permit came through—at least I could gas up and go around Mozambique if the other didn't come in. A BIG thanks to the DGCA staff and especially Mr. Frost, who sent many telexes and faxes to get the permit as quickly as possible. At 8 pm, the second permit was in hand. Phewwww. I now had lots of options. In antic-ipation, I'd already gassed up and filed my flight plan and general declaration. I was planning on departing, but would have cancelled if the paperwork had not arrived.

Tuesday morning, at the airport by 5 am, who would expect Mike and Eddy to see me off at that time? But Eddy drove me to the airport and Mike met us there and they went through all the steps until I was safely in the air. Thanks so much! It's truly been a wonderful stay in the Seychelles. At 6 am I asked for engine startup, but was told to wait five minutes. Then the clearance came through, just as a rainstorm hit and Mike and Eddy were getting soaked waiting for me to depart. I taxied out, did all my run-ups and took off as the orange rays were coming through the clouds to my left. There were small cloud build-ups all around, but it was clear ahead with a nice 12-knot headwind up the runway. The climb-out was actually a little better than normal as I turned to my right, passed over the island, and headed on my way. The clouds were sitting on the moun-taintops like icing on a cake. I wished I could have taken pictures, but was a little occupied. Up to 6,000 feet and on course 224 degrees, southwest; I was headed directly to Mahajanga, Madagascar, not using airway routes this time. There was a big black cloud to my right but a beautiful rainbow to my left; I went between the two and enjoyed the rainbow. Then a second rainbow appeared and I smiled again, it looked beautiful. I have many pictures of rainbows, but the camera just can't capture the vivid colors.

I was checking in with Seychelles control by VHF. They'd asked for an "operations normal" call every 30 minutes (since I wasn't on an airway) and gave me two HF frequencies if I lost VHF contact. Dave and I had actually met two of them, Joseph and Louis, when we were talking with Mr. Orr, the Safety Director, during the week. Their control room was fascinating, but they didn't have radar and relied on position reports to know where all the planes were. I'd told them I'd be talking with them when I departed.

The tailwinds have been a little stronger than forecast and I'm 20 minutes ahead of schedule. The big decision is whether to stop in Madagascar overnight and refuel or to continue on to Lanseria, the GA airport near Johannesburg (or Jo'burg as everyone says). I'm feeling okay, everything is running well, I really don't want to stop after only six hours' flying, although I would like to visit Madagascar, if only for one day. Tough decision.

I'm in contact with Antananarivo Control (good job they shorten that to Tana) and will make the decision when I feel the winds over the Mozambique Channel. As I approach Madagascar from the northeast, I'm at an altitude of 6,000 feet, but I know there's a mountain nearby at 11,000 feet. Needless to say, I'll be watching through the cloud layers to make sure I say clear. The landscape shows brown-tipped hills with little vegetation, big lakes and bays, and a spine of mountains down the middle with green, fertile areas between the base of the hills and the shore. It looks like the trees come right down to the shore on the northwest tip of the island, but as I peer further south, I see beaches, and as I get closer, I see that they are long and empty and beautiful. Also, there are some islands off the coast with some good-looking beaches. Nice place! As usual, there are puffy clouds over the land and islands and it's pretty clear over the water. The tailwinds are holding, so I'm going to continue. Listening to the HF, I note that the Air France flights use French, instead of English, when they are giving a position reports to a French-speaking controller. The controllers switch back and forth between French and English, depending on the plane they are talking with.

The controllers have been making some interesting requests for intermediate reporting. Normally I report the major intersections or navigation aids. The first controller in Madagascar asked for estimated time abeam an intermediate point that was an NDB. That made for some quick calculations, when I thought I should be watching out for mountains. The next controller wanted to know the estimated time when I would be 60 nautical miles outside his VOR, which would be the limit of his airspace. More quick calculations. I wasn't hearing other traffic, so I don't know why they were asking for these additional time estimates—the second one was probably to hand me back to HF control.

The Mahaganja controller asks for my ETA at Lanseria. I give him the GPS estimate with an additional hour to cover headwinds later in the flight. He asks a few questions and seems stumped. Another pilot says, "He can't do that," that it can't be correct and that "he" must have made a mistake. The Mahaganja controller asks when I left the Seychelles, I said 0216 UTC, six hours previously; and when I will arrive in Lanseria, I repeat the time, nine hours hence. He asks my route, and I explain that I'll be passing Maputo. He asks if I'll land there, I said no, just overfly and land in Lanseria. The poor guy is having a tough time and the other pilot isn't making things any easier by continually saying that there's a problem, and it isn't possible, and it can't be correct. The controller finally accepts all the info and relays it to my destination. He says it's "extraordinary" and seems pleased to be handling a unique flight that he can now brag about. Then the two start talking in French, assuming, I suppose, that I won't understand. After listening to them for a few minutes, I finally interrupt and, in French, explain my speed and distance and why it will take me so long to get there. The other pilot starts talking with me directly and after understanding the gas situation he says it's *formidable.* I thought the exchanges were pretty funny. When the Mahaganja controller handed me over to Tana radio he wished me a good trip; I think he was smiling.

The winds are continuing to be good tailwinds and I'm now up to 153 knots even though I'd planned this part of the flight at 120 knots. I know that I'll run into headwinds eventually, but the later, the better. The water is looking very calm. The big problem this flight has been the ANR, Automatic Noise Reduction, in the right earpiece of my headset. I keep hearing the noise canceling and have to continually adjust the ear pad. It's driving me crazy. With the different controllers' accents, it's difficult enough to understand what's being said; now I have to hold my right ear piece with my left hand and write instructions with my right hand—not that easy.

HF contact has been terrific on this leg. Seychelles kept in touch every half-hour. When Tana radio couldn't hear me at first, Seychelles relayed the information. Then I was with Tana radio, then another VHF controller, then back with Tana radio every half-hour. I felt much better than when I was in Indian airspace and out of HF contact for hours on end. Okay, I spoke too soon. HF contact WAS great until Mozambique. On first contact they made sure they had ALL the information, and then didn't require contact again for two-and-a-half hours. Oh well, the first part of the trip had very good communication.

Wow, there are NO clouds. For the first time this trip, no clouds, no horizon, it's blurry out there, changing from dark blue sea to fuzzy whitish horizon to lighter blue sky. I think I like clouds better; at least it gives some relativity to the sky and water. And now the headwinds have finally picked up. I knew they'd arrive sometime, but they didn't have to be higher than forecast, which they are. Oh well, I gained a lot of time in the first nine hours, I can't really complain for the last five or six hours. What I can complain about is no HF e-mail. It had been working great this whole leg and I was sending off and receiving messages. Unfortunately, the PMBO (HF mailbox) in Durban, South Africa, limits usage to 30 minutes a day, and my time is up. I tried to get a message to the operator via another mailbox, but couldn't reach anyone. So, sorry friends and family, I can't receive and reply to your messages or send any updates—it's really too bad, because it makes the trip go better for me.

When you least expect it, good things happen. No, I don't have a tailwind, but the headwind is down and my speed is up to 138 knots. Only 40 minutes to go and I'll be over land again. Then, I'll stay over land from the south to the north of Africa, until I reach the Mediterranean Sea. Although more comfortable than over water, some of the areas are going to be pretty desolate and inhospitable. I'll be doing another oil change and checking the engine when I arrive in South Africa, then again when I arrive in France, and one more time in Scotland before crossing the North Atlantic. Everything has been running well, but I want to keep it that way, so there will be oil and filter change, oil analysis, check spark plugs, and look over all connections.

I'm really getting excited about seeing South Africa. It's enough to get the adrenaline running so that I don't feel tired. I've really,

really wanted to travel around South Africa, and now it's becoming a reality. I can't believe it. I spy the coast of Mozambique and follow the coast to Maputo then turn right towards Jo'burg. Maputo control is a little difficult to understand and I ask for some instructions to be repeated several times. When I'm handed over to Matsapha, Swaziland, it is totally garbled and unreadable. Each time I have to ask for a repeat, sometimes three and four times. I'm embarrassed, but just can't understand the transmission. Finally I'm handed over to Jo'burg control. What a relief to hear clear, concise, precise instructions over a clear frequency. Now I know that flying in South Africa is going to be fun.

Just before Maputo I had to climb to 10,000 feet for obstacle clearance and I turned from southwest to west. Because it was night-time, I was tired, and I was at high altitude, I put on my bottled oxygen to keep a clear head. The winds were forecast to be 25 knots on the nose and were actually higher; my speed dropped to 102 knots. And, it's cold up here! I knew this was going to be the slow part; but it's only 220 miles. Luckily, little by little, as I flew inland, the wind dropped and the speed picked up to over 130 knots. I was handed over to Lanseria tower and was surprised how busy it was, at least 2 or 3 students in the air and others overflying the airport. It was dark and I had a little trouble finding the airport with the city lights everywhere. I was directed on to downwind and with the approach plugged into the GPS, it was easy to see my position. I was allowed to descend to 6,000 feet, and as I turned base and final, there was the long runway straight ahead. Fifteen hours and four minutes in the air, but I'm so happy to be here that I don't even feel tired.

The airport terminal was huge, for a small airport, and immigration and customs were a breeze, thanks to Dean helping me through. I was still in shorts and a T-shirt, everyone else was in pants and a coat; so I quickly donned my vest. Dean said that the temperature was supposed to drop to 0 Centigrade or 32F that night. Brrrrr. Dean is a local pilot who had seen the web page and contacted me by e-mail. He obtained the Mozambique permit and took care of all the local paperwork. He's planned for an oil change later and for meeting local pilots and EAA chapter members. I couldn't be in better hands. I'll also be meeting with Diane from the local ALS foundation.

CHAPTER 13

Hope you don't mind receiving some encouragement from a fellow female pilot based here
in Hawaii. I just found out about you from a Skylines email from Airlifeline. Not sure
where you are exactly at the moment but hope everything is fine or that it soon will be.
What an amazing adventure! You are logging some really exciting flying. Go girl!
All the best from the Aloha State.
Barbara

Two Weeks in South Africa, Namibia, Botswana, and Zambia

What an aviation-friendly country! It's a real pleasure to be here and to fly here. The hotel, only about five miles from the airport, was FULL of pilots telling pilot stories. Every morning at breakfast and evening during drinks and dinner, there were new stories to be told. We had great fun. There was Ray, a professional ferry pilot getting a Cessna 182 ready to take back to Sydney. There was Humphrey, an English helicopter pilot based in Kenya, getting a new helicopter put together and test flown to take back for sight-seeing. And, there was Morey, who lost a Boeing 727—we had great fun listening to that story as it unraveled. Dave had arrived by Air Seychelles several days before me and had already lined up a hangar for the Mooney, and other pilots for a dinner the evening after my arrival.

During the day we were hosted by Ian, who ran Greenwood Aviation Services, and Stan, who operated Out of the Blue Africa Safaris, along with their able assistants, Casandra and Barbara. They had the Mooney washed (which was something that I had desperately wanted to do), organized our country permits, and gave me a desk and software program to do flight planning and filing. With all their help, we got organized for the next legs around South Africa and neighboring countries.

Three colleagues from my previous work life were at a meeting about 100 miles from Lanseria. We had been in e-mail contact and realized that we'd all be in South Africa at the same time. Pat, Ewald, and Jose Carlos all stopped by Lanseria airport on their way to Jo'burg for their flights back home. We had a wonderful 30 minutes catching up and telling stories. The time went by too quickly, but it was GREAT to see them all again.

Ian, Barbara and Stan who helped us enormously in
Lansaria, South Africa

Pat also brought a "care package" for me from the states, including the Orlando Sentinel newspaper from May 11th, 2003, and some US dollars in small bills. An article about my mother, my trip, and me had been printed in the *Orlando Sentinel* on Mother's Day, when I was in India. Kate, the journalist, had interviewed me before my departure and again, by phone, when I was in Australia. She had e-mailed me the text, but I hadn't seen the layout and the pictures—it was magnificent, both the layout and the story. Also, late in the planning stages for the trip, I had mailed Pat a check for $3,000. I said that I'd stay in touch by e-mail and if his trip went as planned and if I needed the cash, I'd let him know. All went as planned and the cash arrived. In many countries I have to pay for avgas with US dollars, cash, and often US dollars are accepted by taxi drivers and at hotels. Having small bills for traveling in Africa came in extremely handy.

Dinner the second evening was great fun. Along with the hotel pilots and Ian, we enjoyed swapping flying stories with Wendy and Paul, both pilots who fly with a precision flying team, have a pilot shop at Lanseria airport, and will be going to Sun 'N Fun '04; Dean and Lynn who helped me though immigration and customs on arrival and helped with recommendations of where to fly in South Africa; Chris and Jean, both pilots with their own planes who are building a Cozy and are probably going to Oshkosh this year; and John who built a KIS, TWICE, as it had an engine failure during early testing. We had a terrific evening.

After two days of learning about South African air space and flight plans (thanks Stan), we took to the air for a short hop to Durban, two hours. From the 4,717-foot Lanseria airport elevation, we climbed to 7,000 feet to cross Johannesburg airspace. It was extremely hazy and dusty. I'd noticed the haze while on the ground and talked about it with Ian. It was the dry season and the fires and burning fields create this haze and poor visibility. At five miles from the airport, we were transferred to 125.80 special use airspace communication frequency. Similar to MBZ in NZ and Australia, each pilot reports his position, direction, and intentions and asks for any conflicting traffic to respond. We flew six miles to the west of Jo'burg Int'l, right over the city. An altitude of 7,000 feet didn't give us much clearance, so I climbed to 7,500 feet. The TCA started at 7,600, so I was still under controlled airspace. Suddenly, there was a BIG jet right ahead and 500 feet higher, headed east to the airport. Wow, that was close. Then another jet was turning just ahead and came over us at about 500 feet separation also. I would have preferred to have been talking with control, rather that with other VFR traffic.

After a few miles, we were out from under the TCA and on our way. The ground was brown and very dry. There were rolling hills and you could see small farm holdings from time to time. Finally the flat brown gave way to small peaks, then mountains to the right and buttes to the left. This went on most of the way to Durban, southeast of Johannesburg, on the coast. About 30 miles from Durban the hills turned to lush green with farmlands and more houses. There were flat-topped mountains with houses or fields, then a massive gorge between them and the next flat-topped mountain. Dave pointed them out and I snuck a peak. I was actually flying under a hood[29] in simulated instrument conditions. I'd been doing so many long flights with the autopilot that I wanted the opportunity to hand fly the Mooney and do some instrument approaches to keep up my precision. The fascinating scenery descended rather sharply in elevation to low hills to the north of Durban. The city was in a valley with small hills on the shore that went straight down to the sea. It was amazingly different and very picturesque. The coast was beautiful. We'd been told that pilots fly along the coast, just off shore, at 500 feet. We followed their recommendations and it was a magnificent sight.

We stayed at a wonderful little B&B within walking distance of the airport. During the afternoon, we sat on the hillside overlooking the golf course and beach, and watched planes on final approach. We walked along the beach and generally enjoyed the views of Durban, the coast, and the bay. The next morning we walked back to the airport. I climbed up to the tower, up steps through a hole in the floor (as it was under construction) and met controllers Eddie and Marius as I filed my flight plan. They were very helpful with communication requirements, ATC boundaries, and how to fly down the coast.

The flight down the coast was magnificent. I took 50 more photos of beaches, what a surprise. They were long and sometimes sandy, sometimes rocky, and empty except for cattle from time to time. On the rocks, the waves would splash up 20 feet. On the beaches, there would be lines of four to five breaking waves rolling in.   Much of the time the shore was relatively flat down to the beach; in other sections, there were cliffs that went straight down to the rocks below. Many rivers flowed from the inland mountains to the sea. The controllers often used these rivers as distance points to their control areas. Unfortunately, the rivers weren't named on the charts. But when I said "unfamiliar with the area" they gave me the DME[30] distance from their airport, and that was sufficient. Although

---

29.   Hood — pilot wears a hood so that she/he sees only the instrument panel and nothing outside through the windows. This simulates being in clouds and is a common technique for instrument training.

30.   DME — distance measuring equipment. Part of the navigation equipment giving distance from a specific radio beacon.

we had been told that the sardines were running and we'd see them in the water with other, larger fish behind, we didn't see any during the two-hour flight. The shore views kept us enchanted the whole time. For about 80 miles in one section there were no towns and very few houses. It's called the Wild Coast, and that is what it was. On the flatter sections of shore, inland of the beach, there were grass strips. It was the only practical means of getting there from anywhere else. What a wonderfully quiet and peaceful place to live.

Port Alfred airport, our next stop, has 3 grass strips, but wasn't that easy to spot with green grass all around. It is at 275 feet elevation, so I climbed higher, up to 1,300 feet, to give me a better view, and finally saw the north-south strip and oriented myself for landing on runway 25. I was amazed at the activity in the air, and when on the ground I realized how many flight schools were located there. I landed gently on the 1,000-meter grass strip and taxied to what looked like a transient parking area. We were to meet Pat, the South Africa Mooney Dealer. We found each other immediately and he told me to startup and taxi over to his hangar. I jumped back in the plane and 'click'—nothing. I rechecked the startup procedure, thinking that I must have forgotten something, tried again and 'click.' Uh oh, a problem. I walked to Pat and explained the situation. I also explained that when I'd started up at Durban/Virginia, the starter had made a weird, abnormal, noise. But, since the engine was running normally, I didn't think anything more of it. We pulled the Mooney over to Pat's hangar, took off the cowl and baffling, and checked it out. Looked like the starter was dead. The problem was that my starter was a light Bendix using 24 volts and the only other starters available were the older versions using 12 volts... Hmmm, we'd look into that after the oil change. With all the equipment available, the oil change took no time at all and Pat gave the engine a quick look-over to make sure that nothing else was loose or broken. Everything looked good.

Back to the starter problem: we started disassembling the components to get the starter off—never an easy job. But with Pat and his two helpers, Dave and Brandon, we had it apart in no time. Pat's mind had been working the whole time and he remembered a plane that had the old style Bendix starter using 24 volts that had been burned in a dispute. He had many of the useable parts in his

Pat, CarolAnn and Brandon after successfully changing the starter

inventory...somewhere. Dave started looking. While we were testing the old starter in the workshop, Dave let out a yell and we all cheered. He had the old type starter in his hand. It tested perfectly. After some work and a little cajoling, Pat finally got the starter into place. A little later, all the baffles and covers were hooked up again. I tested it and the engine started, success! We were all smiling. At 7 pm we washed up and went home with Pat to meet his wife, Janis, who had prepared a sumptuous feast. What luck! My starter fails when I plan to arrive at a Mooney dealer in South Africa, and he happens to have the correct part in stock even though none are used on the Mooneys in the country. I'm counting my blessings. I could have been stuck for two weeks. Also, the weather has been perfect and a week earlier it was raining and miserable. I think I've been exceedingly lucky.

The next day we visit a hanger with numerous planes being built or rebuilt. South Africa is a haven for aviation enthusiast and homebuilders. Phil and Don, pilots and EAA members, who joined us for dinner with Pat and Janis the previous evening, are each building a Jodel. They are about 60% complete and expect to be done in 2004. In the hangar is a deHaviland Rapide that is 80% rebuilt by Don and is looking impressive. There is also an Australian AirVan that Pat is now distributing in South Africa. It's the SUV of airplanes and is simple yet effective. It carries a great load and is stable and fast. There are already six in South Africa with more on the way.

Too soon it's time to say goodbye, and thank you a million times.

The flight from Port Alfred to Cape Town was another visual ecstasy. The green rolling hills slope down to the beach and rocks. Sometimes cliffs appeared with waterfalls. One time there were two whales playing in a bay. Later, as we approached Cape Town, the scenery gave way to mountains on the horizon. I'd heard that they were there, but they were majestic with the clouds on their peaks. It was an awesome site. We turned right, around the last point, and headed north to Stellenbosch, the small GA airport in the wine region outside of Cape Town. A few minutes later we were on the ground enjoying the hospitality of Patrick at the Stellenbosch Flying Club. Ewald, one of the colleagues I'd met a few days before, was taking a few days off to be with his parents in Cape Town. We had a beer at the Flying Club and he took us to a B&B through the beautiful hills and vineyards of the Stellenbosch area.

The next day Chappie and Jackie took us around the region by car to see it from all angles. It was fascinating—the mountains, the extensive farmland to the east, the shore and fishing villages, the towns around the bay, and the Cape Town harbor area. Even though the weather didn't cooperate and it was cloudy and rainy at times, a rainbow seemed to follow us around and kept us cheerful. After a wonderful dinner with more friends, Dirk and Amanda, enjoying the local South African red wine, we said goodbye. The next day we were off to Namibia, or so I thought.

Flying between countries here is not difficult, but requires paperwork, permits, and leaving from and arriving in airports with customs and immigration. I'd planned to leave South Africa at Alexander Bay but found out that they no longer had customs and

Takeoff from Stellenbosch Airport near Cape Town, South Africa

immigration, much to everyone's chagrin. So our only option was to clear at Cape Town International, a short hop from Stellenbosch. I'd been advised to request a spot on the apron (ramp) near international arrivals so that we wouldn't have to walk the full length of the airport and back.

While we were in the air, ramp control gave us a parking spot, A3, and after landing, ground directed us there. It was just outside international arrivals, but how to get to the proper side for clearing? The first guard wouldn't let us in and said that we shouldn't be there; but nicely he told us where to go. We proceeded towards arrivals; only one desk was manned, as there were no arrivals at this time. The officer started to handle the paperwork, but told us that we'd have to clear through departures, and he escorted us there. Departures were efficient and everything was cleared; they then walked us airside. The fuel truck arrived and we received duty free fuel, very cheap, just over $2 per gallon.

Unfortunately, when all was ready and I tried to start the engine...nothing. It turned over, but didn't fire. The new starter was working fine, slower to turn over than the old one, but still turning over. It almost caught a couple of times, but then died. I decided that even if it caught, I was going to the local GA maintenance shop for a check up. I didn't want to proceed north into other countries in Africa with a questionable engine issue. This was the best maintenance I'd have for the next few weeks. Finally I gave up and called the maintenance company to tow me to their hangar. Good timing because the apron people needed the ramp location for a jet arriving in 30 minutes. We were quite a procession leaving arrivals for the GA area. A fire engine led our group. A pickup with Gert driving and Dion in the back holding the tow bar in his hands was second, pulling me in the Mooney, ready on the brakes if necessary. We proceeded behind all the jets down to the south end of the airport (see color photo). I must say, I did enjoy the ride and view.

Checking plugs and magnitos, we found nothing wrong. We did find a loose and leaky induction gasket, which was changed, and the battery was checked and charged. After everything was back in, we had a difficult start, but we started. Dudley and Gert recommended changing my starting procedure to less fuel boost, but throttle full open. That definitely worked better for the following start and the next day—thanks! Dudley and Jenny, the owners, gave me one of their watch caps for the cold mornings, which I wore thankfully at 9,000 feet where it was -5C OAT.[31] Many thanks to all at Cape Aviation. I used the time to file the next three days' flight plans and revise the country permit arrival dates.

It warmed up on our way to Windhoek and is now +5C at FL090 (flight level 090 or 9,000 feet altitude). Cape Town departure was efficient and had us headed north with a wonderful tailwind. After being handed off to Cape Town control, there was no response. I went back to the previous frequency and he said to report periodically, which I did. I hadn't expected to cross the FIR boundary without talking to another person. But three hours later that's exactly what happened. A little later, I heard Windhoek control and started talking with them, only one-and-a-half hours to go. It's desert down there! It's been very dry since leaving Cape Town. There were mountains on the west side, giving way to desert to the east. The river gorges are similar to the Painted Desert in Utah, but without the colors. Trees and shrubs lined the riverbeds, and they were visible as they wound their way through the hills and desert.

---

31.   OAT — outside air temperature. -5C, approximately 20F.

Arrival at Windhoek was the simplest yet. They stamped the immigration form, no visa needed. I filled out their General Declaration form and since we didn't have anything, customs wasn't necessary. Then I was allowed back on the ramp to get what I needed for the evening. I'm now judging arrival procedures by how many pieces of paper I need and how easy it is to get back on the ramp. So far, Eros Airport in Windhoek, Namibia is number one. The next day I was to find that Maun, Botswana, is equally simple and now tied for number one.

While I was preparing to leave Windhoek and doing my preflight, a person who introduced himself as Mr. Erikson approached me. He was from the Civil Aviation Authority and was doing a ramp check. He asked to see my papers. Everything was in order until he asked for the weight and balance for this flight. I explained that I had one with the same equipment on board, but more fuel. I was just lighter on fuel this day. He said that I was required to have a current weight and balance, and if I were stopped in Botswana or Zambia they would want to see one. We talked a while and I learned that he had done his commercial license at Orlando Executive Airport and would be returning in 2005 to do his ATP. I gave him my card and told him I lived just a little south of Orlando. Maybe we'll meet again in a few years. After we said goodbye, I revised my weight and balance papers for the flight.

The flight to Botswana was over mostly barren, dry, flat ground. As we approached Maun Airport, the area became greener and we could see water and the delta area to the north. Checking into the country was simple with very little paperwork. I learned that we needed a VFR flight plan in the system in order to fly to Vumbura airstrip where we would be staying the night. Dave and I wanted to visit one game camp. He had done all the research. My only requirement was that it be the best strip he could find. He finally picked Little Vumbura Camp.

The local charter companies fly in there to drop off and pick up tourists, so I figured I could get in there too. Not much was known about the strip, except that it was about 800 meters long and in okay condition. The camp gave us the lat/longs to find the strip and the frequency to call when we got close. They'd send a truck to pick us up when we called.

I filed the flight plan and we took off again. We had to stay above 2,000 feet when over the National Park area, but descended on the north side. The flood was just starting, and we could see water everywhere. We learned that the whole area would be under water in a few weeks. We called the camp from 20 miles out, found the strip (see color photo), circled, didn't hear any other traffic, and landed, very carefully. It was bumpy but not too bad. I didn't know where to park and it was sandy off the runway. I started off at one point but it didn't look good and I quickly returned to the runway. A guide in a truck drove up and pointed for us to follow. We found the hard top area for parking. I felt better, as I was worried about getting stuck in that sand. Obonnoue introduced himself as our guide and said that it would be about half an hour's drive to the camp. We tied down, unloaded our bags into the truck, and settled in for the trip. Obonnoue started pointing out animals and birds and telling us about the area.

June 6, Marie Garratt's birthday

Mum would have been 81 today; she'd lived a good life and had no regrets. When people said, a year ago, that I would someday start to forget the pain and start remembering all the good times, I didn't think it possible. But, it's happening. Maybe it's this trip, maybe it's talking with people about my mother and ALS/MND, maybe it's just time. But now my thoughts are on the good times we had and not the pain of the last few years.

Many more people have written to me about themselves or family members with ALS/MND. Jackie is in Australia. She can type 14 words a minute on her computer and she loves chat sessions as her primary communication with others. She advised me that June 21st is International ALS/MND Global Awareness Day. She needs caretakers 24 hours a day, but has an extremely positive outlook on life, which is wonderful.

Another person from near my hometown in Orlando, Florida, wrote to say that he's been taking care of his partner for 2 years now, and what a huge learning experience it is for each person associated with ALS/MND. He agrees that much more awareness is needed.

I met with Diane, the chairperson for ALS/MND in South Africa. Her first husband died of this disease. She's working day and night to raise awareness and much-needed support for ongoing research. She says the light at the end of the tunnel is growing slightly bigger as research continues.

On June 6th, I'm in a game park in Botswana. I see many colorful birds, which Mum would have loved; one had light blue stripes on its wings, very beautiful in flight—it's the national bird of Botswana, and the same blue as on their flag. Mum was always bird watching and had books on birds in different areas of the country. She would have loved it, and for me it was a fitting to be here, enjoying the birds, on her birthday.

Obonnoue is an excellent guide. He found a young leopard the first evening, as well as many other animals. He explained about the animals' different habits, mating, migrating, etc., and helped us to understand the Delta animals and way of life. It was fascinating.

That evening we learned more about Botswana. After it became an independent country, a large diamond mine was found. It is estimated that if the wealth were divided among the citizens, all the men, women, and children, each would be worth about $3 million. Therefore, Botswana is a wealthy country and working hard on education, conservation, and health issues.

Dave and I had a wonderful time and returned to Maun the next morning. We parted after six weeks of traveling together. He was to return to Johannesburg and back to the US, I would continue north into Zambia and Ethiopia.

I cleared immigration out of Maun, Botswana and arrived at Livingston, Zambia after a one-and-a-half hour flight. I'd filled the back tank with fuel in Botswana, as I was told that gas would be less reliable as I traveled further north in Africa, and that it would need good draining. This bothered me, because I can't drain the tank in the back seat. I decided to load up at an active airport, and Maun fit the bill. Once I was level, in cruise flight, I ran on the back tank for about 10 minutes to make sure that gas was good; I felt better after that.

The last half of the short trip was exceedingly bumpy. I don't like bumps and was starting to feel queasy. When approaching Zambia FIR, I was asked for my permit number—this was a first. I always put the permit number on the flight plan; this was the first time ATC had asked for it in the air.

I descended to 6,000 feet and saw the Victoria Falls off to my right. Even though I was not feeling well, I couldn't miss seeing them from the air and asked permission to overfly the falls—wow, they are enormous, a kilometer across (see color photo). I can't wait to visit them tomorrow.

Eric, the Airport information officer, greeted me in Livingston. He helped me with the formalities, hotel, porter, and taxi. What service. He explained that with the situation in Zimbabwe, more visitors were coming to the Zambia side and the airport was improving their processes to help the visitors. It was excellent service. At the hotel that evening, I met some locals: Craig, a third generation farmer; his wife, Nancy, from Long Island; and friend Chris. I learned a lot about Zambia, farming, the economy, and life in general in Livingston.

That first evening, while waiting in line for access to the Internet, I listened to conversation of the younger crowd around me. Apparently, a woman had gone to the hospital that day and they had just received word that she had malaria. Whoa... I wasn't currently on malaria medication. I'd taken the course of pills while in India, but stopped, as it wasn't necessary in South Africa. My next set was due to start in several days on my way to Ethiopia. The pills were in the plane. I went back to my room and put on a long sleeved shirt and long pants. Looking at the netting around the bed, that should have been my clue, but I wasn't thinking. I dug in my toilet bag and found one lone pill. I remembered that I'd stopped taking them before finishing the first lot from India. I gobbled that down and figured I'd last another day before getting back to the plane.

The Victoria Falls are magnificent, huge, unbelievably powerful, amazing. You can only see one quarter from Livingston, on the east side. The mist is blowing up from below all the time and at some points you can't even see the falls. There is a walk of about a mile to different viewing points. The people coming out were soaked to the skin, so I rented a raincoat for $1 and stayed dry. The water level is high right now and the falls are at their best; however, when the water is low, you can actually walk across the river and view the falls from the other side. There is also an area called the Devil's Armchair, which is a rock formation that you can sit in with the water falling around you.

The next day I had one more short hop to Ndola before the long leg to Ethiopia. Ndola is in the middle of Zambia, and is not a tourist destination. I chose it only to make the following leg shorter so that I can fly over the Rift Valley in Kenya and Ethiopia during the daytime. It has customs, immigration, and avgas, my only requirements. The short trip to Ndola was bumpy with headwinds, which does not bode well for the next leg to Ethiopia. The weather charts are also showing headwinds and cross winds. After arrival I went to all the offices to talk about departure procedures. Everything looked simple and straightforward. I visited the briefing office to check on my flight plan and Tanzanian permit, the only one missing. Abel, the briefing officer on duty, was extremely helpful; he even called for a hotel and taxi. More wonderful Zambian service. After checking into the hotel and checking e-mail again, I found that my Tanzanian permit had still not come through; therefore an extra day would be required. We had been working on this permit for three months. While I was in Singapore, in early May, I'd received an e-mail from Bo[32] saying that we couldn't get the Tanzanian permit until they received $60 US. I had e-mailed my dad and asked him to wire transfer the money. He'd tried wiring the money and sending a check. We were getting down to the wire here, but Bo felt that it would come through.

The next morning I went through all the procedures again. Being more sure of my next morning's departure, I paid landing and parking, cleared customs and immigration, and confirmed gas for 5 pm. I check-in with briefing, and again Abel was on duty. He'd sent a telex to Dar Es Salaam asking for confirmation for my over-flight, and we filed my flight plan for the next day. All was ready.

The further north I traveled in Zambia the greener it became, and there were large farm fields evident. I read that Zambia now produces enough food to feed its people and is becoming a net exporter. Many of the locals, both in Livingston and Ndola, were proud to tell me that their nation was no longer at war and that peace would last. Zambia is definitely improving on many fronts, and it has been a wonderful nation to visit. Once again, there was too much to see and not enough time. Once again, I'll have to return to this part of the world. Now it's off up north to Ethiopia.

32.　Bo works for the Danish company that was obtaining my permits for different countries.

CHAPTER 14

I have a Mooney Ovation which I fly in Brazil and so have been following your
adventure with great interest.
In the last two weeks I have been worried because there are no updates from
South Africa on.
I hope everything is OK and that I will be soon flying co-pilot with you again on this
marvelous flight which is certainly every pilot's dream.

All the best and good landings
Jean

June 10: Ndola, Zambia to Addis Ababa, Ethiopia, 10th leg flight report

It's been a good morning so far. Up at 5 am as planned, the taxi was not quite ready, but only 10 minutes late. The airport opened at 6 am and I was there at 5:50 am. I talked with the tower controller and Abel, the briefing officer, as they arrived. They let me through and wished me a good flight. I thanked them, especially Abel, for all his work. Out to the ramp, preflight, and takeoff by 6:26 am. It was a nice cool morning, +12C (55F); I needed that for a full gas departure at 4,167 feet elevation. I was on my way again. The controller bid me farewell and "good flight" at 50 miles out, and I was turned over to Lusaka control. I leveled off at FL070 (7,000 feet) wanting to drop weight before climbing further. The scenery was beautiful, with haze over the rivers and swampy areas and the sun just coming up (into my eyes, as I was flying northeast). I could imagine the animals running around below. I passed over the Bamgweulu Swamp and stayed close to the edge; it didn't look too appetizing. I thought I saw some huts on high ground; maybe there are some people living in the reserve area. On the edges of rivers I saw a number of tents, probably game camps for tourists.

As I traveled further northeast I started to see the first hills/mountains in the distance, with the peaks just above the haze/cloud layer. I called Lusaka control, but was out of contact. I tried other stations and the air-to-air frequency to relay, but no one was around. I climbed to FL090 and kept calling. I finally tried Kasama approach, a nearby airport, and relayed my position. I was getting close to the FIR boundary and wanted to make sure

133

Tanzania knew my arrival time and new altitude. With all the trouble I'd had getting the permit, I didn't want a problem flying through their airspace. As I reached the border, I called Kasama for another relay; unfortunately, they were out of range. So, I called Dar-Es-Salaam control directly with my position report. Expecting the worst, I was delighted to have the nice controller wish me a good morning and confirm my position report. He asked for future position estimates and ETA at Addis Ababa. Then he said, "Are you not going to make a landing anywhere?" I confirmed that I wasn't landing.

I keep cross checking the VFR chart with mountain peaks on it against the IFR chart and my airway route to make sure there is nothing ahead at my level. There is one peak above me to my right and two almost my altitude to the left. After I get over this range, the plateau will be at about 4,500 feet and it'll be several hundred miles until I see some towering peaks at over 11,000 feet, one at 14,978 feet, and Mt. Kilimanjaro at 19,340 feet. I'm hoping for clear weather so that I can see them all. I'll have to climb to 13,000 feet later in the flight, but want to use up gas before climbing.

Entering Tanzania, I could see many small towns and some larger villages surrounded by cultivated fields. It seems that they have plenty of water and agriculture in this area. Over the mountains and onto the plateau and it seems dryer, with shrubs, but no noticeable agriculture. It's still smooth air at 10:30 am and I'm hoping that the bumps hold off for a while. Four hours down and I'm a third of the way there. I pull out the breakfast that the hotel had made for me. I'd asked for a little something as the hotel included a full breakfast and, departing at 5:30 am, I wouldn't get it. They'd given me a small package on leaving. I'd expected toast or bread and muffins; instead, they'd prepared bacon, sausage, and two eggs. Not easy to eat with your fingers, but tasty never the less. They'd even included a small package of salt wrapped in plastic. I've found during the whole time in Zambia that they have been very eager to please; this is just one last example.

It's great to see land below and watch it change in topography and vegetation as I pass. I was definitely tired of the long over-water legs and am thankful that the last one is behind me. I think I've taken as many pictures of barren land and I did of beaches in NZ and Australia. It looks different each time I take a picture, but they all look the same when I review them later.

I got a picture of Mt. Kilimanjaro as I passed, not great as there were clouds around it, but I could see the snow-capped flat peak. Coming into "Kili" airspace, I was asked for my Kenya permit. I thought I had the number, as I had a list of all the countries' permit numbers. But I also thought that I'd been told that advanced notification by flight plan was sufficient for Kenya. I looked but couldn't find the permit number. They called back and said they'd found it; I breathed a sigh of relief. There are peaks in the haze and clouds, and I'm constantly checking my position and the peaks—not the easiest flight I've had. As I cross into Nairobi airspace, the controller again asks for my permit number. After looking again, I finally admit that I don't have it with me and will call when I get on the ground. Here I was, worried about Tanzania all the time, and Kenya turns out to be the problem. He clears me straight to NAK VOR instead of overflying Nairobi, which I think is very sensible and saves time. But there are still peaks around. I climb to FL120 and keep a constant watch.

Not much to see on the ground now, as there's a broken layer of clouds below me. Later I have to climb to FL130 because there's a peak covered by a cloud very close to my flight path. As it's hidden and I don't know exactly where it is, I opt to climb. A right turn at the VOR and it's straight ahead to Addis Ababa; only 576 more miles, just less than five hours. It's looking lush and green below, but as we travel further north, it starts to get brown and dry, very dry. When I have Lake Rudolph to my left, it's flat and brown to the right and looks deserted, at least compared to further south where there were lots of villages and towns.

The clouds clear, but it's still difficult to see due to all the haze. Once I cross the border, there will still be a few mountains to pick out and avoid, so I'm hoping it stays clear and less hazy. I'm out of contact with Nairobi control and probably won't reach Addis control until well inside their air space.

I kept calling Addis control, especially after reading on the charts that it is mandatory to make contact five minutes prior to entering their airspace. But, I also continued flying, as I knew there was no way of making contact 300 miles away. I finally heard Addis calling me—phew, at least they were looking for me; but they still couldn't hear me. After another half-hour, we could talk with each other. Cleared to continue to Addis, I descended into the valley, below the clouds and between the mountains. Unfortunately, it was still hazy, but I could see the brown, dry land was giving way to fields and crops. As I approached, there was just one hill higher than me and off my right side. I was cleared down to 8,500 feet and the airport elevation is 7,600 feet, so I didn't have much farther to go. Boy, an 11,000-foot strip is pretty long, especially where there are two parallel runways! I saw it, turned downwind and announced my position. Turned base and final and I was on the ground after 11 hours and 11 minutes of flying. Not the longest, but one of the more worrisome flights I've had. I didn't want to become a CFIT (controlled flight into terrain) statistic, and was constantly crosschecking my position relative to the higher terrain.

After being led to my stand position by a "follow me" bus, I was given time to organize my bags, and was driven to the terminal building. The building was just opposite my position, but they don't want people walking across the ramp and taxi areas. They showed me into the door and told me to go up stairs. It was an impressively large, new, glass-style, empty terminal building with guards sitting around and nothing else. I finally made my way to immigration and explained what I was doing. They stamped my passport, marked that I was crew, and said I'd have no trouble returning to my plane tomorrow. We'll see, I thought... Customs took my handwritten General Declaration document (thanks again Geoff) and accepted that I only had personal belongings. Money change was closed, so I took a cab to the hotel and paid in dollars. That was the easiest entry at a major airport! The terminal building is extremely new and modern; they are just moving into it. The cabby had trouble get out of the parking lot because they'd just opened the new area that day and the workers were still learning how to operate the payment machines.

I finally made it to the hotel, had a beer and a local dish for dinner. Luckily, some Ethiopian friends from Orlando, Nick and Fikirte, had taught me how to eat Ethiopian food. I didn't look like a pro, but at least I knew what to do and how to do it: tearing off the *injera* with my right hand, picking up the *wot* with the *injera*, and putting the whole thing in my mouth. The waiter even brought me some hot sauce after a while—maybe I impressed them enough that they thought I'd want it with their food.

The first day after landing is the obligatory trip back to the airport to check on the airplane and try to understand departure procedures. This was made doubly difficult by the new terminal building and people changing offices or new in their positions. In the old terminal, no one could direct me to ATC (even though the Jeppesen chart showed it was there somewhere). When I finally asked for the Airport Manager I was headed down the right path. I was shown to ATC, filled out the landing, navigation, and parking forms, and paid my parking fee to the finance department—they took US dollars with no problem. Now I had one of the pieces of paper for departure.

While there, I met a Kenyan pilot who told me that I might find GA parking and tie downs by the maintenance area where they also had small GA planes for training new pilots. I walked down there, airside, and was stopped three times because I wasn't in a pilot's uniform. Once I got there, the instructors, technicians, and maintenance personnel were very helpful and showed me where I could tie down. I walked the kilometer back to departures and tried to get through each of the checkpoints to get to the ramp and to my Mooney. Everything was simple except the guy checking airport departure tax stamps. He wouldn't believe that I was crew because I didn't have stripes on my shoulders. Even with crew written on my passport, he asked for identification. Finally, two officers from immigration, who had seen me earlier, saved me and convinced him that I was okay to pass. The gate people let me though and called a van to take me out to my plane. Exceedingly simple except for one person. Next time I'll buy the $1 departure tax stamp!

I taxied down to the GA area and a marshaler showed me to my position. A student pilot helped me to tie down and one of the technical people took me over to the administrative department. The finance person looked up the hangar charges and quoted $248/day. I laughed and said that I wasn't in the hangar, I was tied down outside. Another guy said "What's the difference?" I knew I was in trouble. This continued for about five minutes. Finally the manager came over and explained that they charge a high price to dissuade transient parking. I said that I was dissuaded and would taxi back.

Upon my return, I found some big rocks at the edge of the ramp area and moved them to the plane and tied down. Of all the places I've been, I have met only very helpful people until now. But as I think about it, all the helpful people at airports have been plane people; these were financial types. They were just doing their job. I was actually more relieved, once tied down on the ramp. This ramp was cleaner and quieter; the other ramp was covered in gravel and had people, cars, and buses everywhere. After all that, I felt okay about leaving my Mooney for a week-and-a-half.

My Ethiopian friends in Orlando had mapped out what to do while here, so I went to a tour operator recommended by their family in Addis Ababa and figured out how to make our plan work. After several tries, we found the right combination of commercial flights and days in each location. I couldn't fly privately in Ethiopia, but commercial flights aren't all that expensive. The next day I was off to Dire Dawa. Upon arrival I took a taxi the 60 kilometers to Harer and moved into the recommended hotel. The market going on reminded me of India with people, cattle, cars, goats, and noise everywhere. The big difference was that we are at 7,000 feet and it's cool enough to need a long-sleeve shirt or light jacket. I meet my guide, Abiyu, and we head out. The old town, Muslim, and inside the wall was fascinating in history and life style. The new town, Christian, and outside the wall was not much different, still crowded and noisy. Many kids shout *"Ferengi"* at foreigners. It is a word coming originally from when the French were here. I had been warned about this, but only one taxi driver had yelled it at me in Addis. Here over 90% of the kids yell it at me; it was a game to them. I didn't enjoy it, nor do I enjoy crowds and noise, and was happy to leave Harer, enjoy the countryside during the ride to Dire Dawa, and return to Addis. It almost felt like home returning to my local hotel with the local Internet café across the street!

A day later the longer journey started. First, off to Axum in the north. What an amazing history. The guide, Haile Silassie, takes me from the pre-Axumite history starting in the 5th century BC through the Axumite periods 200AD – 700AD – 1100AD, explaining the time of the Queen of Sheba and her swimming pool and her liaison with King Solomon of Israel. The stone stelae or monoliths, over 3,000 of them, are impressive in stature and construction for that period. In

Giant stelae or monoliths found in Axum, Ethiopia

one of the tombs there is an iron pin (from 5th century BC) holding two stones together. There are tunnels over 150 kilometers in length through which kings sent material and equipment so that invaders didn't know what defenses were being planned. The extent of findings and archeological work yet to be dug is impressive. Unfortunately, there are no funds or museums for display. There are currently teams from the US, France, and England working three months on site each year and nine months at home doing the analysis. There is so much history still covered by earth it's an amazing adventure.

After our day visiting the archeological sites, Haile Silassie invited me back to his home for coffee. Little did I know what that would entail. While one sister brought out the coffee-making equipment, small stool, small charcoal stove, plastic bucket, cups, saucers, tins, and spoons, another brought out a plastic bowl for washing hands. I followed what Haile Silassie did, washing his hands in the bowl as water was poured over them. Then with right hand only, I put *injera* on the plate and his sister spooned *wot* over it. He warned me that it might be hot/spicy. It wasn't bad. Just as I was about to finish, I remembered Nick and Fikirte's warning not to finish first, as the hosts will ask you to take more. I slowed down, but not enough. I said that I had enjoyed it but really didn't eat much and no more, thanks. They had seconds and explained that they would eat the bones, as they were good for them! After another hand-washing, the coffee session started. One sister was already roasting the beans. She had me smell them before grinding. Then she started boiling the water by fanning the charcoal—what a job (see color photo). While the grounds were settling, she put some charcoal in another pot and added incense—the smoke poured out. Then she poured and served the coffee. Just prior, the first sister brought out unleavened bread, which is eaten before coffee. As we drank the coffee, Haile Silassie explained that it is made three times and the sister started boiling the water and fanning the flames again. More bread, more incense, and the second cup of coffee. I had the opportunity to try to make the third round. As the saying goes, a watched pot never boils, but in my case, my fanning technique was insufficient and the sister was getting weary of watching me fail. She added a little wrist action and boiled the water. I washed the cups in the bowl, made the incense, and poured the coffee. I was happy to sit down in the chair after all that—what an experience. It was an evening to remember and an experience you just can't get without a person willing to invite you into his home. I appreciate all that Haile Silassie and his sisters did to give me a real view of life in Axum.

Next stop Gondar, just south of the Semien Mountains—they are majestic and rugged from the air. I was amazed at the number of homes that were dotted here and there, many more than I would have expected in the rugged terrain. King Fasilides moved the capital of Ethiopia to Gondar in the 17th century. What's left of the numerous castles stand inside embattlement walls in the middle of the city. The royal baths are a short walk away. The most famous church in Gondar is Debre Berham Sellassie, Trinity Church of the Mountain of Light, built as were many others on a hilltop and decorated with paintings of scenes from the bible.

Tej is the Ethiopian fermented wine with honey. As I'd read about it before leaving, I had to try some. There were only two places in town that serve Tej. In the Tej bar there were no lights, it was very small, and everyone was sitting on benches against the wall. Johannes, my guide for the day, and I took a seat which happened to be next to the Tej barrel. The woman takes an empty gin or whiskey bottle, fills it from the barrel, and serves you the bottle and carafe shaped glasses. It tastes sweet from the honey and also has some other spices mixed in. We moved outside, where a number of older men were sitting on stone benches. Johannes explained that this tends to be an "older man's hangout." We talked and drank—it was another interesting evening.

The next day was a drive to and trek in the Semien Mountains. They are mystic and magnificent and look like soaring castles and towers, monuments and cathedrals, with chasms that plunge straight down. It was the start of the rainy season and there was a hint of green on the mainly brown slopes. Everywhere the farmers are preparing their fields. I see two bullocks pulling a single plow shear with the farmer usually yelling and using a whip from behind. The land is extremely rocky and where they have cleared it, there are rows of rock walls between the fields. Everywhere the fields are prepared; in one I see a farmer sowing seed. It rained on Sunday when I was in Axum and Tuesday in Gondar, but everywhere is very short of water, as there has been a drought for the past two years.

The journey continues to Lalibela, home of the monolithic churches carved in the ground out of solid rock (see color photo). They really are impressive. Inside there are columns and arches, just like you see in the old European churches. One group of five churches is joined by tunnels also hewn out of rock. Apparently all eleven were made in the same period. It must have taken armies to complete the task. Legend has it that the angels helped King Lalibela at night!

The next morning, it's time for a mule ride up to the top of the mountain (way up top). It would have been easier and more comfortable to walk and when it got steep, I did just that. But it's still amazing what a steep incline the mule can climb with my weight on its back. It's no wonder they are used throughout Ethiopia. The churches carved out of rock on top of the mountain were smaller, but still impressive. Not as well finished: I could see the chisel marks in the walls. The view from the top was inspiring, but in September, when all is green, I'm sure it's even more impressive. There is one road heading to the next town 130 kilometers away, and another in the other direction 180 kilometers. Lalibela has no gas station or maintenance shop for vehicles. It only got electricity, 24 hours per day, about four years ago. Before that they had a generator that provided about six hours per day. Still they have two days per week without power, and hot water is in short supply. The airport, rebuilt four years ago, is 28 kilometers away on the only flat land available.

Life must be difficult in the region. Looking down from above, there is a small village of farmers. They care for the priests and monks in the churches and bring them food. As we walked up and down, I could see lines of people marching down with hay, wood, and other items on their backs or heads, to sell at the market that day. The children also make the trek daily to school in Lalibela. It took us one hour to walk up and 45 minutes back down—now that's a long walk to school everyday!

Last stop on the tour, Bahir Dar, perched at 6,000 feet elevation next to Lake Tana, the source of the Blue Nile River, which later merges to become the Nile River at Khartoum. It is home to some 20 monasteries and churches. Sitting by the lake was very restful; however, changes in the commercial flight schedules proved to be quite frustrating and it was time for the touring to be over.

I returned to Addis the next day and was so happy to see my Mooney on the ramp. I went straight to ATC (Air Traffic Control) to file my flight plan and couldn't wait until tomorrow to get to my plane, so I crossed the ramp and checked that all was okay. Although dirty and dusty, she was ready to fly again. So was I. Tomorrow, we'll be off to Djibouti for a gas stop. Then a long hop to Greece.

More on ALS:

It's heartwarming to see the number of fundraising drives for ALS. I'm sure many of you saw Tom Watson's caddy, Bruce Edwards, at the US Open. What terrific publicity for ALS. I feel sorry for Bruce because I know what he's destined to go through, but let's hope that all this leads to more donations and eventually finding a cure to this devastating disease.

My real work on ALS awareness will begin in Europe, where I'll meet country chairmen for ALS foundations in France, England, Ireland and Scotland; then more after I cross to Canada. Nothing was planned for Ethiopia; however, I had three new e-mail contacts with respect to ALS during my time here.

Max with FSTA in Lusanne, Switzerland, contacted me about

CarolAnn in the pilot's seat, just
before startup the day of departure

Pacific Ocean satellite weather
showing the intertropical
convergence zone of storms

Mooney on the ramp in
American Samoa

The colorful buses in American
Samoa

Flying out over the northern tip of
the North Island of New Zealand

Left: CarolAnn with Mooney in front of
the volcanoes on Lord Howe Island

Above: Debbie and Rick in Melbourne

Above: Flying for hours over
the red sand and desert of
the Australian outback

Right: CarolAnn about five
miles in front of Ayers
Rock in Australia

Top: The group of pilots attending the Aviation Safety Seminar in Singapore

Right middle: Dave and Mr. Tewari in front of the Taj Mahal

Right bottom: View from inside an autorickshaw looking out at other autorickshaws on the street

Opening coconuts to sip the milk
on the shore in Trivandrum

Above: The terraced slopes of the
Himalayas

Right: Dave and CarolAnn
taking an elephant ride

Flying over two of the islands in the Maldives

Above: New Young Eagle, Kalsey, in Seychelles

Top right: CarolAnn in a coconut tree in the Seychelles

Right: Being towed to maintenance, passing behind the jets in Cape Town

The small strip to get to the camp in Botswana

Top: Flying over Victoria Falls,
Zambia, at 6000 feet

Above right: Coffee ceremony in
Axum, Ethiopia

Left: One of many sandstone
churches in Lalibela, Ethiopia

Left: Flying over the cathedral in Vezeley, France

Below left: Being filmed for TV news at the Popular Flying Association Rally at Kemble Airport, England

Below right: Mooney tails and international registrations at the air show in England

Above left: Cousins Angus and Lydia becoming Young Eagles
Above right: The Moher Cliffs on the west coast of Ireland

Top: First sighting of Greenland
— stark mountains

Right: Vividly colorful houses
in Nuuk, Greenland

Above: The Canadian airforce
Snowbirds in formation

Right: The welcome home banner
on my hangar door

my trip. Their previous president of the International Parachute Commission died of ALS a few years ago. It was a blow as well as a learning experience for the whole group. They miss him terribly and support the drive for more ALS awareness and donations. They sent their best wishes and hope that I will be able to visit, which I will try to do.

I also received an e-mail from Susan in Canada. There will be several ALS fund raising and awareness events in September. As I pass through Nova Scotia, New Brunswick, and Newfoundland, I'll participate in as many as possible, especially the walk-a-thon to WALK TO D'FEET ALS. I'll also be visiting the ALS-TD Foundation in Boston, Massachusetts. This is the foundation that my mother chose for donations to go to, as they are doing research on a cure for this disease.

Many thanks to those of you who have made donations to help find a cure for this disease. If you are enjoying these flight reports and haven't yet donated, please consider sending a donation. Just send a check to the ALS Therapy Development Foundation, 215 First St, Cambridge, MA 02142. Thank you.

Top: Grains for sale at the market
Bottom: Women carrying bundles of wood and other items to market

CHAPTER 15

Since you fly VFR you need nothing. Iraklion is 24hrs open, int'l airport.
It's a good idea nevertheless to file your flight plan 48hrs before. Just
remember to advise how long you will stay.

On my side I will inform the head of ATC for your arrival.
Regards.
PS: Tell me if you need something more.
Giorgos

June 22–24: Ethiopia to Greece via Djibouti, 11th leg flight report

In the air again and it feels GREAT. I left Addis Ababa this morning at 10:30 local time with an almost no hassle departure. The only problem was the rain. I had planned to depart at 8:30 but decided to wait for less rain and improved visibility and ceiling. This is only a short two-and-a-half hour flight, mostly "downhill" as I start at 7,600 feet and end at 47 feet, but there are a few mountains around that I need to see and avoid. It starts to clear and I take off, it feels GREAT to be in the air again. What peace and freedom.

I climb and remain only a few thousand feet above the surface, but soon the surface elevation drops and I'm higher. At the same time it becomes very hazy; I see less and less. For a while I feel like I'm in a red cloud, but I can just make out the ground on both sides if I look closely. I don't feel very comfortable, but know that the ground is descending and I'm clear. I thought I would see the Red Sea, and it clears a small amount as I get close to Djibouti, but I can only see a few miles, nothing really. I'm cleared to descend; finally I find the airport, fly the pattern and land. It's HOT. After a cool morning requiring a jacket at 7,000 feet in Addis, it's 43 degrees C (116 F) and very uncomfortable in Djibouti. I clear customs and immigration then start to work with ATC on my flight plan, landing and fees, and met report for the next day.

The departments are close to each other, and after several hours all is worked out and ready for an early morning departure. I only need to gas up at 6 pm this evening. I prefer to fill up when it's a little cooler, rather than during the heat of the day. If the Mobil person had shown up as planned it would have been great; he was an hour late (change of shifts) and it took another hour to refuel from the two 55-gallon drums. So, not much time left for dinner. I had the taxi driver take me to a supermarket where I bought pizza, flan, cookies, juice, candy, and water. That gave me enough for dinner and two meals during the flight. Now, off to bed. I'd found a $20 per night small "hotel." The other alternative was $180 per night US style Hilton or similar upscale hotel. As it was only for one night and it had air conditioning, I opted for the cheap alternative. It was sufficient.

Departure went as planned at 5:30 am local time. Unfortunately, I had headwinds right from the start. When I looked at the met report, it showed 10- to 15-knot headwinds, which would be okay, but 25 to 35 knots is too much. I climbed to 6,000 feet through hazy, still dark skies. I couldn't see the sea below me and even as it got light, I could barely see the land. After an hour into the flight, I'd pretty much decided that I'd need to stop in Luxor for more gas. There were small bumps and a rain shower over southern Eritrea, and the ground speed dropped to 95 knots, I'll definitely need a stop.

The sun came out to my right and the red haze continued. No pictures on this leg, which is too bad because I'd wanted to see the Red Sea. Oh well. When the ground speed went above 110 knots, I cheered, but knew that a stop was still required. The combination of time flown plus remaining estimated time enroute had to be less than 15 hours for me to continue. I only had 17 hours of fuel and I didn't want to have any question about fuel with the last three hours being over the Mediterranean Sea to Iraklion, Greece.

I'm asked to climb to 8,500 feet, which I do, very slowly. After two position reports with Asmera, I lose contact with them. But I'm pretty sure I'll pick them up as I get closer to their main airport, so I'm not worried. When everything is running smoothly and I have no further position reports, I plug in to HF e-mail to see if I can make contact with any stations. Hurray, contact the first time. Unfortunately, since I have a backlog of e-mails to send, I use up all the 30 minutes allotted time immediately and can't send or receive any more. I spend some time updating the web page, then shut off the laptop.

I talk with Asmera control as I get closer and confirm my flight level at 8,500 feet. While I was over the sea, I felt comfortable at FL085, but as I approached land, the minimum safe enroute altitude is 11,000 feet, going up to 11,600 feet. At the next position report, I questioned remaining at 8,500 feet; ATC responded that it was okay. I was vigilantly looking at the land through the haze. It started increasing in elevation, but slowly, so I thought I was okay. I kept looking ahead and down. I was also getting close to the four hours on the back tank and didn't want multiple problems at the same time, so I switched to the right wing tank—one less thing to worry about.

I saw a ridge through the haze, like some of the ridges I'd seen in Ethiopia. Then I saw some higher mountains ahead. I started climbing. With the haze I couldn't see very well and with the weight, I couldn't climb very well, so I opted for a 360-degree turn to give me a better view and more time to climb. I didn't like what I saw: mountains. I finally made it to 10,500 feet which should put me above the peaks, but the minimum safe altitude was 11,600 feet, so I kept climbing and looking. After a long, agonizingly slow climb, I was finally looking down on the mountaintops. As I saw each new peak through the haze, and realized that it was lower than my altitude, I started to relax. Actually, there was less headwind up here and the speed was up to 130 knots, as least one good result of the climb. Only 25 minutes to the next reporting point and at that point, the minimum safe altitude goes down to 8,000 feet; then I can really relax. I tried calling Asmera to report my altitude change, but couldn't reach them. I tried Khartoum center on HF and VHF with no luck. Oh well, I wasn't going to let it bother me, I was safe at 11,600 feet and that's what mattered!

I'm not made for this stuff!! Every time something like this happens, I get a knot in my stomach. I'll be happy to return to the flatlands of Florida and continue flying back and forth to Virginia to visit my dad. And, I know he'll be happy to have me home again. Sniff, sniff. Time to wipe the tears away and get back to the flying.

As I got closer to Port Sudan I tried calling the tower on VHF, and a nice controller answered. He took all the information to relay my position report. No problem—much better than I'd anticipated. Later he called back and asked me to descend to 10,500 for the direction I was flying. The minimum altitude was 10,000 feet so I descended. The wind was still weak and the speed was good at this altitude.

I returned to using the back tank which is going great, every ounce I can squeeze out of there will make the decision to continue to Greece easier. I knew I had at least five hours in the back, possibly up to six hours. When I was in Ndola, Zambia, I'd filled up all tanks. Knowing that Addis didn't have avgas and Djibouti used drums for dispensing, I wasn't sure if Djibouti had a regular fuel line (in which case I could fill the rear tank) or if they'd hand pump out of the barrel into containers and then into the wing tanks (as we did in India), in which case I couldn't refill the rear tank. With that little knowledge, I'd only used two hours on the rear tank on the leg to Addis Ababa, just in case I couldn't refill it. So, I'd flown mainly on the wing tanks. In Djibouti, I had to buy gas by the drum, so I either had 400 liters or 600 liters. I'd opted for 400, as that plus five hours in the rear tank would give me 17 hours endurance, sufficient to fly to Greece with mild headwinds. After I'd filled the wings in Djibouti, I put the remainder of the second drum into the rear tank. That's why I don't know exactly how much is there. I'm over five-and-a-half hours on the back tank and averaging 128 knots, except for when I go over mountain ridges, when it drops to 115 knots. Looks like I should be able to make Greece today. I'm feeling good again, eight hours down and about seven to go.

I'm not yet talking with Cairo control, but another plane starts relaying. They are asking for my permit number. I relay the answer. After a few relays and some waiting time, I receive the message, from the poor Russian Asimov pilot going between me and Cairo, that I'm required to stop at Luxor. I'm starting to hear Cairo, so I thank the other pilot and talk with them directly. They want to know the name of my agent in Cairo; I said that I don't know it. I received the permit information from a company in Denmark that worked through the agent. I didn't know the name. He insists that I am required to stop at Luxor. With my potential gas problem, I think this won't be all bad as I can gas up with cheap gas and continue on to Iraklion tomorrow. Others who have done this trip had even recommended that I make a stop, as the gas is so much less expensive in Egypt than the $12 per gallon (so I'd been told) rip-off in Greece. So, after arguing that my permit was valid, but not really having much choice, I said that I would follow orders and land.

It's the following morning in the hotel in Luxor and I'm not looking forward to today if it's anything like yesterday afternoon—it was exceedingly frustrating as well as unbelievable to be faced with extortion for another flight permit. I don't know if I can adequately explain the events, but I'll try.

Upon landing and parking I was asked for my papers and told to proceed to the tower (by the "nice" man who I later learned was the person trying to make all the money out of me). I gathered my papers and permits and went with him to the tower. It was extremely hot and I was already tired after getting up at 4 am and flying for 9 hours and 23 minutes. The "nice" person said that this would only take half an hour and I'd be on my way.

The tower controller explained that the problem was from the Civil Aviation Authority in Cairo—he was only the messenger. My permit number was not valid and, if I couldn't tell them who my agent was in Cairo, I'd have to pay for another permit along with landing and all other fees and penalties. The "nice" guy told me this would be about 400–500 USD, and I'd have to pay landing anyway, so I might as well pay. I explained that the person/company getting my permits had done the whole world without a problem and he had the information on the agent in Cairo. I only had my permit number that he'd e-mailed to me. I didn't have any other information. After much discussion (round and round the same point) the person in Cairo told me over the phone that my plane was grounded until I gave them the Cairo agent's name.

I bought a phone card from the "nice" guy and called Bo in Denmark. He wasn't there and wouldn't be back until the next day, but the person answering took the message and said he'd contact him. Bo called back and said the agent in Cairo would dispense an agent in Luxor to come to the tower to handle the case. Thinking that the agent would take a while to get here and that this whole thing would take too long to fly any further today, I asked to go to my plane to get some clothes as I'd be staying the night. We trooped down, got through security, got into the "follow me" truck and went to the Mooney. Just as we got there, someone was walking around the plane. After a little confusion, it turned out that he was the agent looking for me. Why at the plane instead of the tower? And, how did he get there so quickly? Much later that night, I learned that he,

Ahmed, is a ticket agent at the airport, was on duty, and received a call to help out. He was already at the airport with a ramp pass.

We trooped back up to the tower. They all talked in Arabic, so I don't know exactly what was said, but the summary was that I had to pay for the permit and penalty, $90 US, in order to leave. Even the driver of the "follow me" truck was in on the discussion—now why should he be involved? I said that Bo, the person in Denmark who got all my permits, had obtained the permit and I wasn't going to pay a second time. I finally reached Bo again; he'd heard from Ahmed's boss. He was as unhappy as I was but said that I should pay or I wouldn't be able to leave. With his okay, I agreed to pay.

Anyway, it took so long to get to this point and I was so tired, that I said I'd stay the night. This meant clearing into the country, then out again tomorrow. During this time, the tower people had been checking for avgas all over Egypt. Luxor, the normal stopping place for most small planes doing this trip, didn't have any. They called everywhere and finally found some at 6th October, the GA Airport near Cairo. The problem then being that they, 6th October Airport, didn't have customs and immigration, so I'd have to make another stop at Alexandria to clear out of Egypt. This was going to be a hassle, especially traveling and landing after one hour with full fuel (if I filled all tanks). I made out the flight plans and we finally left the airport at 7 pm—what an afternoon. Ahmed's driver took us to the Hilton. The only good part was that they charged me $25 for the night and $20 for the ride to and from the hotel. They paid the hotel bill, I paid them. Don't ask me what deal was struck here, but I was happy it didn't cost me too much. The landing, parking, handling, and everything else would be adding up to many hundreds of dollars. I didn't even want to think about it. Weeks later, I found out from Bo that he had paid an additional $500.

I had a beer with Ahmed and called it a night. He wanted to show me the town and make me feel better. But, knowing I needed an early start, I opted for sleep. I had cold pizza left from my flight and ate that. Sleep came quickly.

I'm over the Mediterranean Sea and feeling better, only a slight knot in the stomach, maybe the stress of the morning, or lack of food. I'm eating cookies left over from yesterday's flight. Only two-and-a-half hours to go. Much as I enjoy flying, I just can't wait to get down; this has been a stressful leg.

I felt great when I woke up. Eight hours of good sleep, two hot showers in less than 10 hours, Ahmed is in the lobby, ready to go. Let's hope things work out better today. At the airport, clearances are very slow, but we finally get outside to the plane (that's an hour's hassle condensed). Ahmen had convinced immigration and customs to clear me out of Luxor so that I could leave directly from 6th of October airport, rather than making an extra stop at Alexandria. I don't know how he figured it out, and I was sure it wouldn't work, but later, I was very happy that he did it.

I wasn't allowed to take a picture of the plane or background, which is unfortunate, because it looked good with four armed guards around it, and only one other plane on the huge ramp. I did the preflight, loaded my bags, shook Ahmed's hand, and got ready to startup. Calling the tower, they asked me to stand by. After a while they explained that visibility at Cairo was 2,000 meters. A few minutes later it was 1,000 meters. I got out; this was going to take time. I asked if we could go to the met office and look at the upper level winds. We drove in the "follow me" truck over to the tower. The forecast winds were very similar to those forecast the previous day, i.e., 10 to 15 knot northeasterly crosswinds. I didn't know whether to believe them, given yesterday's experience. If they were really like that, I have enough gas to go directly to Iraklion. I asked the met people about Cairo weather. They said that this time of the year, it's always low visibility in the morning and it would clear in less than two hours. My flight time was two hours. We checked the TAF,[33] and it showed clearing in two to four hours. I decided to wait half an hour, go to the plane, and take off. I updated the departure time on the flight plan, now being over an hour late, and I updated the departure for the second flight plan to Iraklion.

Being patient for 30 minutes was not easy; but I didn't want to put up with all the inevitable questions if I stayed in the Met or ATC offices, so I thanked them and walked outside. Time's up, get in the "follow me" truck to the plane. Ahmed kindly informed me that I would be paying for each trip in the truck. I said that I would much prefer to walk the very short distance to the plane, but he wouldn't allow me. Off we went again. I called for start up. Tower made me

---

33.   TAF — Terminal Area Forecast — aviation weather forecast for a given area.

confirm that I could land with 3,000 meters visibility. I confirmed. Start up, clearance, taxi, takeoff, finally, climb to 8,500 feet. At least it's a little cooler up here and away from all the hassles. I breathe a long sigh of relief.

Finally, I'm on my way to Cairo. As I'm handed off from Luxor to Cairo control, an hour into the flight, Cairo kindly informs me that there is no avgas at the 6th October airport, my destination. Who am I to believe? Three different people, tower, ATC, and Ahmed's boss had confirmed gas at the airport, yesterday. Now this local guy says no gas... What to believe? The winds had been strong headwinds at the start, over 35 to 40 knots making the ground speed 100 to 105 knots. After an hour, it was consistently down to 15 to 20 knots from the northeast, so if I turned on course to Iraklion, it would be more of a crosswind. Based on current speed, I could make Iraklion in just over four hours and had seven hours of fuel left. I asked Cairo if they could amend my flight plan to go to Iraklion. They said that I could stop at Cairo, clear immigration, and proceed to Iraklion afterwards. I explained that I had cleared customs and immigration in Luxor. Luckily, the controller took the time to check with Luxor and approved my flight plan deviation (many thanks Ahmed). I was on my way to Greece. I continuously checked the winds and they were steady 10–15 knots northeast; looks like I'll make it. By the way, the weather had cleared over Cairo, as I passed, and the visibility was over 20 kilometers.

I'm out of VHF radio contact, but have already received a squawk[34] code and the frequencies for Iraklion. Only an hour to go and I'll be in communication again. Unfortunately, I haven't been able to connect through HF e-mail, so Georgis, my contact in Iraklion, thinks I'll be arriving around 5 pm, now it'll be closer to 2:30 pm.

Wow, three ships. The Mediterranean Sea is a little busier than the Pacific! The speed keeps dropping little by little; it's down to 130 knots. But I'm so close I can taste it, and I have plenty of fuel left. Only one hour and 15 minutes to go. No HF contact, so I'll reel in the trailing wire before I forget it. I haven't forgotten yet, but there may be a first time.

---

34.   Squawk — transponder code so that radar can identify the aircraft

I can see the mountains of Crete—beautiful through the haze. But right now, any land would be beautiful to me. Getting closer it looks even better. I finally fly over the tip of the island of Crete, turn left at the VOR, and it's only 50 miles to go. I'm talking with tower and they guide me in. The airport is straight ahead, a straight in approach. I'm down, following another "follow me" truck to the General Aviation, small plane, parking. Wonderful, tie-downs and all. The "follow me" truck leaves, but an Olympic truck picks me up and takes me to their office for processing, then to customs and arrivals. Through immigration and I'm in Greece. Georgis is busy at work, since I'm early. I find a hotel on the beach, on the other side of town, take the bus (for one Euro), and 30 minutes later I'm swimming in the Med![35] It feels GREAT.

The woman at the desk is already taking care of me—she has put a bottle of Retsina (Greek wine) in the fridge to cool. After calling Dad and telling him that I'm okay and about to toast him with Retsina, I call Georgis (VP of the local Aero Club) and we set a time to get together. I return to the pool with a glass of Retsina and a book in hand. Looking over the Med I toast Mum, Dad, brothers and friends, and sip Retsina. I'm finally feeling relaxed. It'll take a little time, but I will recover from the events of the past few days.

---

35.   Med — Mediterranean Sea

Top: Looking up from the runway to the ramp where Flemming is
standing next to his plane.
Bottom: Fying up the Rhône Valley in Southern France

CHAPTER 16

Hi Carol Ann,
I'm an avid aircraft spotter and I saw your Mooney at Kemble this evening. With most foreign aircraft I run a "google search." Wow, what an adventure you have had. I'll be at the Rally on Sunday and if you're still around I'll come over and say hello.

Good luck with the rest of your travels, spend some time enjoying the scenery of Scotland, it's my home country!

I can recommend a few airfields: Oban / Campbeltown / Glasgow / Cumbernauld / Prestwick on the west coast and Edinburgh / Dundee / Glenrothes and Aberdeen on the east coast. Chances are that you have your trip pretty much planned.

Regards
Kieran

Flying in Europe
June 27: Iraklion, Greece to Cagliari, Italy

Ahhhhh, what a relaxing three days in Crete. It was wonderful. Anastasia made me feel so at home in her little hotel that I could have stayed for a week. When she learned that I liked Retsina, she put a bottle in the fridge to cool immediately, while I checked into the room.

Giorgos, the VP of the Iraklion Aero Club, came over the first evening to welcome me and to help out with flying details at Iraklion. We had a great chat. Pilots the world over have been exceedingly helpful. With dinner and breakfast provided at the hotel, I didn't have to do anything but swim and find an Internet café to send my updates. I had planned to fly to the Greek islands to find peace, quiet, sand, and swimming in the Med; but this place had all I needed. So, I stayed and relaxed.

Friday morning I finally said goodbye to the owner and to Anastasia and headed back to the airport. The owner was cleaning the pool the first time I saw him and preparing breakfast this morning. Unfortunately, we couldn't communicate because he couldn't speak English and I couldn't speak Greek. But he seemed like a great, hardworking guy.

The Olympic handling charge, required due to "construction," wasn't as bad as predicted: only 30 Euros, and the avgas was $6.25

In the tower in Iraklion, Greece. The Mediterranean Sea is right outside.

per gallon. Terrible, but only half that foretold. And, at least they had avgas; after Egypt, I'd pay a premium to find avgas. Oil was only sold by the case, but at this stage, I would have accepted almost anything. I was so rested and relaxed after my three days off that I stayed calm through the whole Olympic gas and oil rip-off experience. Nothing could have fazed me at that point.

I had to go to the tower to process the flight plan. The elevator was a black box with no lights; you don't want to be claustrophobic and go in there. I had to leave the door open while I found the right button to push. When I got up there, they were most helpful and told me what to expect for departure and routing.

I waited for takeoff behind two big jets. It was already 11 am (all the processing and gassing took 3 hours) and it was their busy time. I was headed west past the military base of Souda. Unfortunately it was busy there too, and I had to hold twice prior to being allowed to pass through their airspace. At 4,500 feet it was hot, but I was on my way. I'd filed VFR—the tower seemed to prefer that to IFR—and was too low for contact with Athinai (Athens) control, so I wasn't talking with anyone; not a very comfortable position, but I didn't have a choice right now. Only an 8-knot headwind, so I'm averaging 132–134 knots. Less than five hours to go. I'll be in touch with Italy in two hours, then flying over Caraffa (on the toe of Italy), then on to Sardinia.

Well, I've tried all the HF frequencies with no luck. Guess I won't be sending e-mails or talking with anyone this trip. At least there are ships down there. I've counted four so far and although it's a little hazy, they are big enough to pick out. Only four hours to Sardinia and one-and-a-half hours to being over land again. I'll have to climb over Italy, as there are mountains up to 7,000 feet where I'll cross, and up to 10,902 feet on Sicily. This time I'll be happy to climb; it'll be cooler up there, even though the winds will be less favorable.

I'm finally in contact with the world again. It's nice when there's a little concern at the other end. Air traffic control wants me to report "operations normal" every 30 minutes and gave me a backup VHF frequency. I don't feel so alone any more; guess I can quit looking for ships. Boy is it hot, 30 degrees C (90F). I don't want to climb too early because of headwinds, but I do want to cool off. Another 45 minutes and I'll climb to 8,500 feet.

I finally climb and the temperature is down to 20 degrees C (70F). I can see Italy, but it's very hazy. Left turn in 10 minutes and straight to Sardinia. Only three more hours to go. A plane is taking off from Caraffa airport and the controller asks me to stay south of the extended centerline, 270 degrees. The other plane is headed 280 degrees and will report passing 9,000 feet. It's a little disconcerting knowing someone is coming up close behind you. But he finally reports passing 9,000 and I return on course. Most of the pilots and controllers are speaking in Italian, so I really don't know what's going on around me.

Almost abeam Palermo now and in contact with their female approach controller. I was amazed when I was in the Iraklion tower: there were three women and only one man. I also spoke with quite a few women controllers when coming north over Africa. More than I expected, at any rate. It's extremely hazy and I can't see Palermo or Sicily. With less than two hours to go, I'm feeling pretty good. I'm ready for a good Italian meal with Aunt Viv. Not my aunt, a friend's, but we met last October and hit it off very well. She lost her husband about the same time I lost my mum, so it was a difficult time for both of us. I'm hoping that she's doing better.

I tried all the HF frequencies again from 8,500 feet, just in case...but the propagation is no good and I can't make any contacts. I'll reel in the trailing antenna...time to get ready for landing.

It was still hazy as I came across the southern tip of Sardinia, but after a right turn, I was on the ground in another 20 minutes. It's hot, 35 C (100F), but there is a nice wind blowing. The processing is simple within Schengen[36]/European airports. Although I must walk through immigration and customs, no one looks at the passport or any general declaration documentation. As luck would have it, this was the second day in the new terminal. Aunt Viv and I had planned to meet in the departure bar, but in the old terminal, so we had a little trouble finding each other. Within one hour we were together and talking like old times. Viviane gave me a wonderful tour of Cagliari before heading home to a superb Italian dinner.

The temperature was hot, but at the beach, with a breeze, it was comfortable. The mornings were cool and perfect for jogging—which I needed to do, as I was eating a lot of excellent food. Sardinia gets plenty of sun and the fruits and vegetables are juicy and very tasty. We had them at all meals and snacks. I took a bag full in the plane, as Viviane thought I would go hungry during the next four-hour trip.

I was able to spend some time with the pilots of the Aero Club of Sardinia. They were very interested in the voyage, the plane, and the length of the flights. Many thanks to Georgio, a club member, who set up the meeting and Roberto the Vice President, who participated and translated. Pilots everywhere have been a joy to meet. On my web page, I thanked this group in Italian:

Cagliari in Sardegna e di avere il piacere di scambiare delle informazioni concernenti il giro del mondo Mooney. Erano molto interessati alla programmazione del giro, al aero impiegato, alle tappe, alle loro distanze e alle ore di volo impiegati per le traversate, soprattutto quelle

---

36. Schengen agreement between the European countries that signed it. No immigration or customs clearances are required.

oceaniche. E stato un incontro molto interessante e piacevole che non dimentrichero mai per la cordiale accoglienze che ho recevuto.

Ringrazio Giorgio Sarais che e un membro del aero club di Cagliari, e che si dato tanto da fare in cosi poco tempo per organizzare questo piacevole incontro e che mi ha dato l'opportunita di incontrare il vice presidente Roberto Cnrjar e i collighi di volo.

July 1: Cagliari, Italy to Geneve, Switzerland

The exit procedures took 2 hours including avgas—which is even more expensive than in Greece! Again I was "handled" due to parking and needing transportation to the terminal. One doesn't have much of a choice. The handler didn't have any flight plan forms, so that took a while, and then we had to wait for confirmation from Brussels, who modified the route. Tower was efficient with clearances and taxiing and I was off in no time. In some of these airports, although there is a ground frequency, they only use tower. You can find yourself, as I did, calling ground on the hand-held radio for startup approval, and waiting and waiting as no one answers. Finally I called tower and received approval. There are mountains in the north and east quadrants, so circling to climb to altitude was required. I was initially surprised with my climb rate, forgetting that I wasn't overloaded any more. Even with the 32 C (94F) temperature, I climbed well.

ATC kept changing the routing, but it was to make the route more direct, so I gladly accepted the amendments. Finally I was switched over to Marseille control. They just gave me a direct clearance to the French coast, instead of doing two sides of a rectangle around the military airspace. Nice guys! That cuts more than 30 minutes off my trip. Also, with the other pilots speaking French, I can now understand what's going on. The weather is clear blue skies with a few thin clouds at about 6,000 feet and much less haze than previous days. They have rain showers in Geneva, but it should be clearing by the time I arrive. Only two-and-a-half hours to go.

I'm eating well on this short trip, even though I don't need to. Viviane insisted and Nayaghi prepared a sandwich, two packets of cookies, and plenty of fruit. I've just made contact through HF for the first time in many legs. I'm sending off some e-mails and will enjoy reading those that have been waiting for me to collect.

The airspace looks pretty congested on the GPS and on the

instrument charts. I think I'm going to be kept busy over here, although, so far, the communication is pretty light. It's certainly not as congested as Orlando, Florida, airspace. We'll see how it goes. So far, the French have spoken very good English and have been easier to understand than the Italians, who spoke very quickly. I had to ask them to repeat several times.

The coast is in sight, with towns on the flat areas and cliffs rising right out of the sea in other areas. As I fly further north it's green rolling hills with farmlands and lots of small towns and villages with red-roofed houses. I remember that from when I lived in France. Every time I returned from a trip, by commercial flight, I remember the small villages with all the red roofs. It's great to be back in France and flying in my own plane.

As I flew over Marseille and continued north, the communication became more rapid and the controller made numerous traffic calls. Then, it slowed down as I continued further north. It's cold up here; I didn't quite turn the heat on, but I did close the vents. I knew I'd be wishing for the warm weather when I got over the North Atlantic, but I didn't think it would get so cold so quickly. I found out later that the month of June had been very hot weather all over Europe and this was the first cool front that had come through, so it was a relief for everyone.

It was getting cloudier and finally I was IMC.[37] I was handed from controller to controller, remaining at 8,000 feet, which was a safe altitude on the Jeppesen charts. One controller said that I was at my own risk as he handed me off. I checked with the next controller that 8,000 feet was a safe altitude and she said that I was fine. Every time I flew into a cloud I was putting a lot of faith in the Jeppesen altitude and the controllers; obviously I was still a little worried about mountains after my difficulty over Eritrea. I knew there were mountains to my right and I was flying up the Rhone Valley. When I could see the ground, I felt okay. I was switched from Marseille control to Lyon, to Chambery, and finally to Geneva control. He took me off the airway to start vectoring for final approach. The clouds were getting sparser, and I could see the moun-

---

37.   IMC — instrument meteorological conditions - flying in the clouds.

tains to my right and the lake off to the left. What magnificent views. I was on final and the airport was easy to see. Flemming, whom I was to meet, called while I was on final to welcome me to Geneva.

We have a new Number 1 airport for ease of entry—no paperwork and just flash your passport. There is a General Aviation side to Geneva airport and they have customs and immigration for Switzerland and France. It's simple and absolutely no hassle. Going back into France, there is no need to clear at a French airport—I can go anywhere. Flemming, an Earthrounder in his Mooney, and Ray, a Kiwi pilot, met me at the plane and we started talking about flying and swapping flying stories immediately.

Flemming has a wealth of information on flying around the world and had e-mailed me on a number of occasions to give me help and advice. There are five planes currently flying around the world and he has been in contact with all of them. He now gave me information on Iceland and Greenland, which is going to be very useful. Their website, www.honeymooney.com, has the whole story of his and Angela's trip around the world, and he is adding notes from other long trips that he's made to the US and Africa.

We had a wonderful dinner with Flemming and Angela, his wife, and Ray. It was non-stop pilot-talk for several hours. Today it's off to Megeve in Flemming's Mooney. It's a one-way-in, one-way-out, mountain strip. The pilot has to have 10 hours of instruction to be signed off to fly into this *altiport.*

Flemming knows the area very well and I was happy to be in the right seat. It also gave me the opportunity to snap many close-ups of the mountains and glaciers. Due to the clouds, we couldn't get a good view of Mt. Blanc, but the rest of the views were amazing.

The approach into Megeve Altiport was impressive, and it's necessary to be precise. Flemming explained it as he flew and I had the approach plate to follow. The view from final looks very different, and the flare requires a 15-degree change in attitude, something we are not use to. After landing, one must add power to continue up the runway to the ramp on top. It was impressive. We had a French lunch, and then took off to fly down some valleys. Again, the clouds limited our trip, but it was awesome.

July 3: Geneve, Switzerland to Auxerre, France

After a wonderful two days with Flemming and Angela, it was time to move on; only a short one hour and fifteen-minute flight today. Flemming helped me to load up, including lending me his survival suit for the North Atlantic (one size fits all). Startup and taxi went well, but I must have hit a busy time, as I had to wait 15 minutes for departure. That gave me plenty of time to review the departure procedure, as I was headed into clouds and mountains. I had a good climb rate, as I wasn't too heavy, but still was slightly worried about making it over the first mountains, before entering the clouds. Into the clouds I went at 5,000 feet and stayed in at 8,000 feet. It was +3C (36F) and raining, so no ice. I turned right at 7,000 feet and proceeded to Dijon. After half an hour the clouds started to breakup and were broken to scattered for the rest of the trip.

Paris approach gave me "direct to Auxerre" and I was there in no time. I descended to 2,500 feet, which was just below the clouds, and did a visual approach. What was the first plane I saw on arriving? Another Mooney. Later the owner came over and we had a discussion on long distance travel and Mooney airplanes (in French).

The airport was pretty deserted, so I parked in a corner of the ramp and started to clean out the plane—boy it needed it. I separated piles into trash, send back to US, wash, and unload. As I was going to fly friends around, I wanted to take out as much weight as possible. Then I started unloading the 55-gallon drum from the back seat. Within an hour it was out. It attracted a little attention, and one by one, more pilots came over to talk.

After I finished all the work and cleaned the underside of the plane—a horrible job, but necessary every 50 hours or so—it started to look like rain, so I packed up and moved into the Aero Club office. Other pilots were doing the same thing, so about six of us ended up talking about my trip. Actually, the instructor, with whom I'd spoken earlier, had pulled up the web site and several pilots were looking at it. Although I spoke French, I didn't know a lot of flying words in French, but they helped me through and we talked for about an hour.

Gerard and Georges came to pick me up and we talked non-stop all the way back to Sens, about an hour drive. It's good to be "home" where I lived for 8 years. Gerard has a full schedule planned for my stay here. It's going to be fun.

Flying in France

What a joy! *Quelle joie!* This is one of the reasons I planned the trip—to take friends flying. It's been great for me and fun for them. First, I met some very helpful people in Auxerre at the Aero Club de l'Yonne, Christophe; and at the maintenance shop, Bourgogne Aero Services, David and Philippe, who gave me the space and a container to do an oil change. After I finished the oil change, fuselage cleaning, and putting the seats back in, I left for a smaller airport, Joigny, closer to Sens, where I use to live and work. Again, the people at the Joigny Aero Club, President Luc and pilot Hubert, gave me parking space and were helpful with avgas. They and others also wanted to hear all about the trip.

Georges was my first "New Eagle." We flew around Clemecy, Vezeley (a large Basilic church on top of a hill, see color photo), Avallon, and Chablis (lots of vineyards). He helped to determine the route that I would take with future Young Eagles. Francine and Isabelle were next. Although apprehensive, Isabelle held her breath and went for a ride. At the end she enjoyed it.

Young Eagles signing the banner in Sens, France

CarolAnn with a big smile, enjoying giving flights to Young Eagles and old friends

Twins, Thomas and Estelle, were my first French Young Eagles. They were very enthusiastic as were their parents, Philippe and Jocelyne, and friends Robert and Sylvie. My EAA Chapter 74 made me a banner for all the Young Eagles to sign. So, the French youngsters signed it with notes written in French.

Another day I took Gerard and Michelle. Gerard, along with his wife, Francine, took care of me and lent me a car for the whole week. Michelle's late husband, Christian, started my trip by suggesting that I fly my Mooney over to give them a *baptême de l'air*. I was looking forward to taking him flying, but he died of cancer just before my departure from Florida, the end of February. It was moving for all of us, as we remembered Christian during the flight. I know he was with us in spirit.

Then a new Young Eagle, Zelie, and her parents, Charlene and Christian, went for a ride. They had the preflight and loaded in the plane on Sunday, but unfortunately, it wouldn't start. After changing the spark plugs later that day, everything was fine, and they returned Tuesday for a flight around the Yonne region.

This was what I'd looked forward to, and I enjoyed their energy, joy, and enthusiasm with each flight. I thank them all for flying with me. As I move on to England, Ireland, and Scotland, I look forward to introducing more Young Eagles to aviation and taking their parents for a ride as well. It was great to see old friends and colleagues and make new friends. I'm sure I'll be back in France, either commercially or with my plane, to visit everyone again in a year or so.

The wine story:

When I was in Melbourne, Australia, Pamela gave me a bottle of Australian Shiraz and asked me to drink it when I reached France. I shared it with some French friends during a dinner one evening, along with a bottle of South African Pinotage. The French response was mixed to both wines. Some thought they were very good, others thought they weren't full-bodied enough. But, we all had fun taste-testing the wines with dinner *chez Robert et Sylvie.*

July 10: France to England and flying in England

It was another beautiful sunny day when Gerard drove me to Joigny for the last time. It had been a wonderful week of flying, good food and wine in the evening, and camaraderie; I was sorry to leave. We loaded up the Mooney. I had taken out all the heavy items, life raft, ditch bag, survival suit, HF radio, oxygen, etc., in order to fly three passengers at a time. When all was loaded back in, there wasn't room for even one passenger.

I took off to the west into a blue sky with green and yellow fields below. It was calm, serene, peaceful, and beautiful. I'd filed IFR as I didn't want to figure my way around airspace constraints, and was cleared to 6,000 feet. ATC made a few changes to my route, but I was in Dinard, on the north coast of France, in less than two hours. I explained to the arrivals' customs person that I was already in France and came here to clear out of customs, on my way to England. He told me to see him on my way out. I closed the flight plan (as there was no ATC on the field), went to pay my landing fee, filed another flight plan, and went back out through departure customs. They wrote my registration number in their book and I was out. Very quick and easy, no paperwork required.

Back out to the plane, I talked with an English pilot of a LongEZ and his wife, who had just arrived and parked next to me, and were on the way further south in France for a holiday. They went in to customs and I went to start up. Unfortunately, that's when the bad luck started. I'd had trouble with hot starts, but this time it wouldn't start at all. I decided to have lunch and wait two hours for it to cool down, and then try again. Trying to be patient isn't my strong suit, so I checked the battery—no trouble there—and had lunch. Then I filed a new flight plan. I'd planned to go to Jersey for cheap gas— .95 Euros per liter vs. 1.65 to 1.90 Euros in England. But with starting problems, I didn't want to risk another stop. So I changed the flight plan to go straight to Kemble field in southwest England, where I'd been invited to an air show. I was supposed to arrive by 5 pm local and I wanted to make it in that night, before the air show started. I didn't want to arrive at rush hour the next day.

When I tried again, it was no go; there was just no spark. I'd decided ahead of time that it must be the plugs, so I removed the cowling and checked them. They were all wet. I took them out to dry. An hour later, it started like a champ. I was delighted, but somewhat apprehensive about crossing the channel after just replacing the plugs. I was nervous as I climbed and headed out. At first, when I'd repacked the plane in Joigny, I'd put the life raft on the bottom of the back seat, not thinking about crossing the Channel. During the time in Dinard, I moved it to where I could get to it and attached the tethering line inside. No sense having the raft and not being able to get it out in case of a problem. Of course the motor sounded different from normal and, of course I felt vibrations that I hadn't felt before...this wasn't going to be a comfortable trip.

Then I set the radio to Jersey information and started talking with the controller. As soon as I was in contact, I felt better. By the time I left his airspace, I was back to normal and the engine was running fine. I was on a VFR flight plan, but he gave me the next coverage area frequency and sent them the flight information. Plymouth gave me a new squawk code and confirmed radar identification. After Plymouth, I was handed to Exeter and again received another squawk code, then on to Yeovilton with yet another squawk code. This was almost like US "flight following," as they helped me most of the way to Kemble. As I arrived over the coast, just before Plymouth, there were clouds below my 4,500-foot level. I was changing to a northeast direction, so descended, with approval, to 3,500 feet. The haze gave me about 10 miles visibility. I knew that

I was not going to enjoy VFR flying in England. One needs to be low and slow in this stuff and I was not used to it. I would much prefer to be IFR, but the airways are too congested and I'd have to wait a long time for a clearance. So I'd better get in practice and keep a sharp eye out for other traffic. The last handoff was a "free call to Bristol." I didn't understand this terminology and learned later that this means no flight information has been transferred and the next frequency is not aware of my existence.

When I called Kemble Information from 15 miles out, they were ready for my arrival, since they had received my flight plan information. I'd been listening to the frequency and other planes had been arriving, but none were in the pattern as I approached. After landing, I was marshaled to foreign aircraft parking. It turned out that all homebuilt aircraft are together, all foreign commercially built planes are in the same area, and then all British registered commercially built planes are parked in the same area.

At the pilot registration tent, whom did I run into but two Americans from Florida! What a coincidence. Bill and Sue had just flown their homebuilt Lancair over the North Atlantic to come to the show. We became fast friends and did a lot together over the next three days.

And what a fantastic three days they were—I love the atmosphere at air shows; it's all planes and pilots talking planes and flying. The first day I didn't even have time to get around to all the exhibits and tents. After meeting some pilots, I looked at several exhibits and found a pilot who was planning a round the world trip to set a speed record. After my experiences, I spoke with him about some points on his itinerary—especially Luxor, Egypt, with the possibility of no avgas, and discussed entry into major airports in India. I gave him the benefit of my experience and gave him other contacts who had experience in areas into which he'd be flying. For a speed record, he didn't want any hiccups and needed all available information ahead of time.

After participating in a pilot seminar, I met up with Nick, an English pilot, who had e-mailed me lots of information prior to my arrival in England—actually, prior to my departure from the US. Whenever I had a question about an airport or flight rules in England, I'd e-mail Nick and he'd e-mail me the reply. He was flying in for the day and we found each other at the information booth. We spent several hours talking and walking the show grounds. It's so nice to be able to personally thank the people who have helped me along the way. I couldn't have done this trip without help from many pilots like Nick.

Jaqui, the Media Chairperson for the show, had found out about my trip and had contacted me by e-mail before my departure from Florida in February. She told me about the show and invited me to participate. The dates fit almost perfectly with my plans to arrive in England and depart from Scotland, so I agreed to make the show, and set my schedule around arriving one day before the show started and leaving on the last day.

After arrival, I kept checking in at the information booth and media tent, but Jaqui was always running around and not easy to find. Finally, we met and she explained what had been planned for the media...it was to be a media afternoon. First was the ITV television crew. After a short interview, we trooped to the planes and took some footage for the evening broadcast. Bill and Sue with their Lancair went first, then me and my Mooney. We tried not to make each other laugh, but found the staging and takes rather humorous (see color photo). Radio next. One broadcaster interviewed Sue and Bill, and another interviewed me. Each radio broadcaster, after a brief discussion, wrote most of the script and explained how it would go. Then they phoned to the station and made the tape over the phone. The tapes would be edited at the studio and broadcast later that day. It was fast and professional. The broadcasters were very upbeat and enthusiastic during the interviews, with a high energy level. They made it fun for us and I hope the tapes worked out well. Finally we met with a freelance journalist and the local paper. After brief interviews, it was back out to the planes for more photos. We had fun, but were thoroughly tired by the end of the day.

Because it stays light so late in early July, the show and exhibits stay open until about 8 pm. I went looking for some screws and more spark plugs. I'd carried four plugs with me and installed them when I was in France. Now I really wanted to replace the other four. Luckily I found a booth with everything I needed. I wasn't sure about the length of one screw, so the manager let me take several to the plane to see which fit! Nice guy. I finally called it a day and had a beer and fish and chips with Laurie. Flying is more of a social event in England, as it is in Australia and New Zealand, with many Aero Clubs outfitted with a lounge and bar. There is a beer tent at the show, and a live band was planned for the two evenings. Laurie was staying at the local Agricultural College, same as me. He has been running the show for the last 30 years! He's lived with it and helped it to grow from a small event to the impressive show that it is today. It was great to be with Laurie, as we could compare the PFA Rally with Sun 'N Fun and Oshkosh, and talk about planes and flying all evening.

Day two started off at the Scouts' Tent. Stewart had marshaled me to the parking area at arrival and told me that he heard someone was flying the "wrong way" around the world in a Mooney. He invited me to drop in at the Scouts' tent and talk with kids about my trip. I stopped in the first day, but was told that 10 am Saturday would be the best time. We found a globe and I was able to tell them about the trip, the countries, and some of the difficult moments. I think the leaders were more interested than the kids—at least they asked more questions.

Saturday at the show was another beautiful blue-sky day and the crowds were out. It was going to be a good show for sponsors and spectators. I participated in two more seminars and one more interview and photo session. Bill participated in an aerial photo shoot with his Lancair. I kept an eye out for Mooneys and the final count was six: several from England; one German registration but owned by Philippe, a Frenchman; and one other N registration, but I didn't see the owner. After another long day, we settled down for a beer and dinner in the tent, awaiting the awards session. Much to our surprise, I was given the Clive Canning Award for Long Distance Navigation, and Sue and Bill were given the Meritorious Arrival Award. We were honored and delighted. We all agreed that this was a fascinating show with many types of planes we'd never seen before and a great mix of cultures and countries represented. The workmanship of many of the homebuilt aircraft was outstanding, and everyone was happy to talk about their planes and flying. Many pilots had fun with their registration letters. One Brit had given his plane the number G-PPPP—try saying that fast! Swedish registration starts with the prefix SE. Guess what they all use for their next letter?? X!

Sunday was again sunny and warm; another beautiful day for an air show. I stopped in to talk with the Scouts and sat in on three seminars. One of the seminars was on the subject of "Do Women make better or worse Pilots than Men?" Needless to say, there was a lot of debate. The host and editor of *Pilot* Magazine kept the conversation going with pertinent questions and obtained input and responses from the audience. A woman with numerous credentials, including CFI and CFII, was a participating host. She had statistics on accidents and flight hours showing a lower accident rate for women pilots.

Numerous participants indicated that they believe that men are willing to take more risk than women in other areas of their lives and that could carry over to male pilots—indicating that male pilots often take more risk than females. Another participant, who had worked for the US Air Force when they were reviewing whether to let women pilots fly military fighter jets, said that the results of their analysis showed that women dominated in multitasking while men dominated in quick decisions. Each was good at a different area; both of which are needed by fighter pilots. Overall the results showed a similar tendency. People believed that men and women are different in their approach to aviation and women are better in some areas and men are better in other areas. The discussion was excellent.

Late in the afternoon, I thanked Jaqui for the invitation, Tony who got my accommodation, Laurie who drove me back and forth, and everyone else who made this a fantastic show. Just like Air Venture in Oshkosh and Sun 'N Fun, these shows take a lot of work and all the administrators and volunteers deserve a lot of credit, especially as this was a new location and all the logistics had to be worked out for this site. Then I did my preflight and had a LONG, 30-mile, hop to Oxford Airport to visit more friends.

It was beautiful flying low at 1,500 feet over the small farm fields, a perfect summer afternoon for flying. Did I say that I wasn't going to enjoy flying in England? What a mistake, it's magnificent. I couldn't believe that there was no one flying at Oxford when I arrived around 7 pm; a large airport, three runways, and not a soul around. I parked and looked for someone or a phone. I came across one plane that had just gassed up and was leaving, but there was no one else around. I finally found a phone at the security station, called a cab, and went to the nearby village of Thame. Friends Peter and Rita live there. We had a wonderful evening catching up on everything that had happened since we last met.

On returning to the field at Oxford the following afternoon, I found the place abuzz with pilots, students, instructors, and helicopters. It's a very busy place except for Sunday evening. I borrowed a torque wrench and replaced the four old spark plugs. I loaded up with gas and unloaded my survival gear. By the time my hosts/passengers arrived it was 6 pm and cooler; we went for a tour of the local countryside. It was clear, calm, and beautiful with irregular green and yellow fields all around. I don't know how instructors teach "ground reference maneuvers," as there are no square fields and none are aligned north/south or east/west. But, it's beautiful to look at. We went for a tour around the area, and then circled their village of Thame. It's always fun to see things from the air; it gives such a different perspective. Finally we turned west, into the sun, found Oxford, and landed. It's as much fun for me as it is for everyone else to go flying on a beautiful evening. Returning home, we talked, ate, drank, and philosophized late into the night. It was a great reunion and I thank Peter and Rita enormously for being such wonderful hosts.

I'd checked the VFR charts for crossing north of London to the east coast the next morning. If I stayed low, then zigzagged a little, I could miss all controlled airspace and get to Earls Colne airfield without a problem. It worked out exactly as planned. I only saw one other plane, but saw lots of cars sitting in the M25[38] Tuesday morning traffic jam. I was happy to be flying over it all. When I later told the story, people were amazed and envious that I could fly from one side of England to the other in 40 minutes.

Upon arrival at Earl Colne, I found that the local Motor Neurone Disease community had put on a reception for me. I was proud and honored. The local paper took pictures and ran a story about my trip and about MND. All of the people had been touched by MND/ALS in some way—most had lost a family member, or a current family member had the disease. Stanley and Andy, both in wheelchairs, have MND but try to remain in good spirits. Lynn just

---

38. M25 is the ring road around London, notorious for traffic jams.

lost her husband four months ago. The mayor of Colchester joined us to lend his support to our fight against this terrible malady. My mum's old school chum, Jan, had contacted Phyllis, who worked hard to put on this event; I am most grateful to both of them.

The unusually beautiful weather that England had enjoyed for a week finally broke while I was in Colchester with Jan. I was able to take one group flying, but a storm came through the next day and it was very windy and bumpy. The following day was somewhat clearer; however it remained very windy with clouds blowing through at 2,000 feet. Visiting Essex was fun, first I saw the area from the air and got to know the bays and cities, then we drove around and visited some towns, and swam in the North Sea (a little brisk after the Mediterranean). The bays along this coast are amazing because of the tidal activity. At high tide, everything looks normal. At low tide, all the boats are sitting cradled in mud. I would chuckle to myself each time I saw it; it looked so funny.

On the Friday I took another group flying, including Laura, Jan's granddaughter, who is now a new Young Eagle. Because of the

Reception with MND Society of Colchester with the Mayor, right

Boats cradled in the mud at low tide in Wivenhoe, Essex, England

bumps, we cut the trip short. After our goodbyes, I filled up with avgas at 90p/litre (almost $5.50/gallon—get your wallet out for these expensive fuel prices, and it's going to be worse in Greenland) and took off for Biggin Hill, to the southeast of London. The people at Earls Colne had been most helpful. It is a very nice little strip and I thank Victoria and Keith for their help and kindness.

I'd been worried about this short hop. Although it was less than half an hour, I knew that I'd be heading into a busy traffic area. I'd reviewed the charts and knew that if I stayed below 1,500 feet I'd be under the ATC areas. After saying goodbye to Earls Colne radio, I switched to Biggin Hill ATIS for the weather, then listened to their approach frequency. There wasn't much going on: three planes called in for start up, then they taxied and took off, but there was nothing else in the air. I called in and gave them my location and my intentions. I received clearance to do a visual approach, then land. I was guided to the ramp parking, where there were about 10 business jets, and I tied down. Wow, that was easy! I cleaned the plane, revised my baggage packing, and went to the terminal to learn about the local processes and have a cup of tea. As I watched the runway, there wasn't much going on all afternoon. I was amazed and happy, as I'd be returning with family and doing several more trips out of this airport during the weekend.

After an evening with my cousin Jamie and Penny, his wife, we returned to Biggin Hill on Saturday morning for a Young Eagle flight with Lydia and Angus, their children (see color photo). There were scattered clouds at 2,000 feet; it was windy and blustery, but straight down the runway. As we approached the plane, they couldn't believe how small it was. That seems to be the reaction of most people who have followed the trip through the web site. Being next to the plane, after seeing the pictures, makes it seem so much smaller. We flew over their home in Crowborough, but cut the flight short because of bumps and returned to Biggin Hill. Since it was a Saturday morning, the airport was busy with local VFR traffic. We were 4th in line to depart and two more planes joined behind us. Luckily there wasn't too much arrival traffic and we got out relatively quickly.

Believe it or not, while we were having a coffee after our flight, a LongEZ taxied onto the ramp. I joked to my cousin that if the registration was G-EMMY, I knew the pilot and his wife. As the plane turned, we saw the registration, and it turned out to be Mike and Jan whom I'd met in Dinard on my way out of France. What a coincidence!

The next day we returned for more flights; it was still a little bumpy, but better. We went all around Sussex, south to Eastborough on the coast, east along the coast to Lydd, northwest over Bodium castle, then returned to Biggin Hill. The rolling hills, small farm fields, white cliffs and beaches were all magnificent. It's a beautiful country to fly over, when clouds and bumps permit.

Off to Hampton Wick, just west of London, for a day. I caught up on all the news, most importantly the new one-week-old baby of Steph and Eric. Steph's relatives, whom I'd met in Sardinia (sister Danielle and niece Ines), were there. The next morning, after a wonderful English breakfast, we went to Biggin Hill for a quick ride. Ines was very excited about flying, and thinks maybe she'll become a pilot one day.

Bodium Castle in Sussex, England

England is so small; these flights are really quick hops. Forty minutes from Oxford to Colchester, 22 minutes to Biggin Hill, with a headwind, and now 35 minutes to Leicester. I went west from Biggin Hill to stay south of the London control area, then turned right and went north at Farnborough, directly to Leicester. The Farnborough radar controller was busy with a glider competition to the south, but guided me around a few airports and headed me north. The weather was still overcast at 3,000, windy and bumpy with some rain showers, but acceptable VFR. I was getting used to VFR flying again. I kept my head out of the cockpit and looking out the window all the time. Two other planes were heading west, as I was, and there were several others calling in from the airports to the southwest of London. As I headed north, there was a very small, slow plane just below my altitude headed north also. He was difficult to see, so I was glad that I was looking out.

Leicester airport was busy with student pilots in the pattern, but I landed and taxied to parking with no problem. I had a wonderful evening at the pub with old friends and colleagues. Bob, Dave, Hesham, and I had worked together four years ago, and it was a very enjoyable evening of storytelling and hearing all the news.

Bob had followed my trip avidly and knew the answers to all the trivia questions (such as: on which leg did the PTT button break). Wow Bob, that's amazing.

The next days were blustery and rainy. With Vickie and Hesham, I did some bird watching and dog walking, as well as visiting the new work facility that was looking very busy. Unfortunately, although the ceiling lifted, the wind didn't die down. Bob's boys wanted to go flying even though it was bumpy. Luckily they enjoy wild roller coaster rides and the bumpy flight didn't cause any problems, even while circling their house. Their mother, Marion, also enjoyed the flight and became a "New Eagle."

The evening flight to Tatenhill took all of 15 minutes through one rain shower and lots of bumps. After I tied down the Mooney, I found another Mooney pilot, Philippe, and we talked Mooney talk for quite a while. He may well do this RTW (round the world) trip in a few years; he certainly has the right plane for it. Actually, there was a Mooney at Leicester airport also, but I didn't meet the owner. I didn't check out the GA side of the Biggin Hill airport, but so far, from this small sampling, that's over 50% of the European airports with a Mooney!

Bridget, my cousin Gordon's wife, picked me up and took me home for the weekend. More catching up on news on both sides, and they wanted to hear more details of the trip while looking at charts—Gordon is nuts on charts and maps. The next day was a typical rainy English day, so we walked the dog and watched the news and weather. The following morning we got up early and got to the airport by 8:30 am, so that we could fly before the next low pressure system arrived. Although it was a little bumpy with the clouds just starting to build, we had a nice flight around the Staffordshire region and into the peak district. It was beautiful from the air. The whole family was impressed with the green English hills and especially the open fields and hills at the southern end of the peak district—it was a pity we had to return to Tatenhill Airport. As the weather closed in again, we walked Toby, the dog, before the next rainfall.

I had planned to meet a friend, Tim, and his children the following morning to take them flying. His son, William, is an aviation enthusiast. The weather didn't look so good, but we headed off

Gordon (cousin), Bridget and Giles Donaldson in
Stone, Staffordshire, England

to the airport in the hopes that it would improve. Typical English weather that I'm not used to... When we arrived, the airport manager said that the ceiling was 2,000 feet and it was fine weather. Mmmm, not my definition of fine, but I was getting used to it. All the other pilots were out, and most of the planes were leaving the ramp to go flying. We headed out over Litchfield, Stone, and Leek before returning. It was a little bumpy, but we all had fun! Two new Young Eagles happily received their certificates and pins.

July 28: Off to Ireland

Monday morning was time to depart my cousin's home for Ireland. It was a beautiful sunny morning and I thought and hoped it might be a beautiful flight. I was looking forward to seeing Wales and Ireland from the air. But I checked the weather, and unfortunately, there was a front coming in from the west over Ireland. The forecast showed deteriorating conditions for the afternoon. So, I quickly packed and Bridget drove me to the airport.

I had planned to fly from Tatenhill, a small airport to the north-west of Leicester, to Liverpool, and check out through customs and immigration there. When going to Ireland from England, there is an extra step in the process, and what they call Special Branch needs to be notified. Upon arrival at Tatenhill, the chief instructor asked where I was headed, and I explained the process that I had planned to follow. He kindly informed me that I could have checked out of Tatenhill if I'd given them 24 hours' notice. Oh no, that would have been so much easier, especially with my current problem of hot starts. After talking, we decided that there was no downside to calling the local office and asking them, very nicely, if they could come on short notice, especially considering the deteriorating weather in Shannon, Ireland. They called back and agreed to come out to the airport. I was very relieved.

I revised the IFR flight plan and filed it, then did the preflight. When Special Branch arrived, we went out to the plane, I answered all their questions, they looked at my baggage, and we filled out paperwork. Within 15 minutes it was over and I was cleared to fly directly to Shannon. Now I should be able to make it there before the worst of the weather. I fired up, waved goodbye, and took off. Clouds were just coming in over Tatenhill at about 4,000 feet. I called Manchester and they started "working with me." Manchester information gave me a squawk code and cleared me to 6,000 feet. When I was IMC with a traffic call, they diverted me until I was clear, but still the IFR flight plan hadn't cleared. I was unsure of my exact status, but they transferred me to London radar, then London information, and the flight proceeded as if I were on an IFR flight plan, but I was handling my own navigation, and they were keeping me clear of traffic. Over Wales I was mostly on top with a few breaks in the clouds; I could see the hills and valleys, but not much of the Snowdon landscape, which was unfortunate.

As I headed out over the Bay of Cardigan and the Irish Sea, the controller gave me my next frequency, squawk code, and distance where I could reach Dublin radar. I was only out of contact for 30 minutes or so, then back in radar contact with Dublin. I was in clouds and rain most of the time, and that continued over Ireland. The weather at Dublin was 1,000 feet broken, pretty much what had been forecast for Shannon before my departure. I'd had low 6- to 10-knot headwinds over Wales and the sea, but the winds picked up to 25–35 knots over Ireland and my ground speed dropped to 100–110 knots. Every once in a while there was a break in the clouds and I'd catch a glimpse of the green hills and fields, but most of the time I was in clouds. When I was handed off to Shannon, I proceeded directly in. There was another plane on the approach ahead of me who broke out at 800 feet. It was to be an ILS approach, and I was told that it was raining pretty heavily at the airport. I proceeded with the approach and saw nothing at 800 feet. Finally at 500 feet I saw the approach lights and then the runway. The wind was very strong; although my airspeed was 75 knots, my groundspeed was only 55 knots. A few seconds later, I was on the ground and directed to parking. Luckily, it stopped raining and I could tie down without getting wet. Actually, if I'd arrived 20 to 30 minutes later, the ceiling would have been higher, and no rain. It would have been a much simpler approach. But as Paul, an Irishman who just completed his world tour said later, this was good practice for the North Atlantic.

The Airport Operations van picked me up and took me through immigration and customs, then took me to the Operations office. I was welcomed to Ireland by Niall, the Airport Operations Manager, and told that there would be no charges for my stay with them. How nice! He gave me a number to call if I needed anything and wished me a good stay in Ireland. He also told me that he had received information that a newspaper photographer would be out to take my picture. Wow, what a reception.

When I was back in the lounge area, I received a call at Airport Information; it was Carol, my second cousin. She was sorry that she'd missed my arrival, as I'd come in early, but she would come by. She'd called the local papers to do a story! Her father had died eight years earlier of MND/ALS and she felt that more media coverage would help to increase awareness, and maybe boost donations. After two sets of photographs and stories, we went to her house to have tea and meet my mother's cousin, Francis, who was driving down from Birr in the county of Offaly to pick me up. I'd only learned about the Irish family two months before my mother's death. I'd never known my maternal grandmother as she'd died before my mother married. I really didn't know how the family relationship fit together, so we balanced conversation about my trip with discussion on family ties; then Francis drove me 50 miles back

Front row: Maureen (cousin), Patty (Francis' wife), Kathleen (cousin)
Back row: Larry (Maureen's husband), Francis (cousin)

to Birr. Francis and Pattie, his wife, had invited some of the family to their home for the evening, and we pieced together a family tree. We also looked at old photographs, to find any they had that I hadn't seen. Over the next few days, other relatives provided additional bits of information and photographs to put together as much of the family history as we could.

As this was my first trip to Ireland, Francis and Pattie introduced me to many specifically Irish traditions and sites. They have a bog on their land. This provides turf for the stove, used for cooking, and also heats the house and water. I saw how the turf was made, dried, and stored. The top layer of the bog is peat moss that can be harvested for gardens. There aren't many bogs left in Ireland and, as they take many thousands of years to create, some are being preserved in their natural state rather than being harvested. We also visited Killarney, south of Shannon, and went to a show by Brandon Grace, Ireland's foremost comedian. He was excellent. After two more days of visiting with family and completing the family tree as

Cousins Francis, left, and Sean, with the rolling hills of
Ireland in the background

much as possible, Francis and Pattie drove me to Shannon airport.
Francis was interested in a flight and had flown a bit at the local Birr
airport; Pattie preferred the ground. So Francis and I headed northeast over Birr and over the farm. With the bog in the area, he had
no problem finding his farm. We circled and took pictures of the
area, then returned to Shannon via Limerick and held over a castle
while a Citation received priority on his approach. After making
visual contact, I was cleared to base and final, and once again
parked in Light Aircraft Parking.

Paul Ryan, an Irish pilot who had just completed his RTW trip
three weeks previously, met us on the ramp. We had e-mailed back
and forth since he first made contact, when he was in the
Philippines and I was in Ethiopia. We finally met. We had a coffee
in the airport with my cousins prior to saying goodbye to my relatives, and I returned home with Paul. We talked non-stop flying
until late in the evening. We'd decided to do some holds and
approaches the following morning to keep me in good training. I did
one full NDB at Galway after practicing a hold, and then returned
to the hold after the missed approach. Then we flew back to

Shannon for a VOR DME. The whole practice session went very well, and I was on a high all afternoon. I was a little apprehensive of the North Atlantic, where NDB approaches are commonplace. Therefore, I felt much better after successfully completing a full NDB with no problems.

The following morning we visited Foynes Seaplane Museum, which tells the history of seaplane development as the future of transatlantic transportation prior to WWII. It was a small museum, but fascinating. After that, it was pack, redo the flight plan, and head to the airport. Paul had left a life raft at Wick Airport, just north of Aberdeen. As I was headed to Aberdeen, we decided that dropping him at Wick would be about the same, and would give him more time and practice in a Mooney. We refiled the flight plan, filled up the plane with VAT free gas, and headed out over Ireland and Scotland on a very sunny, beautiful day. It was the best weather yet.

We took half an hour to look at The Burren, limestone rock left by the glaciers, and the Moher Cliffs (see color photo) on the west coast of Ireland, prior to heading towards Scotland. Both were fascinating sites, and I was glad the weather had cleared up enough to see some of Ireland. We picked up the IFR flight plan and continued northeast over the farmlands to the coast, with Belfast off to our left. Crossing the North Channel of the Irish Sea to Scotland was very short, with calm water and boats all around on the beautiful bank holiday Monday. Good-bye Ireland, I hope to see you again sometime in the future.

Scotland

Clouds started to increase over Scotland, north of Glasgow. The lowlands to the west were very similar to England and Ireland, but to the north and east, the mountains rose and there were lochs in the valleys. It was a magnificent sight; unfortunately, it was partially blocked by clouds. When the clouds gave way, I snapped pictures. Over Inverness and the Moray Firth, the clouds ended and we could see Wick ahead. We were cleared to descend, then squawk 7000, approach, and land.

Wick was on a flat piece of land jutting out into the sea. As we flew over and started the downwind, I saw a castle to my left on the shore. What a nice view! After I landed, Andrew Bruce, manager of

Far North Aviation, was there with the life raft for Paul. We talked a little, but had to head off, as people were expecting me in Aberdeen. Unfortunately, the hot start problem arose again and it was a no-go. Andrew had a proven remedy for hot starts, which he tried; but finally, we had to park the plane for the night.

I was convinced it would start as always the following morning, but again it was a no-start. We pulled it over to the hangar, took off the cowling and started to check out various possibilities. Andrew was convinced that it was a fuel problem after seeing that it wouldn't drain properly, so we took off the under panel and opened the gascolator to check for debris or blockage. It was clean and clear, no blockage. The mag drop differential had increased slightly during my trip, so we thought that could be contributing to the problem. A check of the timing showed that it was a little off, so we readjusted the two mags to improve the timing. Still no start. Back to a gas problem; the gascolator was not dripping fuel when the plug was pulled, there had to be a blockage somewhere. We put pressure into the tank (blowing into it), and the gascolator cleared and drained. Still no start.

I called Jim and Kelly at Daytona Aircraft Services (they had managed my last two annual inspections). Jim had kindly told me to call anytime, anywhere, if I had a problem. He suggested clearing the fuel line between the boost pump and engine—which I did. Still no start. Next was to check the spark off the impulse mag: it was good. Jim and Kelly were both as mystified as we were—we had fuel, spark, and air; why wasn't it starting? It was exceedingly frustrating; we called it a night. Kelly had given us a list to check the next day; right now I planned to have a beer and sleep on it.

The day had been magnificent—I wanted one like this for crossing to Iceland and Greenland. Later in the afternoon, as I was following Kelly's suggestions, Andrew was handling incoming helicopters. The offshore oilrigs had been closed in with fog and the helicopters, which ferry people from Aberdeen to the rigs, had to stop at Wick until the fog cleared. Thirty-two people trooped into the small terminal. Before they arrived, a small homebuilt had flown in, with two Englishmen who were looking around. While they were there, two airline flights arrived; and after they left, an Italian helicopter showed up. This place was busier than I'd originally imagined. About 5 pm fog started rolling in to the shore from the sea. Andrew believed that it would not come over land, and it didn't. I really want to understand this weather better before crossing. With my current problems, maybe I'll get that chance.

The next morning we cleaned the plugs, insured that gas was reaching the pump with no air in the lines, and tried to start. We had limited success, as it was closer to starting than the previous day. With throttle forward and mixture lean, it would fire and as the mixture was enriched, it would try to keep firing. After many tries, we checked the engine, and only the first cylinder was hot; the others weren't even firing. This led us to believe it was a mag problem. After checking the prices of new mags, I decided to get the old ones checked out at Dundee, the nearest inspection station. It took a while to get the mags off; then I hired a car and drove four hours to Aberdeen to stay with friends for the night. I'd planned on staying with Janet and Brian for the weekend and taking their children, Paul and Stephanie, flying. But for now, it would have to be a quick one-night stay, then on to Dundee in the morning to get the mags checked out and rebuilt.

What despair—this is a real low point. It's been a day of highs and a real low. I left Aberdeen before 6 am to get to Tayside Aviation in Dundee as early as possible. I met Stuart at 7:15 am and he got to work on the mags right away. I couldn't have been happier. Within two hours, I was back on my way to Wick. He'd rebuilt both mags; I'd paid the bill, and was getting an early start on the five-hour drive back. The traffic wasn't too difficult, and by 2:15 pm I entered the gate at Wick Field to see always smiling Andrew and always working Clair at Far North Aviation. After a cup of coffee, I set to work putting the mags back in. I'd worked with EJ at Daytona Aircraft Services during my last two annual inspections and helped him a little, but this time it would be for real. Stuart had coached me before I left Dundee, and again over the phone each time I had a question. After four hours, both mags were back in, checked, timed, and tightened. All tools were put away and we were ready to try a start. I was confident, Andrew less so. We climbed aboard, boosted and cranked. Nothing...how depressing. The second try the starter stalled out. This was unbelievable. We'd checked everything and now put in newly timed mags and not even a kick. Plus I now had to change the starter. I left the field feeling exhausted and depressed. I didn't want to eat and only wanted to sleep.

I also watched the weather while driving for six hours and when I got back to Wick. It was a foggy morning in Aberdeen, and even as I started driving northward at 9 am there was patchy fog. Around Inverness, it was relatively clear and warm with a superb view; as I descended the hill overlooking the bay, it was just a bit hazy. As I proceeded northeast up the northern coast of the bay, the fog was all around and visibility was reduced. It remained in patches most of the way back to Wick, which was socked in when I arrived. Much to my surprise, a small British Airways shuttle landed. Andrew said that visibility was clear at the west end of the runway. As the afternoon progressed, the fog deepened and thickened. An RV and LongEZ were on their way from Reykjavik, Iceland, to Wick. The weather looked worse. At about 5 pm, we heard them on the radio; they decided to continue to Aberdeen. This was what I was worried about in the North Atlantic. The TAF was for only temporary fog, clearing after 5 pm local. Well, it's now 9 pm and the fog is even thicker. As Andrew says, there's no predicting the fog. That didn't make my evening any better.

The next morning I had my list: recheck spark, recheck fuel, and then try to start again. First, no spark; take the P lead off and I have spark. Good. I bleed the fuel as I've done before and check that fuel is getting through the injectors, good. Now to change the starter. Four hours later, I have a new starter in place. Time to try again. She starts first time, but dies just as quickly—lack of fuel. After talking with Tayside, we decide that I should try with the boost pump on. I bleed the system again and try a start with the boost pump on. Crank, put-put-put, she continues put-putting for about a minute with full mixture and full throttle. Finally, the system clears and starts firing properly as I back off the throttle. She runs smoothly. I stop the boost pump and all continues well. I let it run for over five minutes to heat the oil so that I can do an oil change. I'm not going to celebrate until she starts again, hot or cold.

I've already done five oil changes this trip, so the sixth goes smoothly. After that, I pull her to the front of the hangar, cross my fingers, and try again. What a joy, the engine starts up immediately! I call Andrew on the radio, then taxi out to do some patterns. Everything is exactly as before, maybe better. The RPM seems higher, and everything else is running smoothly. After two patterns, I park on the ramp and run back to Far North Aviation. I pay my bill and wish everyone a good weekend. It's Friday evening and I can still get to Aberdeen for the weekend. I call Janet and Rendall and head out. Again, she fires up on the first crank—I'm not used to this! I plan to fly around Moray Firth to Inverness and then to Aberdeen, staying over land the whole way. No sense crossing the 50-mile firth (bay) to save half an hour on the trip, after all the work that's been done on the engine.

I'm listening to the engine the whole way, even though I'm over land, this area is not very hospitable and a forced landing wouldn't be good. Lossy control clears me over some restricted zones and direct to Aberdeen. Another 30 minutes and I'm on the ground. They direct me to park with the business jets, as the aero club parking is full. They then drive me to the ExecAir building where I meet Rendall, president of the Aberdeen Aero Club. He greets me warmly, welcomes me to Aberdeen Aero club, and listens to my week of troubles as he kindly drives me to my friends' home for the weekend. The good news is that they have a local mechanic that works on their planes, who can check out my engine. But, right now, I'm ready for a rest.

We had a wonderful time—the weather continued to be unseasonably warm, which is just perfect around 75 to 80 F in Aberdeen. We walked in the woods and on the beach. One walk took us to a very old, original Scottish house, which is circular and underground with a wooden roof covered in dirt. They explained about "haar," which is their local coastal fog that comes in over the coastline and out again several times a day, or sometimes not at all. One morning, as we are sitting outside drinking tea, I watched it roll in and out two times. Again, this was something that I wanted to understand better before flying in the area. It's normal to see it in spring and fall, but with the unseasonably warm days, they were getting more this summer.

The only downside was that the sore throat I'd had in Wick turned into laryngitis on Saturday morning, and I could only whisper. I wanted to take the family and kids' friends flying, but that would have to wait until I could talk. I tried to stay quiet most of the day, but it's difficult when there is so much catching up to do. On Sunday I could "squeak" a little better, so off we went. The weather wasn't cooperating; there was a scattered layer of clouds at 1,000 feet and a broken layer at 1,500 feet. But we were able to fly over their house and up the coast with all the kids and grownups. We had a great time. As with other visits with friends and family, it comes to an end too soon. It was time for me to move on.

Logistics had been proceeding well and on track all around the world, but unfortunately all my planning seemed to fall apart in Scotland. My last sets of charts were supposed to arrive in Aberdeen. One set got lost in the post (we found out later that it went sea mail instead of air mail) and the other set was sent too late. They were redirected to Greenland. I scrounged enough charts to get to Iceland and Greenland, thanks to Andrew and Paul and I hope to receive the compliment in time to leave for Canada.

The other logistics problem was my Garmin GPS update chip. I'd switched to the International subscription for my trip, which I'd update through my laptop computer. Unfortunately, due to AT&T problems, I had only been able to receive updates a few times, in New Zealand and Australia. After that, the AT&T connection wouldn't work for some unknown reason. I was now in need of the Americas chip prior to my departure from Greenland. My AT&T connection was still not working, and I couldn't use another laptop to get an update. I asked Jeppesen to send me a one-time chip with the latest Americas update to an address in Greenland. This is currently in process. If both plans work, I'll pick up all the neces- sary documentation in Nuuk (formerly Gothab), the capital of Greenland. If not, I still have the minimum equipment necessary to make the crossing, but it will be with fewer backups. As many friends and pilots have remarked, the logistics for this trip have been complex and sometimes very difficult. Let's hope that things fall into place as planned this time.

CA:

I just got your series of notes. It sounds like everything is going very well. I'm sure you're a little tired of it all by now but hang in there. You've just about done it. People are always stopping in my office to ask about you. You're becoming a celebrity! Enjoy your time in Europe. It's got to feel like home after the places you've been. Good Luck!

Love,

PeterJohn

CarolAnn with Diane, ALS Chairperson for South Africa

CHAPTER 17

Dave Ripley, here, in Duncan, OK. I am an AirLifeLine pilot in the Southwest US and am following your trip and wishing you well at each step. I feel a sense of envy and of awe at what you are doing and experiencing. Hope that your last legs go well also.

Regards and good luck.
Dave

Crossing the North Atlantic
August 12: Wick, Scotland to Horafjordur, Iceland, 12th leg flight report

After a wonderful weekend with friends in Aberdeen, I left on the Monday morning for Dundee, half an hour south, to get the engine checked out. Although it was running fine and starting extremely well, I wanted the mechanics to go over the engine before I crossed the North Atlantic. I still had laryngitis when I departed Aberdeen, and although I'd been trying to rest my voice, it still cracked and faded out quite often. I had juice and sweets to keep it lubricated. I followed the coastline down with beautiful views of the cliffs and a few beaches. After I was out of the ATC area and squawking VFR, 7000, I crossed inland, direct to Dundee. The tower brought me in over the airport at 2,000 feet and straight in to the pattern: downwind over the Tay River, base with a good view of the hills rising beside the river, and on to final with the runway alongside the river.

The engineers at Tayside Aviation were all ready to help and Stuart, Neil, and John pulled my plane into their hangar and took off the cowling. They reviewed the mags, tested them again, and pronounced the ignition switch and mags to be looking good. Neil reviewed the whole engine while John made me a new exhaust hanger to replace the one that had broken the previous day. They knew that I was crossing the North Atlantic pretty soon and wanted to be sure that everything was in good shape. We started it one more time, fitted the new hangar, and buttoned up the cowling. They pronounced me ready to go. I very much appreciate all they did to help me out and make sure that my engine was as good as possible. When I was checking the weather to return to Wick, another person

Rugged coast south of Aberdeen

from Tayside Aviation, Bob, gave me his approaches, in case I needed them and got me the latest weather information for the area. As I've said before, people in aviation the world over have been exceedingly helpful to making my trip as safe and easy as possible. I may be doing most of it alone, but it takes all these people to make the trip a reality—it certainly isn't a solo effort. Thanks again to all.

After departing Dundee, I turned almost due north for Wick. The clouds were in layers, but soon broke away and I was in clear sky. The heather covered hills and green valleys were a joy to look at. The last part of the trip was over the Moray Firth. Only 50 miles, but enough to make me gulp after the work that had been done on the engine. I figured that if I couldn't make this, I certainly wouldn't be ready to cross to Iceland tomorrow. So I held my breath, took a picture of the shore, and checked the gauges. It wasn't so bad. After several minutes I started feeling okay again. I called Wick approach/tower and they guided me in. I was back "home." After spending a week here, it felt almost like home.

I started reorganizing the plane for tomorrow's flight. The life raft had to be ready on the front seat and tethered. The ditch bag was right behind. I had the survival suit that Flemming had loaned to me; I'd put that on tomorrow before departing. Graham and I filled the tanks and added four liters of isopropyl alcohol to prevent ice forming in the gas filters. I hooked up the HF radio wires and cleaned the window and leading edges: I'd been through a bug storm and had bug juice everywhere. Then I was ready to go. In the Far North office, I did my flight plan and made sure I had all the charts and approaches.

Back to the Harbour Café B&B for a good night's sleep and one last Scottish breakfast.

The morning was clear but there are clouds moving in from the northwest. The satellite image showed a storm moving over north Scotland, but relatively clear enroute after passing the front, and clear over Iceland. The winds showed tailwinds becoming cross-winds and the METARs[39] and TAFs showed all airports VFR and remaining that way. As I said to Clair and Graham, they were taking away all my excuses, now I had to leave.

I did the preflight, checked the charts, paid my bills, and got ready for the flight. This time I'd be wearing half the survival suit. They are cumbersome, difficult to get on, and hard to move around in. Most pilots put on the bottom half and drape the top over the back of the seat. It worked pretty well, but they are very bulky and I don't know how others fit with two people in the front. Wick tower gave me my clearance and I was off, with less trepidation than I'd imagined. I'd been worried about the North Atlantic legs and thought I'd be very worried the morning of the flight. But instead, I was amazingly calm and ready for this leg. I climbed through clouds that were coming in over Wick and picked up a nice 15-knot tail-wind. As I leveled off at 6,000 feet, the clouds broke clear and the seas were calm. Every once in a while, there was a little bump to make me nervous, but overall it was very smooth. Radar pointed out a helicopter that I never saw, but otherwise it was looking like a short trip at 150-knot groundspeed.

---

39.   METAR — current meteorological report for the local airport and surrounding area.

I knew that I was feeling comfortable when I finally pulled out the laptop, reeled out the HF antenna and tried to send an HF e-mail message. Unfortunately, I couldn't make contact. Oh well, I'll start writing the trip report instead. I lost contact with Scottish radio, but picked up Reykjavik as recommended after crossing 60 degrees north latitude. They came in loud and clear, changed my squawk code, and cleared me to Hornafjordur. It's chilly in the cockpit. I'm wearing a fleece top and haven't put on the heat, but it's a little cool. As I cross the first waypoint and FIR boundary to Iceland, I only have two hours to go. It's really a short trip.

Off to the right are the Faroe Islands. I heard that they are usually cloudy and not a good destination. I met a ferry pilot at Far North Aviation, in Wick, who had stopped there for gas—$10 per gallon. That's the most expensive anywhere! He's not going to stop there again.

The tailwind is down to seven knots with widely scattered clouds below and overcast above; there is a little rain and the temperature is still +2C (34F) at 6,000 feet. The wind moves around to more of a left crosswind and I'm down to 145 knots, which really isn't bad, considering it's usually a headwind when flying westward over the North Atlantic. I just realized that I can't take my shoes off with the survival suit on. I usually take them off when I reach cruise altitude. The next leg will be six hours, so I'd better start without shoes!

I was into the last 150 miles and was studying the NDB approach when I entered some dark clouds with rain and turbulence. My head hit the ceiling once and it's difficult to hold course. It's nothing I haven't been through 15 to 20 times in the states, but it doesn't feel good bouncing around out here over the North Atlantic. After three to four minutes I come out the other side to blue sky and small puffy clouds. That feels a whole *lot* better.

Reykjavik gives me the Hofn weather and it's good VFR. As I get closer, the clouds break up and I can see the town; I descend below the clouds. I see the airport and am given clearance to land. There are mountains and glaciers all around. I'm snapping pictures like crazy to try to capture it all before landing. I can't stop looking at the scenery—it's majestic. I land, taxi, and park, and still can't stop looking at the green hills and dirty white glaciers.

It's cloudy and drizzling. After visiting with the tower controller, I learn that it isn't forecast to clear up in the next few days. It actually looks better to the north. After a trip into town for coffee and a look around, I finally decided to go to Akureyri, further to the northwest. I file to go via Egilsstadir, a town to the northeast, to keep the enroute altitude to 7,000 feet for the first half and 6,000 feet for the second half. I'm thinking that I'll run into icing if I go any higher.

When they give me the clearance, they've routed me direct at 9,000 feet. I explain that I want to stay low, and they revise my clearance to the one I'd originally filed. I circle in the clear around Hofn to climb to 7,000 feet and get some good pictures, then start on my way. The clouds are numerous, thankfully it's only rain in them, but I don't get many clear shots. From time to time I see ice and snow on the mountains and some mountain lakes.

After passing an intersection, the helpful controller asks if I want AKI (Akureyri) direct at 8,000 feet. Again I decline—no sense risking icing.

After I turn the corner and head west for AKI, I descend to 6,000 feet and I'm just below the clouds. The views are amazing—mountain lakes, green valleys with rivers, and sparse mountaintops. There's not much vegetation or habitation. After another bout with dark clouds, rain and turbulence, I'm again in blue sky on the other side and AKI is only 30 miles ahead. This was not going to be a pretty approach, an offset LOC[40] with five descent points, but it looks like it'll be VFR—my lucky day. As I cross the last mountain, there's the wide valley at the bottom of the bay with the town of Akureyri at the end and the airport beyond. It's beautiful—I'm snapping more pictures as I descend from 6,000 feet to sea level. I'm cleared to land and again can't take my gaze off the mountains surrounding the airport.

Iceland is pretty expensive with Guest House accommodation, shared bathrooms, and shared kitchen facilities, at $55/night. Beer at $3/can in bulk! And, Internet access at $6.50 per half hour. But, it's beautiful and sunny, so I decide to stay two nights and get some

---

40.   offset LOC — localizer approach that is not straight in to the runway. A non-precision approach.

updating done. The towns are pretty sleepy and activity is minimal. People are pretty laid back about things and certainly not rushing around—but they are all pleasant and helpful. The one good point is that there is only a landing fee at the first airport and not at each subsequent airport, except for Reykjavik, so all landing and parking is now free after my first payment of $14. Now that's very reasonable. Also, the international entry requirements rank right up there with Switzerland as being simple and easy. Unfortunately, because I came in at a small airport, I didn't get a stamp in my passport. I'll try to get one at Reykjavik.

I've checked in with the tower for tomorrow's departure, sent postcards, and found an Internet café, so I can now tour around and enjoy sunny Iceland.

Thursday morning I'm going to relocate to Reykjavik to prepare for the leg to Greenland. It's up early with the sun—I manage to stay in bed until 6:15 am. It looks sunny and windy. The weather forecast on the TV (that I couldn't understand, but could watch) looked like sun to the north and rain to the west and south. Reykjavik is in the southwest. The 3-day forecast looked like a high coming over Greenland—that would be too good to be true.

With a taxi charge of $11 for the three kilometers to the airport, I can walk. I need the exercise anyway; I haven't been running since Ireland. The woman in the tower is extremely helpful with weather around Iceland and she checks some in Greenland for me. All the airports there are fogged in, so I stick with my first plan to relocate to Reykjavik (RK). I wanted to see the north of Iceland and Isafjordur (IS), a town to the west, if the weather holds, so I planned a VFR flight to IS and an IFR leg from there to RK, as there were clouds and rain in RK. It was still clear and sunny when I took off at 9 am, although there were some high clouds off to the west. The fjord was beautiful, with small villages along the coast and some houses off by themselves. The mountains rose up behind them to 4,000 and 5,500 feet. I turned west over the mountains and climbed to 6,500 feet. It was still above freezing, +2C. I continued west with a crosswind, and RK control gave me a squawk code.

After crossing over the first bay and starting over the second strip of land, clouds were lower, so were the mountains; so I descended to 4,500 feet. I set out across the second large bay.

Unfortunately, the clouds kept getting lower, and, after reaching 3,500 feet, which is lower than the minimum safe altitude when I reach the next landfall, I decided that was enough. I called RK control and started climbing. They cleared me direct RK at 6,000 feet. I felt better. I kept looking west, and it cleared a little, but not enough to have had an enjoyable VFR flight. I'd already seen some wonderful scenery, which would have to do. I proceeded southwest at 6,000 feet into a 40-knot headwind. Every once in a while there'd be a break in the clouds and I'd see land, mountains, fjords, or a mountain lake, but not very often. After half an hour and at 30 miles from RK, I was switched to approach and was guided in. Although the wind was 160 to 170 degrees and there is a runway 19, for some reason they were using runway 13. With 20- to 25-knot winds, this made for quite a crosswind landing. Luckily it was uneventful and I taxied to Flight Services where Sveinn, the manager, proceeded to take care of me.

We gassed up for tomorrow's flight and he got some weather information. It looked like the low would be moving through and I might have a window of opportunity tomorrow for tailwinds over the Greenland ice cap. This is perfect and usually means no fog on the west coast. Good news. But nothing is sure until the next day's weather comes out. So, it's off to find a hotel and look around Reykjavik for the afternoon.

ALS/MND Update:

I recently received another e-mail from Jackie in Australia. She's still writing and fighting ALS/MND and has a new web site of her own: http://55jer.com/jackies%20page.htm where you can read all about Jackie and her family.

I also received e-mails from friends of a new ALS/MND patient. John and Barbara from Canada have a friend Jim who, in his mid 50s, was diagnosed with ALS just 10 months ago. He's fighting, but also living some long-awaited dreams. He took a flight in a Gypsy Moth several months ago, and will surely enjoy some other unfulfilled dreams in the coming months.

When arriving in Earls Colne Field near Colchester, England, I met Lynn whose husband, Derek, died of ALS/MND four months previously. During his early stages, he also lived a dream and did a parachute jump to raise awareness and donations for MND.

While in Ireland, I met one cousin whose husband died of MND 8 years ago. His type of MND progressed very quickly and he died within a year of being diagnosed. It was a tremendous loss for Kathleen and her family. She continues the fight by helping with fundraisers each year at her local church and community.

Many thanks to those of you who have donated to help find a cure to this disease. Some of you have written to me and others have donated anonymously—to all I owe a debt of thanks. If you are enjoying these flight reports and haven't yet donated, please consider sending a donation. Just send a check to the ALS Therapy Development Foundation, 215 First Street, Cambridge, MA 02142. Thank you for your support. I'll be attending fundraising events in Canada and the US over the coming weeks to raise awareness and donations to fight this disease.

August 15: Reykjavik, Iceland to Nuuk, Greenland, 13th leg flight report

It had been raining on and off as I looked for a Guest House and toured a little in Reykjavik yesterday, but it looked nice when I woke up this morning. Some clouds off to the west, but much clearer overall. I had breakfast and headed out into a light shower as I walked back to the airport. Arriving just before 8 am, Sveinn already had all the weather information printed out and it looked very good. Almost clear over the ice cap with crosswinds—Sveinn thought it looked good for crossing and I agreed. We filed the flight plan and I did the preflight. I thanked him for all his help and headed out to my Mooney. I put on the bottom half and the survival suit; remembering to take off my shoes this time, I put them in the back and climbed aboard. This was what I'd hoped for, a nice day for crossing. I called ground and received startup clearance as well as my route clearance. Then I went to start the engine and click-click. I'd heard this sound before; I couldn't believe it. I rechecked everything and tried again—click, click. Oh no...

I clambered out of the cockpit with my survival suit on, took it off, put my shoes back on, and took off the cowling. I was hoping it was a lead somewhere that was off—no such luck. I went in to see Sveinn and he called a mechanic from across the field. While waiting, we discussed Sveinn's hand propping the engine. He said that he was okay with that, and I said that the engine had been

One size fits all survival suit necessary for crossing the North Atlantic

starting on the first turn, so it would be feasible, but...I didn't want to be stranded in Greenland, so I decided against it.

The mechanic checked that power was getting to the starter, so it had to be the starter that wasn't working—how could that be? He told me to take it out and give him a call when it was out. Ludwig, a pilot and Kitfox builder who was wandering around, offered to help me, and together we got it off in 30 minutes. Elias, the mechanic, and I checked it out in his shop and believe it or not, it worked correctly when power was applied—mystery. Maybe it wasn't grounded correctly. We returned and remounted it—click, click, no start.

Elias went over to the operator of the flight school, just next door. Yes, they had a starter in stock that I could have...okay, I'll take it. Elias and I walked back and put on the second starter for the morning.

As we were getting close to finishing Sveinn checked weather and costs to arrive late in Greenland. The weather was good for today, Friday, or next Tuesday (another front was coming through) and to arrive late today, after-hours in Greenland, would be $550. What a choice. I decided to leave. Weather is too iffy and today the weather was just right. Better to pay extra today than be stuck for a week or more. Sveinn filed the flight plan; I paid for the work and new starter and was off. I donned the survival suit (without my shoes), clambered into the cockpit, got clearance, and took off.

I was tense as I climbed out over water and through clouds. This was the leg that made me the most nervous, and I was now starting out late, would arrive late, and had just finished working on the engine. When I finally leveled off at 6,000 feet, the ATC person handing me over wished me a good trip—that was nice of him, and it made me feel better. After 20 minutes, I broke out into blue sky— that made me feel a lot better.

RK control asked if I was HF equipped, as I'd be out of VHF contact. I replied that I was and asked for the frequency. I tried transmitting and didn't hear anything. Something was funny—I checked all the knobs, but something had definitely changed. I hadn't used it in a while and wondered what it could be. I hauled it up on the right seat to check all the connections. Duhh, no antenna connection. After that, it worked very well.

I was in and out of clouds for the first hour, then it was clear ahead; this I took as good news of no clouds over the ice cap. I'd be at 12,000 feet and at -6C (18F) and I didn't want any clouds or poten- tial for icing. I was running about 130 knots with 15- to 20-knot headwinds. I got the oxygen ready. Although only at 12,000 feet, I didn't legally need oxygen, I wanted to be on it as I was tired and had already had a long day. With clear blue sky ahead, and only a scattered layer below, I was feeling better; I realized that I always felt better in clear air than in clouds, especially dark rain clouds. I still haven't seen an iceberg or whale; I hope that will change soon.

The first position report went well. Since I was at 6,000 feet, they advised me that I would have to be at 12,000 over the ice cap. I acknowledged. Only 200 more miles over water, less than one-and- a-half hours. The wind moved around to the northeast and my speed picked up to 142 knots as the headwind component dropped. The second position report also went well, but it was difficult to break in, as many planes were reporting on the same frequency. I heard two planes talking with Gander, Canada. The frequency was definitely more congested than the Pacific.

Ninety miles away, and I can see Greenland. WOW! It looks like a wall of jagged mountains rising out of the sea (see color photo). And, at the same time as I'm snapping pictures, the Kulusuk NDB comes in, straight ahead, confirming my position. There are little icebergs as well. My speed is up to 155 knots as the wind swings around, and my dilemma is whether to stop in Kulusuk or to continue on. If I stop, I'll avoid the $550 overtime fee. But I may be stuck for three or four days, or more. I decide to continue on, and turn back if I encounter icing.

I find that taking pictures of icebergs is like taking pictures of pelicans the first time you go to Florida. You end up with a lot of them; and later, it becomes normal to see them. So, I have lots of pictures of icebergs and mountains, but they are fantastic to look at.

Sondrestrom Radio advises me that Nuuk weather is not good and that I should proceed to Sondrestrom instead. The weather showed that the fog had cleared a little, but was still in the area, with few clouds at 800 feet, scattered at 11,000 feet, visibility 7,000 meters and fog in the area. I accepted the advice to go to Sondrestrom, and plugged in that course. I proceeded over the coast of Greenland to fjords, glaciers and the start of the ice cap. I can see marks in the snow! It was like the first time I crossed Lake Michigan; I kept looking back over my shoulder to see the edge of the ice cap, as all that was before me was white. It looks hazy, like a cloud layer, but there is no icing on the wings. I continue to check anyway. It'll be two hours to complete the crossing of the ice cap. I made a position report and continued on. I was hungry as it was late afternoon and I hadn't eaten since breakfast; I broke into the ditch bag for some beef jerky. Boy, that tastes good; I hadn't had any for five-and-a-half months.

The jet going over leaves a vapor trail with its shadow on the ice cap. That and marks in the snow are all I can see for miles. For me, crossing the ice cap is worse, more worrisome, than my over water legs—or maybe it's just because I had a bad start to the day.

The additional aspects of potential icing and being only 2,000 feet above ground make me more nervous. I keep checking the wings for ice. I've been running the engine at 2500 rpm instead of my normal 2350 rpm, because of the increased altitude and the desire to get this over with.

Sondrestrom calls with my clearance, which I copy and read back. I then ask for Nuuk weather. We have some difficulty communicating and they finally change frequency, understand my request, and give me the latest weather. It's perfect at 10 miles visibility, 12,000-foot broken cloud layer, and strong winds to keep the fog away. I ask to proceed direct to Nuuk. They say that the weather people are still recommending that I go to Sondrestrom, because the weather will deteriorate and I won't be able to leave the following morning. I explain that I'm staying the weekend, won't be leaving the next morning, and would like to divert to Nuuk. They finally accept by request and clear me direct to Nuuk. The left turn gives me a better tailwind, as forecast, and I'm over 150 knots. That still gives me one hour and 40 minutes to go. I give Sondrestrom the new ETA.

While in Europe, I'd thought about returning next year, by Mooney or a commercial flight, to visit family and friends again. At this stage, all thoughts of crossing by Mooney went out of my head—I'll fly commercially with my dad! It's beautiful, breathtaking, surreal, but once is enough for me. I'm hearing strange noises and vibrations, and I can't settle down. I know it's mainly due to the higher power setting, but I'm still pretty tense. I can't hold my breath and sit on the edge of my seat for an hour-and-a-half, so I start checking the approach for Nuuk. I'd already checked out Sondrestrom's before changing my destination back to Nuuk.

On the half hour, just as I was about to call operations normal, Sondrestrom called to ask me to report my position every half hour. I did, and felt better that they were tracking me. I pulled out the laptop and started writing; at least that would calm me down a little and give me something to do. Under an hour to go, what a relief, but the wind has swung around and I have a headwind component.

Looking ahead, it seems that there are mountains on the horizon: how can that be? As I get closer, I see they really are mountains, it's the end of the ice cap and the mountains are higher than the ice. The ice also has what seem to be holes and circles, as it deteriorates near the edge.

I breathe a sigh of relief as I'm snapping pictures of more glaciers and mountains. I can see the fjord and bay and I know that Nuuk airport is in there, just ahead. I call Nuuk at 20 miles out, and they give me the latest weather and say no traffic for descent. I give them the phone number of Allan, who had contacted me by e-mail, and they kindly call to advise him of my arrival.

It's a little bumpy as I come in over the side of the mountain where the runway has been made. Allan is there to meet me and help me through the proceedings. It's cold and I don an extra jacket and hat, both given to me in South Africa. As the storm is supposed to come through that evening, Allan inquires about a hangar. I repack and put my bags in his car. Hangarage would be $160 per 24 hours. We decide to tie down. They have huge concrete blocks and we move the plane to a relatively protected area and tie it down securely, facing into the wind.

Allan shows me his plane, a Grummen AA1C, very nice, in the hangar. There are only about five private planes in Greenland, and it's very expensive to fly. Gas alone is $8 per gallon. We proceed to the tower to pay my dues, but everything is closed, so Allan takes me home. Later that evening, with Else, his wife, we return to check on the tie-downs. All is well. I can sleep peacefully during the storm of the night.

The next day, it's stormy, windy, and rainy with low clouds and mist, and a temperature of 9C (48F). Normally an autumn or winter day for most of us, but it's mid-August in Greenland. When we were talking yesterday evening, Allan said that they'd had good sunny weather a week ago with highs of 20C (70F). Not summer weather for most of us; however, I can see the appeal of the land. The views that I saw yesterday on arrival are majestic. There are mountains and rock formations that take your breath away, and icebergs floating down the bay. Allan and Else made a video of Illulisat and Uummannaq which shows the fantastic panorama of Greenland by plane and boat.[41] We hope to see more by air and car when the weather clears.

During a tour of the town, we stopped by the airport to check on the tie-downs. In the tower, the max winds are up to 62 knots! I

---

41.   Obtain a full 40 minute video directly from Else at elvideo@greennet.gl

was worried—she could take off in those winds! It was only forecast to be a maximum of 45 knots. We added an extra concrete block to each wing, increasing the weight from 600 lbs to 1,200 lbs. I felt better. This was probably the peak of the storm and I was probably overreacting, but the wind was blowing me around and my Mooney was bouncing on the tires and moving the chocks away. I'd never seen a plane tied down in winds that strong and I don't want to see it again. The town is colorful, as are all Greenland towns and cities (see color photo). The buildings are all painted in vibrant colors, a custom dating back to having certain colors for certain buildings: hospitals were yellow, government buildings were red (including the jail), and utilities were blue. Because Nuuk is the capital of Greenland, it has a major hospital, a cultural center, and a university. The harbors are FULL of small boats. There are probably more boats than cars. People use boats for fishing, hunting, and as a means of transportation.

As it drew towards evening, the winds calmed down a little, maybe down to 40–50 knots. When we returned from dinner with Else's sister and mother, a wonderful traditional caribou, the winds were definitely calmer. I felt better and would sleep okay.

The following morning it was calm but still cloudy and misty; I hope it will soon clear.

Some fun facts on Greenlandair: 460 employees, 200,000 passengers/year; planes: 1 B757, 4 DASH-7s, 2 Twin Otters, 1 Beechcraft Super King Air 200, 1 Piper Super Cub and 1 Cessna 172; helicopters: 4 S-61s, 4 Bell 212s, 6 Aerospatiales AS350, 4 Huggies MD500 and 1 Bell 407. Because Greenland has no roads connecting its cities, Greenlandair is the umbilical chord joining the many sparsely populated areas of this vast country. Construction is underway for seven new airports along the western coast of Greenland as fixed wing planes replace ageing helicopters. Needless to say, with the winds that we had, the four planned arrivals into Nuuk were cancelled due to weather.

The next day it cleared, and off we went for some sight-seeing in my Mooney. With Else and her mother in the back and Allan, who acted as copilot so that I could take some pictures, we flew up the fjord, across the low mountains, around to Maniitsoq, up another fjord with lots of glaciers, back down, and then landed at Maniitsoq to return Else's mother to her home. After a tour of that town, we returned to Nuuk. It was an amazing trip that we all enjoyed

August 19: Nuuk, Greenland to Happy Valley — Goose Bay, Canada, 14th leg flight report

The weather was again overcast and windy this morning. Reviewing the weather pages that we received by fax, we could see a low moving over Frobisher Bay in Canada, towards Greenland. The local weather was forecast to deteriorate over the next few days. I either had to get out today or wait for the weekend. Allan and Else kindly said that I could stay as long as I liked, and it surely was a nice, quiet place to stay with magnificent scenery. But the weather at Goose Bay was forecast to be good today and deteriorating over the weekend. So the best choice was to leave today. Luckily, the charts that I'd been waiting for arrived in the morning post. I could have left without them, as I'd "scrounged" enough to get into Canada, IFR. But, I really wanted the VFR charts for my arrival and continued journey.

Allan and I packed and went to gas up. It was cold and very windy. Mentally I set a limit of 35-knot gusts at which I wouldn't leave. The wind was right down the runway, but I didn't know how badly I'd be tossed around. The line guys check the water in the gas prior to refueling, and they ask the pilot to confirm, and sign, that there is no water in the gas. That done, we went to the tower. The woman who was on duty when I arrived was again on duty. She got me the current weather, calculated my bill (very expensive in Greenland) and filed my flight plan. I kept checking the wind monitor. The gusts crept up to 31 knots, then back down to 28 knots. The average winds were only 15–18 knots. I called Canadian customs and was ready to depart. Looking at the winds, I decided that I could go. I told Allan that if the headwinds or turbulence were too bad, I'd turn around and he'd see me that evening.

On with the survival suit; Allan laughed when he saw it! And into the cabin as the rain started again. I double-checked everything, received my clearance, and back-taxied to the end of the runway. A commercial plane had just landed and another was getting ready to leave. The ceiling was over 1,000 feet and winds were down a bit. I took a deep breath and advanced the throttle. We took off quickly, and then were bounced around a lot in the first few minutes. I held a steady runway heading and climbed to 6,000 feet. There was a mountain to the left, but nothing ahead and to the right. Two other planes were coming in, but were still 30 and 50 miles away. The turbulence subsided after I passed 3,000 feet although the clouds and rain continued. At least it was relatively calm now. The strong 30-knot headwinds at the surface dropped to 20-knot headwinds at 6,000 feet. After 45 minutes, I was between layers with good visibility and no rain. That was much better than I'd expected.

At one hour and ten minutes the sky really cleared, and I could see blue sky and blue water ahead—it looked great. It reminded me of my departure from Kissimmee, five-and-a-half months ago. The local weather was poor, but once I got out of it, it was clear and blue sky. I was comforted that my decision had been the right one. I knew that I'd find good weather; I just didn't know it would be this soon. At one hour and fifty minutes, I ran into clouds again, which was disappointing, but it didn't last long. As I continued, there were waves of clouds and rain and sections that were clear and dry. The wind varied from a 35-knot headwind component to a 15-knot headwind. But the average speed was higher than planned and the trip looked like it would be five hours and 40 minutes versus the planned six hours.

The HF position reports went well, but I couldn't raise any ham operators on the HF channels and my HF e-mail was still not working. As the flight progresses uneventfully, I started feeling a little down. This is almost the end of the trip. I'm ready to come home, but it's hard to believe it's almost over. A lot of people have asked me recently, "What now?" Well, now it's really that time, what AM I going to do?

Two hundred miles out, and I'm in VHF contact, with barometric pressure given in inches of mercury! I can put away my conversion chart, from hectopascals, which I've had with me for five months. Just off the coast of Canada we run into strong headwinds, clouds, and rain again. But it's still supposed to be clear in Goose Bay. I can't see much coast or inland, just glimpses through the clouds from time to time. Finally it clears, and I can see the pine trees and numerous lakes of Labrador. It's flatter than I'd anticipated—I thought there'd be more mountains. Not around here. I see the big lake, Lake Melville, and finally pick up the airport and land into a 20-knot headwind. It's a huge old air force base with very few planes in evidence. Apparently there are air force planes in all the hangars. I choose Woodward Aviation, one of five FBOs, as my handler, and taxi to their ramp. The service is wonderful (as I find out later, for CAN$75), and they refuel right away and get me a B&B for the night, as well as driving me over there. It's WARM for the first time in (what feels like) weeks. I put on shorts and go for a long awaited run. It feels GREAT.

I'm sitting in Canada, contemplating the end of this trip. It's been an absolutely amazing adventure. At the start it was all planning, distances, legs, and endurance. Then packing, weight, volume, and minimal requirements—what can I leave behind that I don't really need. I never once imagined all that I would live and learn. It's been a mosaic of people, places, and flying, but mostly of supportive aviation enthusiasts who've unwaveringly gone out of their way to help me with parking, a home, food, charts, maintenance, and anything I needed that they could provide. When doing the seven months of planning, I never once thought of the people side, but they, more than anything else, have made this trip the most outstanding adventure of my life. Two types of e-mails kept me going during the low points of the trip. One set came from pilots who said that I was living their dream—I couldn't let them down, so I kept going. The other came from ALS patients and families. They told me their different and difficult stories, wished me the best on my adventure, and were supportive of the cause to raise awareness for ALS. I thank all my e-mail supporters and am glad that I had very few low times and many more high points during this trip.

I've only a short time to go and I don't know what I'll do when I return, but I do know this: there are a lot more positive things going on in this world than negative, and I'm going to continue to help people see the positive side in everything when I return. I'm going to talk to school children, Young Eagles, Scouts, EAA chapters, and other groups about my trip, and accent the positive nature of people all around the world.

Top: Flying over Lunenburg, Nova Scotia
Bottom: Accepting a gift from Brian,
President of the ALS Society of Nova Scotia

Chapter 18

Dear CarolAnn,

Hi, My name is Debbie Ragan. I live in Cairo, GA. I read about your journey around the world in my husband's company newsletter. Your brother put the story in with your web site! I read what you have done so far and I am so jealous! I wish that I could be with you. I love to travel and Ron and I have hosted 18 exchange students from around the world someday we hope to visit most if not all of them.

My best,
Debbie

Canada and the Last Legs Home to Florida
Nova Scotia and Newfoundland

Departing from Goose Bay was simple. Woodward Aviation had requested all the information the evening before, and had a complete package ready when I returned the following morning. I gave them the flight plan, which they faxed in, paid my bill, and was on my way. It was a beautiful, blue-sky day with a few puffy clouds. As I traveled south, I enjoyed the unbroken acres of trees up and down the hillsides. There were very few roads, lots and lots of lakes, and several rivers. This went on for two hours. I arrived at the Gulf of St. Lawrence and the Ile d'Anticosti. The St. Lawrence Gulf is much wider than I'd imagined, about 200 miles at the widest point.

My destination was actually Shearwater, the military base just south of Halifax, Nova Scotia. I was to participate in their annual air show. I had received the arrival procedures and filed IFR to UAW, the designated arrival point for Shearwater, and had my PPR #[42] in the remarks section of the flight plan. Unfortunately Shearwater was below VFR minimums and didn't have any instrument approaches. A front was moving across Nova Scotia and, one after another, each of us arriving for the air show was told to go to Halifax and cleared for the ILS 24 approach. We were directed to various FBOs, and each was full of military aviators trying to figure out what was going on. We were finally told that no one would be going to

---

42. PPR # — approval number showing that the plane has been approved to participate in the show and to land at Shearwater.

Shearwater that evening and start time for the air show the following morning had been pushed back to noon to allow for our late arrival. I received an 8:30 am slot time for the Saturday morning departure to Shearwater. I called Lori, from the ALS Society of Nova Scotia, who had organized our participation, and she picked me up and took me to Judy's house. Judy's husband, Dave, died of ALS a year ago, and she kindly offered to house me during my stay. She lives only 10 minutes from the Shearwater airport, which made it a wonderful location.

Saturday morning was foggy. I arrived before 8 am to preflight and be ready, but couldn't even see the runway when we heard a commercial plane land right in front of us. It was somewhat clear at Judy's home, but the airport is in a valley, and fogs in more than the surrounding areas. The military pilots started arriving, and all the slot times came and went with everyone stuck to the ground. At 10 am it started lifting and at 10:30 am the military pilots headed for their planes and helicopters. I decided to wait until the rush was over. When everyone else was out, I headed to my Mooney, got taxi clearance immediately, took off, turned left to Shearwater, base, and final, and I was there. A "follow-me" truck led me to my space on the display ramp and I shut down. There I was in the middle of all the military planes...this show was going to be fun.

Lori found me and we put out the pamphlets and pictures and I blew up the inflatable globe that I had bought. We were ready. By Sunday evening, we were sunburned but happy. We'd talked with hundreds of people. More than one-third knew about ALS, and the others learned about it. Many were interested in my trip and a few had flown Mooneys. During the air show itself, we watched lots of military jets, helicopters, a Pitts, Extra 300, and the superb Snowbirds, Canadian precision aerobatic team.

I also finally got to meet Bob Ringer. Bob is a pilot who had seen my website and e-mailed me many months ago. He'd offered to show me around when I arrived in Nova Scotia. We had time to chat during the air show. He also contacted the local FBO to get me hangar space and fuel after the show.

The show set a new record with more than 65,000 attendees, and we raised awareness for ALS and talked with lots of very nice people. On the Monday we had an interview by ATV for their local news *Live at Five*. Paul, the broadcaster, did a good interview and

Lori and inflatable globe at the Shearwater Airshow to raise awareness for ALS in Nova Scotia

worked hard to make a thorough coverage of ALS, my flight, and the goal to increase awareness. We saw the coverage that evening and were very happy with the results; thanks Paul and ATV.

Lori and Chris, her husband, took me around the area, showed me Acadia valley to the north and Keith's local beer brewery, and we had a reception for more than 30 people in the area associated with ALS. I explained about my trip and the support I'd received by e-mail from pilots and families touched by ALS. I spoke with most of the participants and we shared our stories. I was touched and pleased to have been able to participate, and I believe we have done something to help those with ALS in the Nova Scotia area and to raise awareness of this devastating disease.

Judy and Lori were originally from towns in Newfoundland and strongly recommended visiting the island, pronounced New-fn-LAND (like we say un-der-STAND). I enjoyed their stories and Judy's Newfoundland baking so much that I had to visit. The flight up the east coast of Nova Scotia was beautiful. There were trees down to the water, with rocks on the coastline. There were a few towns, like Lunenburg, which were brightly colored and had been old fishing and fish processing towns. Tourism is now their main source of revenue.

In Newfoundland, I chose to visit Stephenville, on the southwest coast, because I wanted to see a small town and meet the local people. Also, a flight up the west coast is supposed to be outstanding. There was a front moving across Newfoundland, and although the weather was sunny elsewhere, I had to do a full approach into the airport. It was very good practice. As I became visual at 1,000 feet, I could see tree-covered hills to my left and finally picked up the runway lights two miles ahead. Tom, at the FBO, was very helpful and friendly. He booked me a B&B and said that a ride would be provided when I was ready. He then brought over Glenda, from the local newspaper, and we had a quick interview and photo session (in the rain) to get a story on ALS into the local paper. It was my luck that the Snowbirds would be putting on an air show the next day, thus the reason for media being present when I arrived.

Actually three Snowbird planes had already arrived—I'd heard them talking with Gander center while I was still 50 miles away. While I was there, the remaining eight Snowbirds arrived, did a low approach, landed, and lined up with the rest. What a beautiful sight; I couldn't wait to see them perform again. The forecast is for a sunny day tomorrow, so we hope to get a great show.

The Newfoundland accent is very strong and the people are very open and friendly. The small town of Stephenville has a population of about 8,000, down from 12,000 several years ago as people move to other provinces for better job opportunities. One of the schools has closed and another is scheduled to close next year. As the Snowbirds were scheduled to do an air show, many teachers had planned to do tours of the airport or other aviation related events that morning.

The coast was magnificent. There were some valleys and bays and lots of cliffs and wooded mountains up to almost 3,000 feet. There were small lakes on top of the mountains and apparently plenty of caribou and moose, which I didn't see. Near the bays and river mouths there would be some houses, and in some areas there were major towns. Overall, it was sparsely populated. The shores were mostly rocky with cliffs coming straight down to the sea. Not too many sandy beaches around here.

I also learned that this is one of two areas in the world where the earth's mantle, normally 100 miles below the surface, had been pushed up and can be studied by geologists. The brown mountains, where there were no trees, were that area. It was definitely different from the rest of the area, but interesting as I flew by, and now I understand why.

When I returned from my flight up and down the coast, there was a class of children at the FBO. Since the hot air balloon rides had been cancelled due to high winds, the teacher asked me to talk about my trip. I happily obliged and talked about my Mooney, the flight, and the various countries that I visited during my trip. The kids asked questions and I had fun. I also had another interview with the local paper, thanks to Tom, who wants to make sure we spread the word about ALS.

That afternoon, it was time to watch the Snowbirds again—wow, am I lucky to see them twice in one week. Actually, pilot number 4, Steve, was in the FBO when I was there and I told him how much I enjoyed their performances.

I was outside with my camera, ready to watch and take pictures of the Snowbirds when the airport manager's van came up. The airport manager, another Tom, invited me to ride with them to the show line. We got a front row seat, in front of the crowds, and out of the wind, to watch the show (see color photo)— it was fantastic!

After the show, it was time to take some Young Eagles for a ride. Daughters from the B&B where I was staying, Laura, Stacey, and Nicole, had watched the Snowbirds and were eager to taste aviation in a small plane. We walked through the preflight and piled in. As we were getting ready, the Snowbird pilots walked by and wished us well—what a treat. I flew over the bay and up the coast with the daughters, as well as circling their house. Although bumpy, it was great fun.

Afterwards, Linda, who runs the B&B, invited me to share a typical Newfoundlander jigs dinner of salted beef. And the desert was also a typical regional fruit crumble. They were both delicious, and just what I had wanted to do—experience local cooking and life.

I had a terrific stay in Stephenville, Newfoundland, and very much appreciate the hospitality of all the people, especially Linda and Bill at Wood'N B&B and Tom, Larry, Tom and Carolyn at the airport and FBO. Time to fly back to the US and meet old friends.

Back to the US — Maine and New Hampshire

It was a beautiful sunny morning, windy and cool as usual, for my departure. Although the low level winds would be strong headwinds, it looked like crosswinds to slight tailwinds at higher altitudes. I wanted to fly low and see the whales and seals, but started out at 4,500 feet over the water until I got to the Bay of Fundy. The air was clear and I picked up the Nova Scotia shore before losing site of Newfoundland. It was a beautiful flight. I crossed Prince Edward Island (PEI, as the locals call it), which looked lush and fertile, and continued west to the Bay of Fundy, which has the largest/highest tidal movement in the world. As I approached, I could see an enormous area of brown, it looked like a muddy bay. Then I picked up wave movement, and it seemed that the tide was coming in. I descended to 2,500 feet and hit the 15- to 20-knot headwinds, but couldn't see any whales. I thought I saw two pods below the surface, but couldn't be sure.

The shorelines were spectacular, with lots of trees and cliffs plunging to the bay. There weren't too many houses and few roads. As I traveled southward, the number of houses, small towns, and boats started to increase. Before crossing the US boarder I was transferred to Boston Center and received the most wonderful welcome. The response was, "N220FC, Boston Center, CarolAnn, welcome back to the United States of America and congratulations on a great accomplishment and a job well done." Wow, can you believe that? I thanked John, as his name turned out to be, and we talked a little. He is an Angel Flight pilot also. He invited me to get together if I had time...as it would turn out, we met several days later. I was so touched, I couldn't stop smiling—it was such a wonderfully warm and unexpected welcome return to the US. I was still smiling as I approached Portland and landed over an hour later. But I couldn't figure out how he knew that I was returning and that I had flown around the world...how did he know that I was coming into his airspace?

CarolAnn being interviewed upon arrival at Laconia Airport, NH. Airport Manager, Diane, and Jim, who lent his hangar to Carol Ann for the weekend, are behind

After completing the customs requirements, I was really back in the US. I taxied to the other side of the field and called in to the local FBO. I'd planned to visit our old neighbors from when we lived in Pennsylvania. When our family first moved to the US from England in 1964, these people were our first neighbors for eight years. Although my parents had stayed in touch with them and visited several times, I hadn't seen them in over 30 years. It was a wonderful reunion. We were all looking older, but reconnected very quickly. They wanted to hear about my trip, and I wanted to hear about their life after leaving Pennsylvania and how all the children were doing. Although Bob had lost his eyesight in an accident over 20 years previously, he had rebuilt their house in Portland and spent his relaxation time building model wooden boats. It was a touching and memorable reunion.

I received an e-mail from John, the ATC controller who welcomed me to the US, and invited me to visit him in New Hampshire. Well, that state is right next to Maine, so I said I'd be happy to join him. His friend, Jim, lent me his hangar to house my plane. Diane, the Laconia Airport Manager, welcomed me to

John trying on CarolAnn's Mooney for size (John's a Cessna driver)

Laconia and organized some press coverage; and another friend Chuck, an actor and B25 pilot, joined us for dinner. What an amazing coincidence—Chuck had played the role of the doctor in the movie about Lou Gehrig and his fight with ALS.

We shared lots of flying and ATC stories and talked about anything and everything, especially the merits of Mooneys vs. Cessnas. John is a Cessna driver; his boat is named Sea Cessna. It was a beautiful return to the US with new friends sharing some time together. Overall, the weekend epitomized my whole trip. Aviation people, who don't even know me, going out of their way to help me. This happened in most countries mainly by aviation folks, but also by people not tied to aviation. It has given me a very positive outlook on the world and humanity in general. It has been a most fantastic trip.

After a wonderful weekend of boating, kayaking, and lots of talking with John and his friends, I finally had to depart for Boston. I was to visit the ALS Therapy Development Foundation on Monday morning and needed to fly to Boston's Bedford Airport Sunday evening. It was an uneventful short trip, but the traffic was intense.

A NASCAR race was ending just south of Laconia and the jets and large twins were lining up to depart. A little Mooney waiting in line was not what they wanted. As I arrived in Bedford, Boston approach was talking a mile a minute and six of us were in line for the Bedford approach. It was a busy 45-minute flight in congested airspace.

During the weekend, John finally answered the question about how he knew I was completing a round the world trip and entering his airspace. My brother, Andy, a corporate pilot in Atlanta, wanted to do something special for my return. He'd contacted Boston Center to see if they could help. Andy spoke with John, and together they worked out my welcome home. Thanks to both of you! It was a memorable welcome back to the US.

Boston — ALS Therapy Development Foundation

On Monday morning I arrived at the ALS Therapy Development Foundation office and labs in Boston. As this was the foundation that my mother had chosen for donations, I had maintained contact with them during my trip. I wanted to visit the

CarolAnn and Chuck who played the doctor in the film about Lou Gehrig's life

facilities, meet the people, and learn the current status of research into cures or medicines to help control ALS.

Jennifer and Lawler met me and talked a little about ALS and what they were doing. Then Phil and Chris gave me a lab tour, explained the process of determining which drugs to test, and showed me the animal testing area (extensive tests are done on mice with the ALS gene). It was absolutely fascinating—I had no idea this was the direction that research was taking, and that they were in clinical trials with two drugs as well as testing over 80 drugs on mice. It gives one hope that a drug will be found that could limit the degeneration caused by the disease, and further research could lead to a cure or finding the cause for this debilitating disease.

ALS is considered an "orphan" disease; i.e., it doesn't affect enough people to have future cash generating potential to interest the BIG drug companies in drug development. However, its neurological process and progress is very similar to Alzheimer's and Parkinson's, so much research can be shared between the various groups studying the different diseases. The advantage of this particular lab is that they are testing drugs that have already been approved for other diseases. Therefore, once the drugs are found to have successful prolongation of life in mice, they can proceed to clinical trials almost immediately. All the people I met were very focused on their research and driven to find a cure to this devastating disease. It was an enriching and encouraging visit.

All this research takes money. By buying this book, you have already made a contribution. Sometimes it doesn't seem to make a difference, but they showed me some new lab equipment that they had just been able to purchase—it really DOES make a difference. If you are enjoying this book and want to do more, please send in a tax-deductible contribution to the address listed in the back of this book. Thank you.

New York and jump to Virginia

The owner of my hangar in Florida resides in NY state in the summer, and even before I'd left, last February, he'd invited me to stop by Mt. View, NY, on my return journey. Capt. Bob is a retired airline pilot with tons of experience. He'd e-mailed me throughout my trip with tips, support, and encouragement.

It was cloudy between Boston and Sullivan County, NY, so I'd filed an IFR flight plan. Actually, with the uncertainty of TFRs[43] popping up, I preferred to fly IFR for everything except short hops. Due to low clouds, I was set up for an ILS 15 approach. By the time I reached the outer marker I was already VFR, so I announced my position, descended, and landed. Bob was talking to me on final and welcoming me to MSV. John of Woodstock Aircraft Services provided me space in his hangar. Many of Bob's friends and students stopped by to say hello. It was a very warm welcome.

With Nancy, Bob's wife and pilot of her own Cessna 152, we had a wonderful evening of catching up and chatting. At midnight, I finally had to go to sleep. They live out in the country with no one and no lights around. It's pitch black. It was cloudy, so we had no stars or moon either. It was a very peaceful night.

I'd received an e-mail from my dad that evening; actually, I hadn't connected for several days, so some were old. He'd had pneumonia and wasn't doing so well. In addition to that, we'd been watching the weather, and hurricane Isabel was headed his way—he lives in Virginia on the North Carolina boarder, but inland from the coast. First thing the next morning, I called him. He sounded very weak and sick. Bob and Nancy could tell from the conversation that I would be leaving immediately. He felt terrible, he was out of medication, and the storm was headed his way. What a situation.

Bob drove me to the airport, gave me a flight route and altitude that would get me around the major cities without deviations, and kissed me goodbye. I was off again, much quicker than planned. It was a beautiful day, but I couldn't enjoy the scenery, and took very few photos. I was worried about Dad. We'd agreed that I'd land at Oxford, NC, and put the plane in a hangar, but he'd also talked about evacuating. During the flight, I thought it would be better if I landed at our local airport, especially if we were going to evacuate. I sent off a quick e-mail, as he was going to get someone else to pick me up at Oxford, half an hour's drive from home. I hoped someone would check their e-mail before I arrived—well, they did, but too late. Ed had already headed out to Oxford. I landed in Marks Municipal and

---

43. TFR — temporary flight restriction — put in place when the president and other top officials travel around the country or put around major sports events.

hitched a ride to my dad's house. In a small town, people are very friendly and Buddy, who picked me up, was no exception. He said if we needed anything else, he'd be happy to help.

Dad was not doing well when I arrived, so we went to the clinic right away, then to the pharmacy for new medicine. The next day he was already doing better. We continued to watch the weather and news. We were forecast to be in the zone with 50–60 mph winds. After much discussion, we decided to stay put. I flew the Mooney to Oxford where they had hangar space; we cleared the patio, and put all loose items in the garage. We did one last shop, filled up water bottles, and got out the flashlights and candles. If the electricity went out for an extended period, we'd drive southwest to a motel.

The wind was increasing in speed and force. Unfortunately, it was coming straight down the bay—that left no protection for the house. Being familiar with previous hurricanes that had passed the North Carolina coast, Dad explained that the winds had come from the south and east, affording the house a lot more protection. I'd never been in the house during a hurricane passage before, so it was all new to me. Every once in a while, there'd be a thud as a branch fell on the roof. I'd jump up and take a look to see what had happened. There was one tree on the windward side that was almost dead and leaning toward the house. Needless to say, I wished that we'd cut it down earlier in the year. Dad was lying in his chair, covered with a blanket, trying to sleep. He still wasn't feeling well and was trying to conserve strength in case we needed to leave.

When the strong gusts and rain hit, it was full force on the side of the house with all the windows. After all I've done this year, I thought, this is a fine way to end the trip! At noon, we watched the latest update on the news. The coast was getting the 100-mph winds. We still had five to six hours before the high winds would pass us. I finally relaxed. As when flying over the ocean, I couldn't jump at each noise and I couldn't hold my breath. Better to relax, try to do something, and keep my mind off it.

My brother, Richard, and sister-in-law, Di, called from California to see if everything was okay. They'd been watching the news and weather, but couldn't tell how close we were. At 3:46 pm we lost electricity. As we looked out a side window, we could see two trees at a sharp angle. They weren't down all the way, but had definitely toppled. Later that evening, we lost the phone line. The winds continued to blow hard and the gusts were noisy and forceful. The next day I was to learn that peak gusts were 65 knots. On the gas stove, we cooked lamb chops, potatoes, and broccoli—it was a great candle-light dinner. From my safely supplies, I had a miner's lamp type flashlight that sits on my head so that I can use both hands. It worked great, and it was nice that it finally came in handy. By 8:30 pm we both thought the winds had died down a little. It certainly wasn't as noisy. We made it an early night.

The next morning was blue sky and calm. Quite the opposite of the previous day. I could see a third tree had gone down and the first two were across the driveway. They would have to be cleared before we could get out. Cleanup work lasted for 5 days.

During my stay with Dad in Virginia, I got to meet some of my devoted followers, a Thursday morning coffee group of retired men who e-mailed their support during my trip. Joe, a pilot, Ken, a ham radio buff, Mark, and the others have been following my trip from the start and made sure that the local papers informed the community of my adventure. Each paper has now completed a follow-up story. I joined the Thursday morning coffee group on several occasions. They'd read every flight update and practically memorized my trip, thus had numerous questions—which I was happy to answer; and I added more stories. They've asked that I prepare a more formal presentation for the community, which I will happily do. I just made a presentation to the local Danville Civil Air Patrol and a Clarksville elementary school. I'll be making one to my local EAA Chapter 74 in Orlando when I return. This is something that I'm looking forward to doing—sharing this experience through giving more presentations to schools, flying organizations, and anyone else who is interested.

The stay in Virginia also afforded me the opportunity to say thank you to one of the hospice nurses who helped my mother during the last six months of her illness. Pam has a son, Taylor, who loves flying and wants to be a pilot and fly in Alaska. We were supposed to go flying a year ago, but weather got in the way and we'd cancelled at least twice. This time it was a perfect blue-sky day without much wind. We flew for about an hour over the area, their home, the lake, and the John Kerr Dam. Taylor has a good feel for the controls and will soon be taking lessons. All the best Taylor, you'll be a great pilot.

Virginia to Atlanta and Florida — HOME

Departure from Clarksville was a local ABC TV event. Don and cameraman, Ted, came up from Raleigh, NC, to interview me and film the takeoff. My Mooney was on a small grass strip and I was going to fly to Marks Municipal for the interview the morning of my departure. I'd left the heavy equipment in my dad's car for loading after the interview, as I was to take Ted up for a flight to get departing shots. The weather wasn't great, but was predicted to clear and was already VFR at the local airports that have weather reporting. Dad and I did the preflight; I started and taxied to the end of the strip. Dad always stations himself three quarters of the way down the strip to watch the takeoff and wheel retraction. As I climbed and turned towards Marks, I noticed some low scattered clouds that I climbed above. I was amazed to see a cloud layer over the town and surrounding area. Just to the west was clear and where I'd come from was clear. I descended VFR over the lake and started towards the airport; however, the clouds got lower and lower and the visibility deteriorated; there was no way to see the airport.

Later Mark, who was waiting for me at the airport, said that he could hear me but not see me. It seemed as though the cloud was hanging just over the field and town. I circled again and was going to try a second approach but realized that it was futile. I followed the lake east; after two miles I had clear skies above me again and I landed back on the grass strip. I'd called my dad on his handheld radio and told him I was returning, which he acknowledged.

Dad's car arrived followed by the ABC van and Mark. They were going to do the interview from the grass strip. Don and Ted set up, wired me, and the film rolled. What fun! Instead of filming from the cockpit, they got me loading the plane, doing the preflight, explaining the cockpit to Don, receiving a home-baked cake from Dad, and giving him a departing hug. It was Election Day, so other stories precluded them from showing the video clip that day; however, a week later it aired and looked very good.

After takeoff, I circled the airport a few times, and then took off for the southwest. Or so I thought. My HSI[44] wasn't in agreement

---

44.   HSI — horizontal situation indicator — an instrument that gives heading information, more accurate than a compass or heading indicator

with my GPS. This had happened to me once before when practicing holds in Florida. I freed the HSI then re-slaved it and it found
the right direction; now both were in agreement again. It's okay if
this happens when I'm VFR but I'd be pretty lost if it happened in
the clouds. At least I know that it's the HSI that gets "mixed up."

I had a beautiful short VFR flight to Asheboro, NC, for relatively
cheap avgas, $2.32/gal. I rechecked weather, which was still poor in
the Atlanta area, and had a nice chat with Dean, the FSS briefer. After
waiting an hour for the weather to be clearer for my arrival, I finally
took off, received my IFR clearance, and proceeded into the clouds.

Unfortunately, there wasn't much rain. I was hoping my
Mooney would get cleaned off before my arrival, but no such luck.
Two hours later, I picked up the Griffin Spalding AWOS, which was
reporting 2,900-foot overcast. I actually wanted to go into a private
grass strip, Eagles Landing, 5GA3, but had filed to Griffin Spalding
because the ceiling was forecast to be lower. Three planes were all
arriving to do an approach at Griffin Spalding at the same time. I
was second in line and was advised to slow down as the plane in
front was on an eight-mile final and hadn't yet cancelled IFR. I
advised the controller that if the ceiling was as reported, I'd cancel
and proceed west VFR to a private strip.

As I descended to 2,000 feet, I was under the clouds and the
visibility was greater than six miles. I cancelled IFR and proceeded
northwest; the strip was five miles away. Luckily, I'd checked the
lat/longs on AirNav.com and plugged them into the GPS.
Everything was green and it was very difficult to pick out runways
from fields. I found and circled the strip. It was just as Janet and
Carolyn had explained in an e-mail, so I prepared for an uphill
runway 32 arrival. It went very smoothly, and I stopped at the
hangar at the end of runway 32 on the left, as described by Janet. I
chocked the Mooney and walked to the house. It was open but no
one was around. I walked around, no one. I walked to the strip, no
one. I returned to the patio and sat for a while. I began wondering
if I'd landed at the wrong strip. The chart shows about five private
strips in the same area. Finally the "gang" arrived from shopping—
I'd come in early and they were still preparing for my arrival. We all
exchanged hugs and started chatting.

Janet runs the Ambassador Chapter of the 99s. The members
communicate by e-mail and there are no regular meetings;
however, they get together when someone is in town or as they

travel to towns or countries where other members reside. There are about 90 members in a number of different countries. After my stay with Kathryn, a 99s member in Darwin, Australia, Janet heard about my trip and included me on her e-mail list. In the last monthly e-mail, I noticed a remark about Atlanta, and I sent a return e-mail that I'd be passing through Atlanta the following week. It all started there!

Janet invited me to her home and invited others to join us. We had a wonderful evening talking about my trip, their planes and careers, flight training, and any number of topics. Marsha, not yet a pilot, but wonderful artist, joined us and drew a picture of me! It is beautiful. The next morning she captured my Mooney in Janet and Kyle's hangar on the strip. How wonderful to have a sketch of my Mooney. It was a magical evening and continued the next morning as Carolyn, the neighbor across the strip, returned with other neighbors. It was so much fun; I can see that an airpark community may be in my future.

Unfortunately, the weather wasn't cooperating the following morning, but Janet and Kyle were driving north and dropped me off at my bother, Andy's, home. Debbie, my sister-in-law, was there, getting ready to leave for work. Auntie CarolAnn was the baby sitter for 3-year-old Andrew Junior for the afternoon! We had fun reading, playing on the swing set and in the sand box. During naptime I got my e-mails done, then we had more sand box time! Andy finally arrived home just in time for the diaper change; that's my limit of baby sitting: playing, and not changing!

Andy and Debbie had already signed up for a 3-day bike ride south of Atlanta for the weekend. So, if I was going to spend any time with them, it was going to be on a bicycle seat. We picked up a rental bike close to the ride, and Debbie outfitted me in her clothes. Then I relocated my Mooney from Eagles Landing to Newnan, where the ride was to take place. One more goodbye with Janet, Kyle and little Lauren, but I'm sure I'll be back and will be flying in and out of Eagles Landing in the future.

It was perfect bike-riding weather, cool in the low 70s with overcast clouds to keep the burning sun out. We did 52 miles on Friday and 63 on Saturday. My legs were okay but my butt was very sore. I was happy I didn't have to ride on Sunday. Andrew was the star of the ride, as everyone knew him and cheered him on. He was

CarolAnn with 99s in Atlanta. From left: Linda, Carolyn, Janet, CarolAnn, baby Lauren (Janet's), Susan, and Marsha

towed behind Andy and Debbie's tandem. It won't be long before he's peddling his own weight!

Sunday morning was again cloudy with forecast rain for my route. I filed IFR, but the ceiling was high enough for me to pick up the clearance in the air. Andy drove me to the airport and, after a big hug, I was off again on the final leg to Florida. After I broke through the 4,500 to 5,000 foot overcast cloud layer, I was in bright sunshine. It was brilliant and beautiful. Since it was a Sunday, the MOAs[45] were cold and I didn't get the usual deviations around them. As I continued it got cloudier, and I climbed to 7,000 feet. Finally I was in clouds and rain for a while. All of a sudden, I saw a big spider in the cockpit—I hate spiders. Not wanting it to re-appear during an approach or other critical time, I found a tissue and caught it: another problem dealt with.

The clouds cleared as I crossed the Florida/Georgia border, but there was a layer below me. Airports were calling for 400-foot

45.   MOA — Military Operating Area — protected airspace.

broken. The forecast had been for clear skies at Lakeland. Actually, I had been invited to land at Fantasy of Flight (FOF), but had filed to Lakeland in case it wasn't VFR upon arrival. Fantasy of Flight has the world's largest aircraft collection and two beautiful grass strips. It's usually not permitted to land there, but they'd invited me to stop in just prior to my final arrival at Kissimmee. I couldn't pass up that opportunity.

I could see the clouds breaking up, and the ATIS at Lakeland was announcing scattered clouds at 300 feet and broken at 10,000 feet. I cancelled IFR after passing Zephyrhills and turned left towards FOF. Unfortunately, there were still clouds to the east. I couldn't go under, so I opted to fly over at 1,500 ft and follow Highway I-4 northeast, knowing that FOF is just to the north of the highway. The clouds were getting a little thicker, but just then there was a huge open area with the grass strips and museum of FOF. I couldn't believe it. I'd been calling their frequency with my distance and altitude, but had not received any response. I started the approach, continuing to call my position, and kept the airport in sight the whole time.

What a magnificent 5,000-foot grass strip; it was a pleasure to land on it. As I turned off the runway, onto the ramp, Jerry was there waiting for me and Pam from FOF came over.

Jerry first contacted me by e-mail early in the trip, but was sending me two to three e-mails a day as I closed in on my return to Florida. He had organized the Fantasy of Flight stop, a lunch in Lakeland mid-week, a return to FOF the following Saturday, and flying kids with cancer at Sebring that Sunday. He was really becoming my PR person! After a big hug, we got to know each other and had lunch with Pam in the FOF restaurant. Jesse, VP of Fantasy of Flight, joined us and showed us around afterwards. Jamie, editor of *The Flying Life* Magazine, arrived in time for pictures and an interview. It was a happy morning and a great welcome "almost home."

As it closed in on my final departure time, I checked weather again. It had cleared somewhat and I could most likely make it into Kissimmee without the IFR clearance that I'd filed. I said my final goodbyes, fired up, checked everything, and took off. Orlando approach gave me a squawk code for advisories, but indicated that the weather was VFR at Kissimmee (ISM). I spied the field from 15 miles out and checked the AWOS. Since I left, there is a new TFR over Disney. So I had the ORL VOR plugged in to make sure that I didn't come close. No sense getting busted on my last leg.

I couldn't stop smiling as I got closer to ISM. Home! The airport looked great. At 10 miles out, I called tower and received a very warm welcome home. I proceeded to a right base leg. It was wonderful to return to my home airport—I knew where everything was! After seven months of flying into new and different airports, this felt terrific. I turned final and touched down on runway 15 feeling great. Tower advised me that I'd been requested to taxi to Marathon FBO, and turned me over to ground. Huck was the controller on ground. He has a deep voice and is one of the few controllers I can recognize over the headphones. It was so wonderful to hear his voice as he also welcomed me home and told me to taxi to Marathon. I couldn't stop smiling! Huck had been working tower the day in February when we did a low fly-by to check the angle of the 100-foot trailing HF antenna. He'd given us priority over the other aircraft in the area as we did the low pass and he told us it was hanging down at about a 45-degree angle.

The "follow me" truck led me under the overhanging canopy and right in front of the FBO where the TV cameras and newspaper reporters were waiting for me, along with a small group of friends. I could barely complete the shut down checklist, as I wanted to get out and hug everyone. It was a wonderful welcome home. The TV people were eager to get rolling, so I didn't even get to talk with everyone before their interview. It aired on the 6 and 11 pm local news, and they did a pretty good job. Huck came down from the tower and gave me a big hug. Even though I'd been flying at Kissimmee for three years, we'd never met; we'd only talked over the radio. He had to return to work and I had to return to the interviews, so we really still haven't met!

Melissa, from the *Orlando Sentinel,* took her time and listened to all our chattering. She actually got her story more from our discussions about the trip than from an interview.

We decided to go to my hangar on the south side of the field. There I could finally sip the wine that Jeanne and Bob, from Marathon FBO, had opened in honor of my trip and arrival.

More friends, Wes and Sandy, were on the south side and they'd hung a banner on my hangar door (see color photo). They'd worked on my HF radio installation for the last four weekends and the last night before my departure. They were supposed to be off sailing today; I don't know how they materialized in Kissimmee for my arrival. We talked even more and sipped wine, finally! They all helped me unload my plane's contents into the car. It's quick work with lots of people doing the to and fro with each load.

Finally we pushed my Mooney back into the hangar—I think we both smiled and let out a sigh of relief (me and my Mooney).

Mooney in the hangar with friends Chuck, Wes, Sandy, and Don

EPILOGUE

A week after my return, I was at Fantasy of Flight, the World's Greatest Aircraft Collection, near Lakeland, Florida, on the ramp, talking about my trip and signing autographs. FOF asked that I give a presentation about the adventure to the crowd during lunch, and I happily obliged. The next day I was flying kids with cancer, a special program as part of Young Eagles. What strength of character these kids have. I thoroughly enjoyed taking them flying, explaining about how the controls work, and talking with each of them.

A month after my return, I finished developing a presentation for the many EAA Chapters and other flying clubs who were asking for me to talk to their members. I gave it to our Orlando Chapter 74 first and it went well. Before our monthly Young Eagles flight, my EAA Chapter gave me a water gun salute and Color Guard arrival, along with a proclamation from the Mayor of Orlando. It was quite a reception.

Two months after my return, after Christmas and New Years with family, I was still learning all that had happened at home during my seven months away. There were new stoplights on the local road, a huge new car showroom at the major intersection, babies had been born, people had died, and I was still catching up with the community and news.

Six months after my return, I've completed over 20 presentations, raised an additional $6000 for ALS/Lou Gehrig's disease research, totaling $17,000, and I've completed writing this book and am ready to go to print. Most pilots go through a depressive type feeling after a journey such as this—I have been reliving my adventure through presentations and through writing the book so that I haven't had time to let life "go back to normal." It probably never will.

My Mooney passed the annual inspection in December, now has 2100 hours on the engine, and is getting me to and from all the presentations. We'll need an overhaul of the engine next year, most likely. Then, after running the new engine for a year, we'll be ready to go again! With a new prop, good weather, and a little luck, maybe we could even try for a speed record... me and my Mooney.

Gerard and Michelle after our flight remembering Christian
(who died of cancer in February 2003)

GLOSSARY

ADF - Automatic Direction Finder. A piece of radio navigation equipment in the airplane that senses and indicates the direction to the non-directional beacon (NDB) ground-based transmitter.

ATIS - Automatic Terminal Information Service. The continuous broadcast of recorded non-control information in selected terminal areas. This usually gives weather, airport conditions, and expected approaches in use, and it is updated hourly.

DME - Distance Measuring Equipment. A piece of equipment in the airplane used to measure the nautical mile distance from the plane to the emitter on the ground, based on the frequency dialed in.

EAA - Experimental Aircraft Association. A group dedicated to homebuilt aircraft, restoring aircraft, and helping members to build their own planes.

FBO - Fixed Base Operator. A business based at an airport that provides services, fuel, etc. for local and transient aircraft.

FIR - Flight Information Region. An airspace of defined dimensions within which Flight Information Service and Alerting Service are provided. For instance, Oakland Radio FIR covers from the coast of California to 05S latitude. Auckland Radio covers most of the south Pacific.

GA - General Aviation. That portion of civil aviation which encompasses all facets of aviation except air carriers holding a certificate of public convenience and large aircraft commercial operators. GA covers most small, private planes and company jets.

IFR - Instrument Flight Rules. Rules governing the procedures for conducting instrument flight; this covers altitudes, airways, communication, etc.

ILS - Instrument Landing System: precision equipment permitting a pilot to descend through clouds down to 200 feet over the runway to make an approach. This is the most precise approach for general aviation pilots.

IMC - Instrument Meteorological Conditions. Meteorological conditions expressed in terms of visibility, distance from cloud, and ceiling less than the minima specified for visual meteorological conditions.

LOC - Localizer. One component of an ILS, which provides course guidance to the runway.

METAR - Aviation Routine Weather Report. This gives the weather report for a specific airport at a specific time. It includes the wind, visibility, cloud cover, temperature, dew point, and altimeter setting.

NDB - Nondirectional Beacon: a low or medium frequency radio beacon transmits nondirectional signals whereby the pilot of an aircraft properly equipped can determine bearings and "home" on the station.

OAT - Outside Air Temperature

Over Gross - Each plane has a design maximum gross weight, over which it is illegal and irresponsible to operate the plane. With an FAA endorsement and specific requirements, it is possible to legally operate over gross weight.

SAR - Search and Rescue. If a flight plan has not been closed within a specified time, a search and rescue operation will be initiated to find the pilot and plane. This service seeks missing aircraft and assists those found to be in need of assistance.

SOCAL Approach - Southern California Approach, an extremely busy air traffic area.

TAF - Aerodrome Forecast. Aviation weather forecast for a given airport. For a specific airport and valid period of time, this gives the forecast conditions of wind, visibility, and cloud cover.

TFR - Temporary Flight Restrictions. An FAA imposed flight restriction over a specific area to protect persons and property in the air or on the surface.

Unicom - A non-government communication facility which may provide airport information at certain airports.

UTC - Universal coordinated time, also known as zulu time. The standard time in Greenwich, England. Used for all aircraft departure, enroute, and arrival times, worldwide.

VFR - Visual Flight Rules. Rules that govern procedures for flight under visual conditions. Also used to indicate weather conditions greater than minimum VFR requirements.

VOR - Very high frequency Omni-directional Range: VHF output giving the pilot 360 degree indication of his position relative to the beacon.

Zulu time - also know as UTC, universal coordinated time, see above.

REFERENCES

Weather web sites:

http://aviationweather.gov and go to Satellite - Intl on the left hand side
http://www.goes.noaa.gov/WINDS/windsNHIRW.html

FAA information on countries and airports:
www.faa.gov/ats/aat/ifim/ifim2tc.htm

Web site for this flight and preparation details
or overview of flight leg statistics:
www.kerrlake.com/mgarratt/prepare.html
www.kerrlake.com/mgarratt/overvw.html

Other earthrounder flights:
www.earthrounders.com

ALS web site:
www.als.net

CarolAnn with Janet and Brian after their flight up and down the Aberdeen coastline.

(Photo by Colin Rennie of The Press and Journal, *Aberdeenshire, Scotland)*

How to Obtain Additional Copies of

Upon Silver Wings: Global Adventure in a Small Plane

Books may be ordered three ways:

1. Please send a minimum contribution of $25 to cover shipping and handling ($30 for overseas donations) to ALS-TDF.
    a. Telephone: 617-441-7270, please have your credit card ready.
    b. Send check, payable to ALS-TDF to 215 First St., Cambridge, MA 02142. Please write **Attn: J. Oken** on the envelope and **Silver Wings** in the memo section of your check.

2. To receive an AUTOGRAPHED copy, please send a minimum contribution of $35 ($40 for overseas donations) to ALS-TDF and receive a book signed by the author and a confirmation of your tax-deductible contribution.
    a. Telephone: 617-441-7270, please have your credit card ready.
    b. Send check, payable to ALS-TDF to 215 First St., Cambridge, MA 02142. Please write **Attn: J. Oken** on the envelope and **Silver Wings** in the memo section of your check.

3. Amazon.com

    Please note: Contributions made directly to the ALS Therapy Development Foundation in excess of $25 will be tax deductible to the extent allowed by law. All revenue will go directly to ALS-TDF.

    When you buy from Amazon.com, 15% of the list price goes to Amazon as commission and the remainder, minus shipping and handling, goes to ALS-TDF. These purchases are not tax deductible.

Please tear out this page and give it to a friend.

ALS
AMYOTROPHIC LATERAL SCLEROSIS
MOTOR NURONE DISEASE (MND)
LOU GEHRIG'S DISEASE

ALS is a chronic, progressive disease that is marked by gradual degeneration of the nerve cells in the central nervous system that control voluntary muscle movement. The disorder causes muscle weakness and atrophy which paralyzes the entire body, yet leaves the mind untouched. The vast majority of ALS patients die within two to five years of diagnosis. There are no effective treatments and there is no cure.

There are an estimated 30,000 ALS patients in the US today with over 5,600 new patients diagnosed each year. ALS has roughly the same incidence rate as Multiple Sclerosis. Statistically, someone you know will contract ALS in the next 10 years.

Most people who develop ALS are between 40 and 70 and it is 20% more common in men than women. Lou Gehrig, with whom ALS is most commonly associated, first brought national and international attention to the disease back in 1939 when he abruptly retired from baseball after being diagnosed with ALS. However, ALS is not just Lou Gehrig's disease and it knows no boundaries. The disease has cut short the lives of such notable and courageous individuals as Hall of Fame pitcher Jim "Catfish" Hunter; creator of Sesame Street, Jon Stone; actor, David Niven; Senator Jacob Javits; and most recently Tom Watson's golf caddy, Bruce Edwards.

ALS Therapy Development Foundation is a nonprofit biotechnology company focused on finding treatments and a cure for today's ALS patients. It was founded by the brother of a patient with ALS. A number of scientists and associates who work for ALSTDF have been motivated by a loved one with the disease. Please donate today.

How to Obtain Additional Copies of

Upon Silver Wings: Global Adventure in a Small Plane

Books may be ordered three ways:

1. Please send a minimum contribution of $25 to cover shipping and handling ($30 for overseas donations) to ALS-TDF.
    a. Telephone: 617-441-7270, please have your credit card ready.
    b. Send check, payable to ALS-TDF to 215 First St., Cambridge, MA 02142. Please write **Attn: J. Oken** on the envelope and **Silver Wings** in the memo section of your check.

2. To receive an AUTOGRAPHED copy, please send a minimum contribution of $35 ($40 for overseas donations) to ALS-TDF and receive a book signed by the author and a confirmation of your tax-deductible contribution.
    a. Telephone: 617-441-7270, please have your credit card ready.
    b. Send check, payable to ALS-TDF to 215 First St., Cambridge, MA 02142. Please write **Attn: J. Oken** on the envelope and **Silver Wings** in the memo section of your check.

3. Amazon.com

    Please note: Contributions made directly to the ALS Therapy Development Foundation in excess of $25 will be tax deductible to the extent allowed by law. All revenue will go directly to ALS-TDF.

    When you buy from Amazon.com, 15% of the list price goes to Amazon as commission and the remainder, minus shipping and handling, goes to ALS-TDF. These purchases are not tax deductible.

Please tear out this page and give it to a friend.

ALS
Amyotrophic Lateral Sclerosis
Motor Nurone Disease (MND)
Lou Gehrig's disease

ALS is a chronic, progressive disease that is marked by gradual degeneration of the nerve cells in the central nervous system that control voluntary muscle movement. The disorder causes muscle weakness and atrophy which paralyzes the entire body, yet leaves the mind untouched. The vast majority of ALS patients die within two to five years of diagnosis. There are no effective treatments and there is no cure.

There are an estimated 30,000 ALS patients in the US today with over 5,600 new patients diagnosed each year. ALS has roughly the same incidence rate as Multiple Sclerosis. Statistically, someone you know will contract ALS in the next 10 years.

Most people who develop ALS are between 40 and 70 and it is 20% more common in men than women. Lou Gehrig, with whom ALS is most commonly associated, first brought national and international attention to the disease back in 1939 when he abruptly retired from baseball after being diagnosed with ALS. However, ALS is not just Lou Gehrig's disease and it knows no boundaries. The disease has cut short the lives of such notable and courageous individuals as Hall of Fame pitcher Jim "Catfish" Hunter; creator of Sesame Street, Jon Stone; actor, David Niven; Senator Jacob Javits; and most recently Tom Watson's golf caddy, Bruce Edwards.

ALS Therapy Development Foundation is a nonprofit biotechnology company focused on finding treatments and a cure for today's ALS patients. It was founded by the brother of a patient with ALS. A number of scientists and associates who work for ALSTDF have been motivated by a loved one with the disease. Please donate today.

How to Obtain Additional Copies of

Upon Silver Wings: Global Adventure in a Small Plane

Books may be ordered three ways:

1. Please send a minimum contribution of $25 to cover shipping and handling ($30 for overseas donations) to ALS-TDF.
    a. Telephone: 617-441-7270, please have your credit card ready.
    b. Send check, payable to ALS-TDF to 215 First St., Cambridge, MA 02142. Please write **Attn: J. Oken** on the envelope and **Silver Wings** in the memo section of your check.

2. To receive an AUTOGRAPHED copy, please send a minimum contribution of $35 ($40 for overseas donations) to ALS-TDF and receive a book signed by the author and a confirmation of your tax-deductible contribution.
    a. Telephone: 617-441-7270, please have your credit card ready.
    b. Send check, payable to ALS-TDF to 215 First St., Cambridge, MA 02142. Please write **Attn: J. Oken** on the envelope and **Silver Wings** in the memo section of your check.

3. Amazon.com

    Please note: Contributions made directly to the ALS Therapy Development Foundation in excess of $25 will be tax deductible to the extent allowed by law. All revenue will go directly to ALS-TDF.

    When you buy from Amazon.com, 15% of the list price goes to Amazon as commission and the remainder, minus shipping and handling, goes to ALS-TDF. These purchases are not tax deductible.

Please tear out this page and give it to a friend.

ALS
Amyotrophic Lateral Sclerosis
Motor Nurone Disease (MND)
Lou Gehrig's disease

ALS is a chronic, progressive disease that is marked by gradual degeneration of the nerve cells in the central nervous system that control voluntary muscle movement. The disorder causes muscle weakness and atrophy which paralyzes the entire body, yet leaves the mind untouched. The vast majority of ALS patients die within two to five years of diagnosis. There are no effective treatments and there is no cure.

There are an estimated 30,000 ALS patients in the US today with over 5,600 new patients diagnosed each year. ALS has roughly the same incidence rate as Multiple Sclerosis. Statistically, someone you know will contract ALS in the next 10 years.

Most people who develop ALS are between 40 and 70 and it is 20% more common in men than women. Lou Gehrig, with whom ALS is most commonly associated, first brought national and international attention to the disease back in 1939 when he abruptly retired from baseball after being diagnosed with ALS. However, ALS is not just Lou Gehrig's disease and it knows no boundaries. The disease has cut short the lives of such notable and courageous individuals as Hall of Fame pitcher Jim "Catfish" Hunter; creator of Sesame Street, Jon Stone; actor, David Niven; Senator Jacob Javits; and most recently Tom Watson's golf caddy, Bruce Edwards.

ALS Therapy Development Foundation is a nonprofit biotechnology company focused on finding treatments and a cure for today's ALS patients. It was founded by the brother of a patient with ALS. A number of scientists and associates who work for ALSTDF have been motivated by a loved one with the disease. Please donate today.